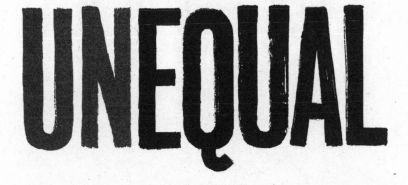

A
STORY OF
AMERICA

UN

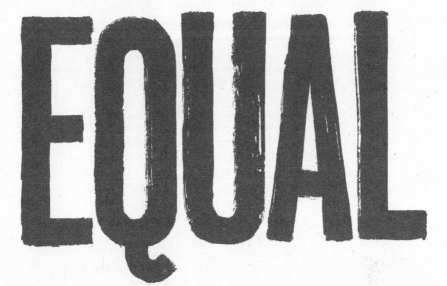

EQUAL

MICHAEL ERIC DYSON
& MARC FAVREAU

LITTLE, BROWN AND COMPANY
New York   Boston

Little, Brown and Company
Hachette Book Group
1290 Avenue of the Americas, New York, NY 10104
Visit us at LBYR.com

First Edition: May 2022

Little, Brown and Company is a division of Hachette Book Group, Inc. The Little, Brown name and logo are trademarks of Hachette Book Group, Inc.

The publisher is not responsible for websites (or their content) that are not owned by the publisher.

Library of Congress Cataloging-in-Publication Data
Names: Dyson, Michael Eric, author. | Favreau, Marc, 1968– author.
Title: Unequal : a story of America / Michael Eric Dyson, & Marc Favreau.
Description: First edition. | New York : Little, Brown and Company, 2022. | Includes index. | Audience: Ages 12 & up | Summary: "Interconnected stories present a picture of racial inequality in America, showing systemic discrimination in all areas of society and showing the unbroken line of Black resistance to this inequality." —Provided by publisher.
Identifiers: LCCN 2021058473 | ISBN 9780759557017 (hardcover) | ISBN 9780759557024 (ebook)
Subjects: LCSH: African Americans—Civil rights—Juvenile literature. | Civil rights workers—United States—Biography—Juvenile literature. | United States—Race relations—Juvenile literature. | Civil rights movements—United States—History—20th century—Juvenile literature.
Classification: LCC E185.61 .D995 2022 | DDC 323.1/196073—dc23/eng/20220103
LC record available at https://lccn.loc.gov/2021058473

ISBNs: 978-0-7595-5701-7 (hardcover), 978-0-7595-5702-4 (ebook)

Printed in the United States of America

LSC-C

Printing 1, 2022

For Marcia Louise Dyson, who has made, and conquered, history in eight decades, and to our grandchildren, Layla, Mosi, and Max, citizens of hope for a redemptive future

—MICHAEL

For Doris Cammack Spencer, who lived so much of this history, and triumphed over it, and for her grandsons, Owen and Emmett, who are already blazing a path toward a different future

—MARC

CONTENTS

★ ★ ★

PROLOGUE

★ ★ ★

A NOTE TO READERS

This is a book of truth. So we'll start by telling you the stone-cold fact that there are many people who do not want you to read it.

They may say that the stories found in these pages could be dangerous to your mental health. That readers will feel victimized or collapse in a puddle of guilt. Some of those people will undoubtedly try to ban this book. Please know that what they are trying to ban is the truth.

All of this may sound unreal. We have a hard time imagining that anyone would want to make history illegal in the United States of America. But that's exactly what's been happening in 2021.

And why now? It's no accident, we think, that this new attempt to whitewash history follows the largest protest movement in American history—a movement for racial justice and equality that had white supremacy back on its heels. The forces of inequality and white supremacy in America have always been afraid of history, because the truth is not on their side.

The real story of racial inequality—and resistance to it—is the prologue to our present. You can see it in where we live, where we go to school, and where we work. It's reflected in our laws, in our system of government, and in who gets to call the shots. It's even in the water we drink and in the soil we till. It's why George Floyd died on a sidewalk in Minneapolis. It's why Breonna Taylor was shot in her own bed in Louisville, Kentucky. And it's why millions of Americans turned out in the streets in 2020 and 2021 to push America in a new direction and to change its history for good.

History seems like it's behind us, and sometimes it is. Other times, though, the things that happen in the present are simply the latest episodes in a show that's been going on for years. We're surrounded by history's unfinished business, by story lines that will be wrapped up only when new characters step in—step up—to finish the plot.

After the Civil War, African American people and their allies tried to make genuine equality a reality for all Americans. Long after the war had ended, for the next 150 years, thousands of people, Black and white, dedicated their lives to making the promise of freedom real. Even if we have forgotten their names, their dreams live on.

We believe that all of us should remember the names,

and the dreams, of America's freedom fighters. *Unequal* is their unfinished story—and our own.

Some people in America, very powerful people, would prefer that you didn't know this story. They've tried for almost 150 years to stop stories like this from getting out, and today they are trying very hard, in cities and states across America, to make it illegal for you to learn about what is contained between these two covers.

These people believe that some knowledge is so dangerous that it should be kept from you at all costs. With knowledge, you may decide to act differently, or to make different choices about your life. You may question the world around you or the things you've been told since you were a young child. Perhaps you'd make connections that you wouldn't have made otherwise—or even join the fight to make freedom and equality real for all Americans.

That's our hope, at least.

CHRISTIAN COOPER, a Black man, out for an afternoon of bird watching in Central Park, had asked Amy Cooper to put her dog on a leash in a place where it was forbidden for dogs to roam free. Amy pulled out her cell phone and started to dial.

"I'm taking a picture and calling the cops....I'm going to tell them there's an African American man threatening my life."

Amy had decided to remind Christian where he was. This was a white place.

On April 29, 2018, a white woman named Jennifer Schulte aimed the same message at a Black family picnicking in a park in Oakland, California. Do what she says, she ordered, or she'd call the police. Two Black men in Philadelphia arrested for simply being in a Starbucks. Black people followed in stores, Black drivers trailed by police in white parts of town. No American, Black or white, is surprised when stories like these make the news, because we all take these color-coded places for granted, even though America pretends to be color-blind.

White places are parks, streets, stores, neighborhoods, even schools—anywhere white people decide that they should be in control. Black people are careful to teach their children about color-coded places; being color conscious is a matter of safety for kids who might get mistaken as a threat. Black parents learned it from their parents, who learned it from theirs. Color coding and the battle against white spaces are part of the story of America.

Mary Church in the 1880s.

CHAPTER ONE

★ ★ ★

MARY CHURCH TERRELL
Fights Back
Against Segregation

Sixteen-year-old Mary Church lingered on the bustling train platform in Bowling Green, Kentucky, clasping a first-class ticket to Memphis. When her train approached, Mary asked a white porter for directions to the first-class car. But after mounting the steps, she discovered that his instructions led her to the wrong place. She found herself on a train car separated by a wooden screen into two parts: the front, where white men sat in the smoking section, puffing on pipes and cigarettes, and the back, where African American men and women squeezed uncomfortably onto crowded benches.

It was the fall of 1879. The Civil War had ended fourteen years earlier. Slavery was abolished in 1865, but for most of Mary Church's young life, Americans—in Congress, in the South, and all over the country—had been arguing and battling over whether Black people like her could finally enjoy the rights and freedoms promised by the Constitution. By 1879, most white Southerners were hell-bent on saying *no*.

People like Mary's father, Robert Reed Church, however, were not going to take no for an answer—and he taught the same lesson to his daughter.

Born into slavery, Robert Church survived the Civil War only to be shot in 1866 by a white mob rioting against Memphis's increasingly prosperous Black community. He survived again, and refused to let the attack slow him down. In a few short years, Robert Church managed to build a thriving business along the Mississippi River, buying up land and attracting customers, to become the South's first Black millionaire.

Church understood as much as anyone that freedom was not simply the absence of slavery.

- It was about safety and the right to move freely without harassment.

- It was about building a future, through wealth and property.

- It was about the ability to make a living.

- It was about finding decent housing.

- It was about building great schools to educate children.

- It was about standing proudly as equal citizens.

And to secure all that, African Americans needed to represent themselves in the halls of power.

White southerners piled on with other assaults on Black freedom, beyond the attack in Memphis. They founded the Ku Klux Klan in 1866, a vigilante army meant to keep Black people out of politics and to force them back onto white-owned plantations, and they passed the Black codes—a set of state laws that seemed ominously like slavery. But four million free Black people, and their white allies in Congress, weren't having it. Backed by the federal government in the form of constitutional amendments, new laws, and federal troops, they pushed back hard against white supremacy.

"Reconstruction," as their new movement was called, upheld the right of all men (it was still restricted to men) to vote, hold office, serve on juries, and perform the other basic responsibilities of citizens—regardless of race. It was a simple idea: For the first time in its history, America approached something like a true democracy by protecting the rights of all people, Black and white. For this reason, some historians have even called Reconstruction the "second American Revolution."

In Memphis, where Mary Church lived, nearly 40 percent of voters were African American in the 1870s and 1880s, and they elected more Black legislators than would hold office again until the 1990s.

In 1870, Hiram Rhodes Revels of Mississippi became the first Black person to be elected to the US Senate; in 1874, he was joined by Blanche K. Bruce. Since that time, no African American person has held that office in Mississippi.

In total, more than 1,500 African Americans held political office in the South, including Governor P. B. S. Pinchback of Louisiana, the only Black person to hold a governor's office until well over a century later, when Douglas Wilder was elected governor of Virginia.

To those who lived through it, Reconstruction was like the world turned right side up.

By 1876, however, many white people across the United States had begun to think twice about their commitment to democracy and to protecting equal rights. In 1877, the federal government withdrew the very troops who made sure that Black and white people received equal treatment under the law. Former enslavers and their allies now felt free to launch their counterattack—and when they did, they targeted Black voters.

White supremacists stuffed ballot boxes with fake votes for white candidates. They intimidated African American voters at polling places. And when all else failed, the Ku Klux Klan stepped in to remove democratically elected governments by force.

Reconstruction was not destroyed in a day. Instead, white politicians, planters, and militia chipped away at it, year after year.

———◇———

As Mary Church entered young adulthood, Black and white Southerners were locked in a battle of wills—and sometimes battles with actual guns—over whether the South would be governed by democracy or by white supremacy. And the places where Black and white people mixed, especially trains and streetcars, were quickly becoming flash points.

"Instantly I knew this was the Jim Crow coach which I had never seen but about which I had heard," Mary said, using the common expression for racial segregation. And it was exactly the place that her father had sought to keep his Black daughter away from, by buying her a first-class seat.

As the conductor made his way down the aisle, Mary explained the mistake to him, hoping he might direct her to the first-class car.

Instead, he gave her a look "calculated to freeze the very marrow of my bones," Mary remembered.

"This is first class enough for you, and you stay just where you are," the man sneered. She tried to leave the car but the conductor blocked her way.

Mary weighed her options. Her father had paid for a first-class seat, but was it worth the fight?

"As young as I was," she remembered, "I had heard about awful tragedies which had overtaken colored girls who had been obliged to travel alone on these cars at night."

When the train approached the next stop, Mary told the conductor that she was getting off. It was a huge risk for an African American girl, at nighttime, in the South. "But of the two evils," she thought, "I decided that leaving the train was the less."

"I am getting off here," she said, "to wire my father that

you are forcing me to ride all night in the Jim Crow car. He will sue the railroad."

Mary's stubborn protest angered the conductor, and he struggled to pull her suitcase from her hands. "I held on to it with a vise-like grip," she said. But when their tug-of-war began to attract the notice of the few passengers remaining on the car, the conductor relented at last.

"You can go into that car if you want to," he begrudged her.

Mary Church made it home safely, but her first encounter with Jim Crow changed her. She returned to Oberlin College after break, and three years later became one of the first Black women in American history to graduate from college. While at Oberlin, she met the legendary civil rights activist Frederick Douglass, and she followed his example into a life of speaking up against the forces of white supremacy.

———◇———

For most of Mary's young adulthood, white people enforced racial segregation erratically on trains, in streetcars, and in other public spaces. White southerners believed that this patchwork left too many holes open where Black people— people like the proud Robert Church and his well-educated daughter—might squeeze through. By the 1890s, the time had come, they believed, to close the gaps.

Segregation didn't just happen naturally: It was part of a plan by white supremacists to return Black people to a second-class status, one as close to slavery as possible, and to unravel the last remaining accomplishments of Reconstruction.

What finally turned the tide fully against Black people, not only in the South but everywhere in the United States, was the very institution whose job it was to uphold the rule of law.

In 1896, the nine justices on the US Supreme Court handed down their decision in a case titled *Plessy v. Ferguson*. The case had originated with a Black plaintiff named Homer Plessy, who attempted to ride a whites-only streetcar in New Orleans and was arrested, tried, and convicted for this "crime." Plessy's lawyer, Albion W. Tourgée, appealed that decision and argued before the court that segregation's "only effect is to perpetuate the stigma of color." The court affirmed Plessy's conviction and ruled that, despite the promises of the Fourteenth Amendment to the Constitution (declaring "equal protection of the law" to all citizens, regardless of race), it was perfectly acceptable for states to establish racial segregation. From then on, "separate but equal" would be the law of the land.

Before the court's decision, Black people could at least attempt to claim their constitutional right to equality: equal schools, equal homes, equal employment opportunities, and more. But after *Plessy v. Ferguson*, the nation swapped its patchwork of laws and customs for the ironclad rule of racial inequality.

——◇——

With the law on their side, white southerners leapt at the chance to clamp down on Black people's desire for freedom and independence. Segregated streetcars and trains were only the beginning. White schools fired Black teachers. Black students, where they could attend school at all, met in drafty, unheated structures. Hospitals turned away Black patients, and libraries closed their doors to Black borrowers. Theaters created separate entrances for Black people, forcing them to sit apart, in the worst seats. Restaurants hung signs that read WHITES ONLY. Laundries were segregated by race.

They even tried to make God co-sign white supremacy: Black people had to swear on separate, segregated Bibles in southern courtrooms.

Outdoor spaces offered no refuge. John W. Brown recalled that as a child in Virginia, "anything that was public was also white. For example, the public park, the public playground, they were white." Especially in the hot summer months, pools and beaches kept Black people away, often under the threat of violence.

As the campaign to exclude Black people heated up, segregation seeped into even the smallest crevices of daily life.

"The Jim Crow law made friends into enemies overnight," Mamie Garvin Fields recalled. As a young girl growing up in South Carolina, Mamie played marbles and ate lunch with her white neighbors from across the street. Their families helped one another: "When they didn't have sugar, or they didn't have tea or coffee, they'd send over to borrow some."

"Now here comes Jim Crow," she said. When the first segregation laws passed, her neighbors took to calling her "ni——." White children threatened to shove her off the sidewalk. Fights broke out between Black and white students from the local school.

"The law made it that we weren't really neighbors anymore," she said.

Black people learned that segregation demanded a new kind of etiquette—from Black people only. When the legendary Black intellectual W. E. B. Du Bois, a northerner, accidentally bumped into a white woman on the street in Nashville when he was a student at Fisk University, he removed his hat and apologized sincerely. The woman screamed at him in response, leaving Du Bois, the first Black person to earn a PhD from Harvard, at a loss for words.

"Was it because I showed no submissiveness?" he wondered. "Did I fail to debase myself utterly and eat spiritual dirt? Did I act as equal among equals? I do not know. I only sensed scorn and hate; the kind of despising which a dog might incur."

Reminders of their new legal status haunted Black people everywhere. Black people could not enter a white home through the front door. They had to step off the sidewalk if a white person passed by. At a local post office in Mississippi, postal workers scratched out the words "Mr." or "Mrs." on letters addressed to African American recipients.

No Black person believed for a moment that "separate" could ever be "equal." Racial segregation was meant to demoralize, dehumanize, and destabilize Black people.

When African Americans found life in the South suffocating, a train trip to the North, even in a segregated car, offered some breathing space for people who had grown tired of daily slights and injustices.

The North, however, had its own racial rules, although they were not always written into law. In fact, white people in the North pioneered discrimination against free Black people before 1865, and many of these lessons were simply imported by the South after the Civil War.

Black people in the North endured racist insults and violence. In the summer of 1919, a Black teen went swimming in Lake Michigan and accidentally crossed an invisible color line on a Chicago beach. Before he could turn around, a group of young white men hurled stones at him until he drowned. A young boy named Dempsey Travis recalled how this terrifying event affected his family. "I was never permitted to learn to swim," he said. "For six years, we lived within two blocks of the lake, but that did not change [my parents'] attitude. To Dad and Mama, the blue lake always had a tinge of red from the blood of that young black boy."

Beaches from Boston to Los Angeles were no safer. Pools routinely barred Black swimmers, except, in rare cases, on specially designated days. Amusement parks like Cincinnati's Coney Island were off-limits to Black children.

Away from the big cities, "sundown towns" lurked in nearly every state. These all-white places required African Americans to leave before sundown, some posting signs warning Black people to stay out—a practice that continued as late as the 1970s. (One of us vividly remembers being warned against getting caught after dark in suburban Dearborn while growing up in Detroit in the 1960s and 1970s.) In 1909, the town of Anna, Illinois, became all-white after a nearby lynching; in 2018, residents of the town openly admitted that its name stood for "Ain't No N—— Allowed."

Black people were extra careful when traveling anywhere by car; a wrong turn could mean running out of gas too far from a friendly gas station, sleeping on the back seat, or worse. Many Black people traveling any distance depended on the *Negro Motorist Green Book*, a special travel guide that listed hotels, gas stations, restaurants, and other establishments that welcomed African American guests.

Segregation steamrolled the nation, forcing Black people into tighter and tighter spaces. But still they found ways to push back. The growing restrictions were concrete evidence of how hard African Americans resisted the new limits on their freedom.

In 1905, the resistance took shape when Black leaders, including W. E. B. Du Bois and newspaper publisher William Monroe Trotter, organized the Niagara Movement to advocate for equal rights for Black people. By the time an anti-Black riot erupted in Abraham Lincoln's hometown of Springfield, Illinois, three years later, the Niagara Movement had swollen to 170 members in thirty-four states. The violence in Springfield convinced the Niagara Movement's leaders that it was time to forge an interracial alliance of people to fight white racism. In 1909, Black leaders from all over America joined with white allies to found the National Association for the Advancement of Colored People (NAACP).

Mary Church (by now Mary Church Terrell) was one of the NAACP's founding members. Through the darkest days of Jim Crow, NAACP activists—and ordinary people across the country—took extraordinary risks to resist white supremacy.

———◇———

On January 27, 1950, seventy years after challenging the train conductor in Bowling Green, Mary Church Terrell waited her turn at the entrance to Thompson's Restaurant in Washington, DC.

At eighty-six years old, Mary was one of a dwindling number of people who could remember the days before segregation. She had spent her entire adult life under Jim Crow. But all around her, the segregated city buzzed with thousands of white government workers, politicians, taxi drivers, and streetcar operators, all of them insensitive to the racial inequalities that still afflicted the capital of the world's largest democracy. Even the restaurant in the US Capitol building refused to serve African American diners.

None of this was new to Mary Church Terrell; she understood that America's capital city was also the capital of American racism. In February 1915, in the White House, President Woodrow Wilson hosted the premier of the wildly popular silent film *The Birth of a Nation*, which celebrated the triumph of white supremacy over Reconstruction—and depicted African American men (played by white actors in blackface) as rapists. In 1919, white mobs attacked the city's Black neighborhoods; Black veterans of World War I joined local citizens to prevent a massacre. It took a daring First Lady named Eleanor Roosevelt to finally desegregate the White House in the mid-1930s, but she was in a distinct minority of white people. In the 1930s and 1940s, spectators in the gallery of the US Senate could hear the likes of Mississippi senator Theodore Bilbo, who hurled racial epithets openly while his colleagues looked on and said nothing.

Backed up by the highest court in the land and by America's most powerful politicians, Jim Crow backed down only when a movement of brave citizens decided not to give up on democracy.

Three companions joined Mary that afternoon as she crossed the threshold into Thompson's: Reverend William Jernagin, Geneva Brown, and David Scull. The small band made their way through the cafeteria line, picking out cake, salad, and other bites to eat. When they reached the cashier, a waitress standing nearby called over a man in a white uniform. He introduced himself to the group as the restaurant manager.

Then he told Terrell and her friends they could not eat there.

"Why not?" Jernagin demanded.

"Because we don't serve colored people here," the manager replied.

"Do you mean to tell me that you are not going to serve me?" Mary asked.

Terrell's question was a carefully rehearsed ploy. She had remained an activist into old age, looking for every opportunity to undermine the power of Jim Crow.

With the help of two lawyers, Mary and her friends had staged the episode in order to file a lawsuit, one that would strike at the heart of the city's segregated society. The real drama would play out not in Thompson's segregated dining room but in a Washington, DC, courtroom.

Harking back to an earlier era—a time when Mary was still a young child—Mary's legal team revealed that Washington still had two laws in force that no one seemed to remember. Passed in the 1860s and 1870s, the laws stated that all restaurants, theaters, bars, and hotels had to admit "any respectable, well-behaved person without regard to race, color or previous condition of servitude."

Defenders of segregation liked to argue that keeping the races separate was only natural—a practice that reflected people's desire to live apart. But DC's "lost laws" revealed that the opposite was true: that white supremacists had imposed segregation's unequal rules on people who longed to live as equal citizens.

On June 8, 1953, the US Supreme Court ruled that Mary Church Terrell—and all people—could eat, sit, or ride anywhere they wished. It was a quiet victory, compared with the momentous decision the court would hand down eleven months later, when *Brown v. Board of Education of Topeka, Kansas*, declared "separate but equal" unconstitutional, over-ruling *Plessy v. Ferguson* once and for all.

Mary Church Terrell lived just long enough to learn about *Brown v. Board of Education*, drawing her last breath at ninety years of age, two months after witnessing the last gasp of legal segregation in the United States.

———◇———

Seventy years after Mary's quiet victory, the ghosts of Jim Crow still stalk America's public places. Legal segregation is long dead, but Black people are still watched, followed, and policed in spaces that are designed for relaxation but expose them to discrimination.

Instead of relying on laws to do the work of segregation, America has built an ever more elaborate system for main-taining America's white places. Police harass Black motorists and pedestrians. Real estate agents steer Black buyers away from white neighborhoods—a practice that also serves to keep neighborhood schools segregated. White people call the police whenever a Black person seems "out of place," which usually means anywhere that is majority white. Color coding is as real and as dangerous as it was more than a century ago.

Black Americans today, no less than Mary Church Terrell as she boarded her train in Kentucky, understand the intended message of these encounters with police, businesses, and their own neighbors. When people respond by declaring that Black Lives Matter, their words echo the arguments of Terrell, the early NAACP activists, and thousands of other people who have devoted their lives to banishing segregation's long shadow.

They know that the promise of Reconstruction—of a nation where race plays no role in how Americans are treated—is still an American dream.

AHMAUD ARBERY liked to run. His days as a high school football star were behind him, but he kept fit with long workouts that trailed through the neighborhoods near his home on the outskirts of Brunswick, Georgia.

It was hot on that February afternoon in 2020. Did Ahmaud stop for a drink of water? A video camera in a nearby house, which was under construction and empty, showed a man passing through and back again, tracing a path to an outdoor faucet.

Two white men, a father and son, grabbed their guns, jumped into a pickup truck, and raced after Ahmaud. A third man joined the fateful chase in his truck to cut off Arbery's route of escape. When they caught up with him, Ahmaud and the son scuffled. Gunshots echoed through the quiet streets.

One thing was certain. The white men were still alive, and armed. Ahmaud Arbery lay on the sidewalk, dead.

And then nothing happened. The local authorities decided not to charge Gregory and Travis McMichael with a crime. They walked away, free men. It took a video of the killing, national outcry, multiple changes in jurisdiction, and three months for charges to be brought against the three men who were eventually convicted of murder.

Some in the media, and some politicians, argued that Arbery's killing was a simple accident. But when the same thing happens again and again, in the same ways but with small variations, a pattern starts to emerge. For centuries, Black men and women have been killed for crimes they did not commit. Or for talking back to a white person. For being too proud or too successful. Or, simply, for being in the wrong place at the wrong time. For being thirsty and looking for a drink of water.

There is a uniquely American word for that pattern: *lynching*.

Ida B. Wells, circa 1893.

CHAPTER TWO

★ ★ ★

IDA B. WELLS
Exposes America's Lynching Epidemic

If she went ahead and published the article, trouble would find her. In the spring of 1892, Black people in the South found themselves jailed, shot, or hanged for less. Ida B. Wells knew this to be true; she was born into slavery in 1862 and had no illusions about white people. But this time she had no choice. This time it was personal.

White people had murdered Ida's friend Tom Moss.

It all started a few weeks earlier, in the middle of the night of March 9, when seventy-five masked white men surrounded the Shelby County jail in Memphis, Tennessee. Despite the jail's imposing walls and iron fence, nine members of the mob managed to slip inside and find their three victims. They dragged Calvin McDowell, Will Stewart, and Tom Moss into the muddy street, then hauled them to the nearby Chesapeake and Ohio railroad yards. While newspaper reporters and other witnesses—including the Shelby County judge—looked on, the masked men riddled McDowell, Stewart, and Moss with bullets. McDowell was killed by a point-blank shotgun blast. The bullet aimed at the resisting Stewart lodged in his neck. When Moss was asked if he had any final words before he was shot, he replied: "Tell my people to go west. There is no justice for them here." The killers then mutilated the dead bodies with a hail of gunshots. Reporters scribbled down every gruesome detail and made sure that the story appeared in the morning papers on March 10.

Like every Black person in the South in 1892, Ida knew the word for what happened: the three Black men had been *lynched*.

Never one to worry too much about her own safety, Ida started digging into the facts behind the murders. After all, she hadn't become the first Black woman in America to own a newspaper by hiding in the shadows. Though she was a young Black woman under five feet tall, living in a city ruled by powerful white men, Ida didn't scare easily.

Once, a railroad conductor in Memphis tried to toss Ida off the ladies' car, scolding her that it was reserved for whites only. During the tussle that followed, Wells bit the man's hand. Only when a group of white passengers came to the conductor's aid did he succeed in ejecting her from the train at the next station. Another person might have simply walked away; Ida responded by filing a lawsuit against the Chesapeake, Ohio and Southwestern Railroad for assault and discrimination. Although she lost, she taught her people a valuable lesson about persistence in the face of bitter odds when she pursued the case all the way to the Tennessee Supreme Court.

The South had a way of throwing obstacles in Ida's way, dragging her into fights that she didn't start. And something inside Ida always made her fight back.

Ida had recently invested her every penny in her own newspaper, the *Memphis Free Speech*. White people may have taken away her right to vote and segregated the streetcars and trains in the city she called home, but Ida was determined to control her own destiny. Under her ownership, the *Free Speech*'s circulation increased to more than four thousand subscribers. It was enough to make a living. It was enough to keep her independent.

Like Ida, Tom Moss had struggled to carve out a life for himself, out from under the thumb of white people. With his friends Calvin McDowell and Will Stewart, Tom had helped found a successful grocery store in Memphis, the People's Grocery, that catered to the city's thousands of Black residents. He also belonged to the Tennessee Rifles, a Black militia and fraternal organization. He often wore a tan uniform emblazoned with the letters TR.

Even though the door seemed to be closing on freedom for Black people in the 1890s, Tom, like Ida, believed that independence was possible, if you fought for it. No wonder the two had become close friends.

Ida's investigations revealed that the success of the

21

People's Grocery made Tom enemies among his local white competitors. They couldn't make a case against such an honest businessman in court.

Ida had seen her share of racism, but Tom Moss's murder opened her eyes to a completely different reality. She thought that she knew the South. She believed that she understood how to rise, and to help lift up her community. With grit and determination, Black people could get ahead even in places like Memphis, where white people held the upper hand and still longed for the days of slavery.

Now, she realized, all that was changing. Something evil was brewing. Ida called the lynching in Memphis "our first lesson in white supremacy." In Memphis and throughout the South, Ida wrote in her newspaper, lynching was becoming "an excuse to get rid of Negroes who were acquiring wealth and property and thus keep the race terrorized and 'the n—— down.'"

The pages of the *Free Speech* crackled with new revelations, criticisms, and venom aimed at the city's white leaders, whom she suspected of complicity in the lynchings. She named names. She placed prominent people at the scene of the crime and also later exposed one of Moss's white competitors as the devious purchaser of the People's Grocery at a bargain-basement price.

All that spring, she turned up the heat—until, on the eve of a trip North, her enemies believed that she went too far with her accusations.

Ida was on her way to New York City when she learned

that a white mob had forced its way into the *Free Speech* office, ransacked it, and destroyed her printing press. Some of Memphis's "leading citizens" joined in the attack. And in case she mistook the attackers' intentions, they left behind a note that read, "Anyone trying to publish the paper again will be punished with death."

A fellow journalist, T. Thomas Fortune, met her at the station in Jersey City and broke the news. "Now that you are here, I'm afraid you will have to stay."

Ida would not return to Memphis, or to the South, for thirty years.

The destruction of the *Free Speech* left Ida penniless. Still, she threw herself into investigating and writing about lynchings. To her surprise, more and more readers eagerly awaited what she had to say.

With the help of her many admirers in the African American press, Ida published articles, pamphlets, and books, which found their way into the hands of readers all over the United States. When Ida wrote a seven-column exposé of lynchings in T. Thomas Fortune's *New York Age*, the paper sold ten thousand copies—including a thousand on the streets of Memphis alone. Invitations to speak piled up in her mailbox. She traveled to England and toured the country, giving lectures about the horrors of lynching in America. In a few short years, her campaign made Ida the most famous African American, man or woman, of her generation. And little by little she made sure that no American could ignore the horrors of lynching.

She had her work cut out for her. A region already notorious for violence seemed to turn a dark corner in the 1890s. Mobs of white vigilantes singled out Black people for the smallest perceived offense, torturing and murdering them in broad daylight.

One victim accidentally walked into a room where three white women were seated. Another bumped into a white girl on his way to catching a train. Others spoke back to a boss or dared question a police officer. Almost anything, it seemed, could get a Black person killed. The common denominator was being in the wrong place at the wrong time, and just being Black—which was considered a crime in itself.

Victims of lynching had not been convicted of any crime, and no member of a lynch mob was ever arrested for murder. These murders were not perpetrated under the cover of darkness. Lynchings in the 1890s and 1900s attracted thousands of onlookers, who treated the events as public entertainment.

White spectators snapped pictures of men and women suffering slow and agonizing deaths. Some of these ended up on memorial postcards and became ghoulish items for sale in drugstores and curio shops. In one example, the photos show white parents and their children standing near the charred corpses of victims. A few of these survive to this day, complete with postage, and notes scrawled to friends. One of these reads, "Well John—This is a token of a great day we had in Dallas March 3rd."

The tormentors cut off victims' fingers, toes, and ears, and even removed their internal organs, distributing them to the crowd as souvenirs. Men and women were burned alive or dragged through the streets.

Ida struggled to comprehend these almost unimaginable acts of violence. After months of investigation, she discovered that white people hid behind a myth. In many cases, they falsely accused innocent Black men of raping white women and girls. Ida was the first journalist in America to investigate these claims and to show that in nearly every single case, they were lies. "Nobody in this section of the country believes the threadbare old lie that Negro men rape white women," Ida declared in indignant ink.

The *New York Times* chafed at the notion that white women would willingly consort with "Black brutes," and tagged her a "slanderous and nasty-minded mulattress." So much for journalistic objectivity.

Something very different was happening in the 1890s, Ida concluded. Lynching didn't have to do with punishing crimes committed by Black people; it had to do with suppressing Black power. Like Tom and Ida herself, Black men and women everywhere claimed rights as citizens. They filed lawsuits. They started businesses. They fought back.

Some white people decided that it was time to send Black America a message. The goal of the lynch mob was to strike terror into the hearts of Black people everywhere, telling them that nowhere was safe from the threat of white violence. In all, between the end of Reconstruction and 1950, lynch mobs murdered over four thousand African American people in the South.

Ida realized that she could not turn back this wave of terrorism. But she had weapons of her own. If the white South was going to fabricate a story about Black people, Ida was going to set the record straight. Before cell phones and viral videos, she exposed the truth about the violent mobs that attacked innocent Black men, women, and children. Lynch mobs wielded ropes, guns, and torches. Ida fought back with her razor-sharp pen.

White people argued that lynch mobs brought justice to Black criminals. But Ida corrected that history all by herself, telling the truth about racist violence in America and presenting her evidence in the court of public opinion.

———◆———

Vigilantes stalked Black people throughout most of the twentieth century, even when public authorities discouraged lynchings and the killers were forced back into the shadows.

In 1955, they lynched Emmett Till, a fourteen-year-old Black boy, for allegedly whistling at a white girl. They assassinated civil rights activists in the 1960s and buried them in unmarked graves in Mississippi.

Sometimes the murderers wore the white cloaks of Ku Klux Klansmen, but more often they dressed as ordinary citizens—and even as officers of the law.

Today, threats of violence hang over all Black people who find themselves in the wrong place at the wrong time.

A seventeen-year-old boy named Trayvon Martin was visiting his father in Sanford, Florida, in February 2012. One evening he walked out to a nearby convenience store to buy a package of Skittles and a can of iced tea. On his way home, an armed vigilante named George Zimmerman accosted Trayvon on a sidewalk and began following him home.

Shots rang out. Trayvon Martin lay dead on the sidewalk with a bullet wound to the chest.

The police detained but then released George Zimmerman (who had been carrying a handgun that he used to kill the teen), because Zimmerman claimed it was in self-defense. It took a national protest movement for the local prosecutor to reverse course and eventually charge Zimmerman with second-degree murder.

In the months that followed, right-wing bloggers and many news stations went out of their way to depict the unarmed, innocent Trayvon Martin as a dangerous criminal—even though he had no criminal record. The picture they painted of Trayvon was eerily similar to the way lynch mobs depicted Black men a century earlier.

In July 2013, a majority-white jury in Florida declared George Zimmerman innocent of any crime, and he walked away a free man.

The same story is repeated again and again—and as with George Zimmerman and the men who shot Ahmaud

Arbery, the perpetrators are charged with a crime only when protesters force the government to act. When a Black person is killed under suspicious circumstances, white people move quickly to assign guilt to the victim, not the perpetrator. These false stories—much as they did in lynching's heyday—serve to fuel the cycle of white violence.

———◇———

Ida B. Wells-Barnett (her married name) died in Chicago in 1931, but her work continues to this day.

On June 30, 2021, a ceremony was held in Chicago to dedicate the Ida B. Wells-Barnett monument, the first one in the city honoring a Black woman. The monument, crafted by renowned artist Richard Hunt, rises from the ground where the infamous Ida B. Wells public housing project was once erected.

In attendance that day was renowned journalist Nikole Hannah-Jones, whose Twitter display name is "Ida Bae Wells" in honor of her pioneering journalist role model. "We are actually fighting against the same type of tyranny and white supremacy that Ida B. Wells was fighting against all those years ago," Jones noted.

Ida's work also continues through the National Memorial for Peace and Justice in Birmingham, Alabama, the first memorial and museum dedicated to the memory of lynching victims in the United States. What is sometimes referred to as the "lynching museum" reminds Americans of what Ida uncovered more than a century ago, namely, that the struggle for equality is also a struggle for safety—for the ability of Black people to move without danger through America, free from fear and free from the terror of white supremacy.

THE NET WORTH of an average white family in America today is ten times the net worth of an average Black family. A recent study captured how extreme the difference is, revealing that "Black families whose heads graduated from college have about 33 percent less wealth than white families whose heads dropped out of high school."

In this country, having wealth is part of what it means to be free. It's what we have left when we subtract all our debts—the money and resources that let us pay for our homes, our bills, and other essentials. If there is money left over after we cover the bases, maybe we can pursue a dream, start a business, take a risk on a new career.

Wealth isn't necessarily the same thing as being rich: it's not about having too much, but rather about having enough—enough to live a stable and happy life. Today, very few Black families have enough.

However you slice it, the math is straightforward: America has a racial wealth gap. It gets wider each year. And the heavy truth is that even when two people have the same level of academic achievement, the same degrees, and the same job prospects, if one of these people is Black, he or she is likely to have less money in the bank. There's a simple reason for this: Most of the wealth people have comes in the form of an inheritance. An inheritance could be money given to you by a parent or grandparent; it could be a home or other property left to you in a will; or bills paid on your behalf. Whatever its source, an inheritance is something you didn't earn yourself; our family histories powerfully influence our lives, and our wealth, in the present.

As a community, Black people had their inheritance stolen. Why this is true begins with slavery, but the story does not end there.

Left: Portrait of Buck Franklin, Nashville, Tennessee, 1901.

Calvert Brothers Studios, Tennessee State Library and Archives

Below: Smoke rises over Tulsa during the 1921 massacre.

Alvin C. Krupnick Co., photographer, Library of Congress Prints and Photographs Division, Washington, DC

CHAPTER THREE

★ ★ ★

BUCK FRANKLIN

Bears Witness to the Destruction of Black Wall Street

The People's Grocery lynchings taught Ida B. Wells a lesson that Black people would face again and again for the next hundred years and beyond. The new system of white supremacy was set up to steal from African Americans. The racist myths, the KKK robes, and the angry white faces in the crowd hid resentment—and greed.

Black people, many of whom had toiled as slaves before 1865, knew in their bones what it meant to have the fruits of their labor stolen. For that very reason, perhaps, they didn't let the lynch mobs stop them. Even though segregation made inequality the law of the land, some Black people managed to thrive in separate, all-Black worlds they had built from scratch.

In Richmond, Virginia—the former capital of the Confederacy—Black businessmen established a bustling neighborhood in the Jackson Ward, boasting its own news-papers, banks, department stores, and the Southern Aid and Insurance Company, the first Black-owned insurance company in America. In Durham, North Carolina, more than two hundred African American businesses lined the street of the Hayti neighborhood (Hayti survived Jim Crow, only to be bulldozed by the federal government to make way for a new highway, in 1958). "Sweet Auburn" Avenue in Atlanta, Georgia, was a hub of religious, cultural, and economic life for Black people for much of the twentieth century; it was once dubbed "the richest Negro street in the world."

Black people even launched their own westward migration in the late nineteenth century, heading in growing numbers to frontier settlements where they could carve out lives totally separate from the hostile world of Jim Crow. Little towns like all-Black Nicodemus, Kansas (which still stands today), provided a refuge from racism.

African Americans built businesses, churches, homes, and other community institutions in defiance of Jim Crow. But they couldn't escape it completely.

All across the United States, wherever Black people had managed to accumulate wealth and property, white America seemed determined to tear it down. In the early decades of the twentieth century, a wave of destruction set back the clock for tens of thousands of aspiring Black professionals and entrepreneurs.

The Black community of Wilmington, North Carolina,

once known as "the freest town for a negro in this country," was the first to feel white supremacy's jealous wrath. In November 1898, a white mob riled up by Southern Democratic leaders moved through the streets of this elegant coastal city in a carefully planned operation to burn down the offices of Black newspapers, remove Black officeholders from power, and destroy Black-owned businesses. White gunmen cut down Black citizens at will, murdering more than sixty people.

More large-scale attacks on Black neighborhoods and towns followed: Atlanta, Georgia, in 1906; Springfield, Illinois, in 1908; and East Saint Louis, Illinois, in 1917.

In the summer of 1919—named "Red Summer" by civil rights activist and author James Weldon Johnson to mark the flow of Black blood that year from more than three dozen attacks—racist mobs terrorized Black residents of Chicago, Charleston, and Washington, DC. In the small town of Elaine, Arkansas, one hundred Black people were massacred in a single attack.

For many ambitious Black people, it seemed like a race against time. How far could they go before Jim Crow yanked them back toward slavery?

———◇———

Buck Franklin decided that he had had enough.

In the winter of 1921, he left his family behind in tiny Rentiesville, Oklahoma, bound for the booming city of Tulsa, seventy miles to the north. Buck's son John Hope, who later became a renowned Harvard-trained historian, was only six years old. He realized that his father wasn't coming home only when the latter didn't show up for dinner. "It seemed that my world was suddenly crumbling," he recalled.

But Buck Franklin had no intention of abandoning his family for good. Tulsa was a place large enough for his dreams, and he planned to build a new legal practice, and when the time was right, he would bring his family up from Rentiesville.

Franklin's ambitions led him to a part of Tulsa called Greenwood.

Greenwood was the wealthiest Black community in America—a "Black Wall Street" with hundreds of Black-owned businesses and homes. Some of Greenwood's Black residents had made their fortunes in the state's new oil industry. Others catered to the growing population of African American residents with stores and restaurants that lined the neighborhood's streets.

The Williams Dreamland Theatre, with 750 seats, welcomed Black moviegoers. Restaurants such as the Bell and Little Café catered to an upwardly mobile Black clientele. Dance halls, a skating rink, posh hotels, and every kind of business—from dentists to barbers to record shops—thrived with the support of thousands of Black patrons.

The granddaughter of a Greenwood resident recalled, "My grandfather often talked about how you could enjoy a full life in Greenwood, that everything you needed or wanted was in Greenwood. You never had to go anywhere.

"He talked about seeing Black success and how his sense of identity and pride came from Greenwood," she added.

In Greenwood, an energetic Black lawyer like Buck Franklin could make his way in life.

In the spring of 1921, Buck finally sent his family word that they should join him. For the young John Hope, the world was about to right itself again.

Before they could board a train, however, terrifying news had traveled the rails from Tulsa all the way to Rentiesville.

On May 30, a young Black man named Dick Rowland was accused of assaulting Sarah Page, a white woman. A group of white men approached the Tulsa courthouse with the aim of lynching Rowland, but they were thwarted by Black defenders. The details were still murky when rumors began to ripple across the white neighborhoods that surrounded Greenwood. Terrified Black residents loaded their rifles and waited for the attack they were sure would come.

As night fell on May 31, Buck Franklin heard pops in the distance. It could be fire signals, he thought. But then the noises grew louder. Buck rose from bed and went down to the street to investigate.

"About midnight," he recalled, "I arose and went to the north porch on the second floor of my hotel and, looking in a north-westerly direction, I saw the top of Standpipe Hill literally lighted up by the blazes that came from the throats of machine guns, and I could hear bullets whizzing and cutting the air. There was shooting in every direction."

Under the cover of darkness, white attackers converged on Greenwood from all sides.

Seeing that the police had abandoned them, many of Greenwood's residents fought back with guns. Bullets zipped and ricocheted through the streets. Several biplanes—most likely crop dusters recruited for the attack—made bombing runs over the neighborhood, firing indiscriminately at residents and dropping explosives. Buck Franklin witnessed several planes dropping flaming turpentine balls on rooftops, which quickly ignited.

For twelve long hours, the neighborhood looked like a war zone. Dead bodies lay in the streets, some of them charred beyond recognition. Hemmed in on all sides by the attack, Greenwood's Black population found few places to hide. National guardsmen who arrived on the scene treated Black survivors like enemy prisoners of war, forcing them to march through the burning streets with their hands on their heads.

"For days we did not know if my father was dead, injured, or unharmed," John Hope Franklin later recalled. "Finally, we received a letter, in which he gave our mother some details of the tragedy and assured us that he was alive and well."

Buck Franklin witnessed scenes of terror. "One was a woman on the opposite side of the street," he recalled. "She was traveling south—hair disentangled and disheveled—in the very path of whizzing bullets. She was calling wildly to a little tot that, a few minutes before, had dashed in panic before her." From the same direction, Franklin saw three men escape from a burning building, lugging a trunk. All three were murdered in a sudden hail of bullets.

Others described similar tragedies all over Greenwood.

Dr. A. C. Jackson, who had a reputation as "the ablest Negro surgeon in America," was shot and killed as he fled his burning home, his hands raised in the air in surrender.

Olivia Hooker's mother hid her children under an oak table in the living room while white men ransacked their home. Three-year-old Olivia froze in terror as she caught glimpses of the destruction.

"They took a hatchet to my sisters' piano," she recalled. "They took all the silverware that Momma had just got for Christmas, coffee pot, teapot—you know, that kind of beautiful stuff. If anything looked precious, they took it."

In all, the looters emptied out over twelve hundred Black homes, stealing millions of dollars' worth of private property.

One by one, attackers set Greenwood's homes on fire. Flames spread to every structure in the neighborhood, including churches, hotels, restaurants, offices, and even the local hospital. Anything that remained after the white looters had done their work was burned to the ground. In all, the arsonists destroyed eighteen thousand homes.

"For fully forty-eight hours," Buck Franklin reported, "the fire raged and burned everything in its path and it left nothing but ashes and burned safes and trunks and the like, where once stood beautiful homes and business houses."

"And so proud, rich, black Tulsa was destroyed by fire," Franklin said.

The attackers completely destroyed forty square blocks, nearly the entire neighborhood of Greenwood. In less than two days, more than nine thousand Greenwood residents became homeless refugees.

Today, historians and researchers estimate that the Greenwood mob murdered as many as three hundred Black people. No one knows for certain where all the victims are buried; as recently as 2019, archaeologists believed they had identified mass graves, not far from the location of the attacks.

The local police and the federal government refused to investigate the attack or its perpetrators. Instead, the ruins of Greenwood became the site of a second crime: a historical whitewash.

The story of the Tulsa massacre did not appear in Oklahoma's history textbooks for another eighty years. Most American students still don't learn about it in school; when the attack was dramatized in the HBO series *Watchmen* in 2019, many viewers believed that it was fiction.

But the survivors never forgot what they witnessed or what had happened to their homes, businesses, and families.

The massacre in Tulsa was seared into John Hope Franklin's memory. He resolved to make sure America would remember as well—and to bring justice for the victims of the attack and their descendants. But rather than following in his father's footsteps to a legal career, John became a historian. His book *From Slavery to Freedom* has become one of the most respected books on African American history ever published.

In 2003, Franklin helped bring a lawsuit against the city of Tulsa and the state of Oklahoma, seeking reparations for over one hundred then-living survivors of the massacre and three hundred children and grandchildren of victims. A federal judge dismissed the case, but it helped set in motion a much wider movement to remember what happened in 1921 and to heal the historical wounds of that violent day—a movement that remains unfulfilled.

"The wealth gap," according to the historian Mehrsa Baradaran, "is where the injustices sown in the past grow imperceptibly in the present." It's hard to know how much wealth, and how many months and years of sweat and toil, were erased in a single day in Tulsa.

A report commissioned by the state of Oklahoma detailed nearly $2 million in insurance claims from the Greenwood massacre, which would be valued at nearly $30 million today. The total financial impact on victims was likely much higher, as many victims, fearing for their lives, fled the city without attempting to recoup their losses.

But even these numbers don't capture the deeper meaning of the loss of Greenwood.

"What if we had been allowed to maintain our family business?" asked one woman, whose grandfather's shoe shop was destroyed by a white mob. "If they had been allowed to carry on that legacy, there's no telling where we could be now."

The wave of violence did not break in Tulsa, either. Other so-called race riots crushed Black businesses and communities in the years that followed. In one especially shocking example, white mobs demolished the entire town of Rosewood, Florida, in 1923. The only building left standing was a general store, and the entire Black population fled the area; estimates of the number of people killed range from six to several dozen.

When the mob violence of these years finally ebbed, hundreds—perhaps thousands—of Black people had been murdered and many more injured. The ruins of Black homes and the rubble of businesses littered the streets of American cities, awful reminders of how quickly—and with so much violence—years of hard work and savings had been stolen by white people, or had simply gone up in smoke.

President Joseph Biden went to Tulsa on June 1, 2021, to commemorate the hundredth anniversary of the shameful events. Biden was direct: "My fellow Americans," he declared, "this was not a riot. This was a massacre, among the worst in our history, but not the only one. And for too long, forgotten by our history." Biden said that great nations "come to terms with their dark sides. And we're a great nation. The only way to build a common ground is to truly repair and to rebuild."

Black people never stopped building better lives for

themselves. In Tulsa—helped in many cases by the lawyer Buck Franklin—they quietly pieced together new homes and business. But what was taken from them in the massacre was never returned. Those who began again, the children and grandchildren of the enslaved, had to start at square one.

The seeds of inequality sprouted in Tulsa in 1921 and, in countless communities across the country, grew and grew.

WHEN HE WALKED into the break room at work one morning in 2007, Ron Law found a noose hanging from the ceiling.

It might have seemed like a joke—except that it kept happening again and again at the shipbuilding company where he worked. People left racist graffiti on the bathroom walls, and supervisors made racist remarks within earshot of Black employees. Black workers noticed other patterns, too. They were passed over for promotions and training and routinely harassed by their bosses.

To this day, simply getting a job is harder for Black applicants, due to outright discrimination. Résumés with "Black-sounding" names end up in the reject pile in large numbers; darker-skinned applicants have a much harder time getting hired than do lighter-skinned applicants.

For those Black people who do land jobs, the uphill climb is steeper than for most white people. Black people with equal qualifications make less money than white people, are promoted less often, and are the first to be fired when a company needs to lay off workers.

The destruction of Black wealth in Tulsa and other cities is only one part of a larger story of financial inequality. For much of the past 150 years, most Black people never even had the chance to break out of poverty.

Black people have fought their way into every American workplace, and over the past century, Black individuals have become leaders in business, medicine, law, education, engineering, science, entertainment, military service, and in every other profession and industry. But the successes of some must not distract from the struggles of many, and the history of a time when Black people everywhere suffered from legal discrimination still hangs heavily over the present.

Ned and Viola Cobb and their first child,
Andrew, circa 1907. Tallapoosa County,
Alabama.

CHAPTER FOUR

★ ★ ★

NED COBB
Confronts Racial Inequality at Work

On a Monday morning in 1931, Ned Cobb's worst fears came to pass.

A white landowner named Watson had persuaded Ned to borrow forty-five dollars for farm supplies, but it was just a ruse. When Ned paid him back in cotton, Watson claimed that it wasn't enough. It was his word against Ned's. A white landowner against a poor Black farmer.

"He was goin to take what I had if I owed him; if I didn't owe him he was goin to take it," Ned said.

Watson had the law on his side, and he sent a deputy sheriff to seize Cobb's livestock to pay off the supposed debt.

Ned Cobb didn't have a plan, but he knew what he had to do. Losing his cattle and mules would mean not making a living or feeding his family that year.

Ned Cobb lived and farmed in the Black Belt of Alabama,

named for the dark, fertile soil that helped make cotton the South's main export crop and the source of most of its wealth. But the money made from cotton did not trickle down to poor families like the Cobbs, who scraped a living from the soil and hauled bales of the fluffy white cotton bolls to the local marketplace.

The problem came down to who owned what.

Watson owned the land on which Cobb grew his cotton, and the tools he used to grow it. Each year, when the time came to sell the crop, Cobb owed a portion of it to the landowner.

"But who's the man ought to decide how much?" Ned asked. "The one that owns the property or the one that works it?"

The arrangement was known as "sharecropping," but in truth, it was about taking, not sharing. Even in good years, a white plantation owner chiseled away at a sharecropper's earnings with his pen: some here for rent, more there for groceries purchased at the plantation store, still more for fertilizer, seeds, and tools, all bought on credit. The planter kept the ledger book, and it always added up in his favor.

Sometimes, to Ned Cobb, debt felt almost like slavery.

After the Civil War, Black people in the South desired above all to stay independent from their former owners. They refused to work in gangs on cotton plantations and resisted any attempt to pick cotton under the direct supervision of white people. Their determination transformed the way the southern economy operated for the next one hundred years. Instead of being grown on plantations that looked a lot like they did under slavery (which is what many white people would have preferred), the South's main crop, cotton, grew on small plots of land farmed by Black families.

African Americans clung to their hard-won freedom. But in the words of one historian, they had "nothing *but* freedom." White people still owned most of the land and controlled the banks and the stores that made farming possible. If white people couldn't bring back slavery, then they were determined to exploit and control the South's Black labor force any way they could.

Sharecropping was the most common method, but it wasn't the worst.

On March 30, 1908, a Black man named Green Cottenham was arrested in Alabama because a white sheriff suspected that Cottenham didn't have a job—a so-called crime devised by white politicians after Reconstruction. A local judge sentenced Cottenham to thirty days of hard labor in a local mine. And because he couldn't afford to pay the fines imposed on him by the judge, Cottenham ended up serving nearly a year, working for no money in brutal conditions.

Cottenham's predicament wasn't an isolated case. In Alabama alone, more than two hundred thousand Black people toiled for no pay in mines, on plantations, and in factories. They were caught in this new system of "convict labor" by a web of new laws, racist sheriffs, and corrupt judges, whose only goal was to force as many Black people as possible to work for nothing.

Once captured by the system, Black people learned that it functioned exactly like slavery. They were bought and sold by different plantation owners. White overseers subjected them to all kinds of physical punishments, including whipping. They were fed only enough to survive, and often worked in rain and snow without appropriate clothing. Anyone who tried to run away (or anyone who helped a runaway) could be beaten, whipped—and sentenced to an even longer term. Many died, only to be buried in unmarked graves.

In all, Southern states forced hundreds of thousands of African Americans onto chain gangs as late as the 1950s—almost a century after emancipation was supposed to have wiped involuntary servitude off the map. For these men and women, the history of slavery was not a thing of the past but a powerful force that shaped their chances of getting ahead in the twentieth century. And like so many chapters in this history of inequality, the convict-lease system and chain gangs were kept out of the history books.

When a journalist named Douglas A. Blackmon painstakingly retold this story in his 2008 book *Slavery by Another Name: The Re-Enslavement of Black Americans from the Civil War to World War II*, his revelations hit like a bombshell—and earned him the Pulitzer Prize for his work. The true story he told of Black people being imprisoned and exploited for their labor was deemed so controversial by prison authorities in Alabama (the state that had been the worst offender) that they banned prisoners from reading the book. Blackmon retorted by arguing that "this is the kind of history that helps us understand why things are the way they are today, and it could help inmates understand the world they live in, whether they're white or black."

Blackmon revealed that chain gangs, as much as sharecropping, were the key to understanding how millions of Black people had been prevented—by force and by violence—from achieving the American dream.

———◆———

Men like Ned Cobb could be found all over Tallapoosa County, Alabama, all over the state of Alabama, and everywhere else in the South. Sharecroppers provided the labor that fueled the South's economy. They received very little in return.

They were trapped. Trapped by the white men who owned the land. Trapped by Jim Crow. Sharecropping seemed like a way for poor people to make a living; in reality, it was a system designed by white people to steal from Black workers like Ned Cobb.

The only way to keep white people from stealing from Ned was to stay out of debt—yet staying out of debt was almost impossible for a Black man who depended on white people for supplies, who paid rent to white landowners, and who sold cotton to white buyers.

No, Ned Cobb wasn't going into debt, because debt was the opposite of freedom. His own father had been born into slavery not far from here, and had worked the land for fifteen years as someone else's property. The Cobbs inherited their last name from an enslaver, but received little else for their years and years of unpaid work. They knew the price and the value of freedom.

That same year, Cobb had met a group of people who felt the same way he did about sharecropping. They belonged to a new, secret organization called the Alabama Sharecroppers Union. The union's goal was simple—to give sharecroppers more of a say in their daily lives, reasoning that, together, they would be stronger than alone. Together, union members might own land or share necessities. They could negotiate for fairer prices from plantation stores. They could stand up for one another.

Opinions such as these were dangerous in Alabama in 1931. Union members had to meet in remote cabins, by lamplight, sharing stories and lessons and dreams for a different future.

"We was taught at our meetins that when trouble comes, stand up for one another," Cobb said. "Whatever we was goin to do, whatever that was, we was goin to do it together."

A rumor was spreading through Cobb's neighborhood that Watson was coming to confiscate his neighbor's livestock— and that Cobb was next. And so, that Monday morning, when Cobb heard that a sheriff's car had rolled up to his neighbor's house, it was time to stand up for what was right.

Cobb had slipped a .32-caliber revolver into his pants pocket. But when he casually approached Deputy Logan, he followed the instructions of his union organizers who warned him to avoid confrontation with white authorities.

"Be quiet, whatever we do, let it work in a way of virtue," Cobb recalled. "They got a song to this effect, did have years ago: 'Low is the way to the bright new world, let the heaven light shine on me.' Low is the way, humble and low is the way for me.

"I tried to go by the union's orders," Cobb said.

"Mr. Logan, please sir," Cobb pleaded, "don't take what he got. He's got a wife and children and if you take all his stuff you'll leave his folks hungry. He aint got a dime left to support em if you take what he's got."

Deputy Logan wasn't having it. "I got orders to take it and I'll be damned if I aint goin to take it," he growled at Ned.

Some of Cobb's fellow union members had gathered in the distance, but as soon as they sensed a showdown brewing between Cobb and the deputy, they scattered into the woods. Cobb was all alone, but he didn't budge. Something had awakened inside him.

Somebody got to stand up, he thought. If he had to do it all alone, so be it.

"Well, if you take it," he said to Logan, "I'll be damned if you don't take it over my dead body. Go ahead and take it."

A Black man didn't speak like that to a white police officer in Alabama, or anywhere at all. Deputy Logan informed Cobb that he had reason enough to kill him on the spot.

Cobb responded, "Well, if you want to kill me, I'm right before you. Kill me, kill me. Aint nothin between us but the air. Kill me."

53

Ned's single-minded determination seemed to cut through the tension in the air. The deputy and his men stopped what they were doing.

"I didn't think about gettin shot and I didn't think about not gettin shot," Ned recalled. "I thought this: a organization is a organization and if I don't mean nothin by joinin I ought to keep my ass out of it. But if I'm sworn to stand up for all the poor colored farmers—and poor white farmers if they'd takin a notion to join—I've got to do it. Weren't no use under God's sun to treat colored people like we'd been treated here in the state of Alabama. Work hard and look how they do you. Look how they done my daddy in his time and look how Mr. Watson tried to do me."

Ned's voice was steady as he spoke to the deputy and his men. His feet were planted on the ground and his gaze fell firmly on Logan.

At last, Logan backed off. But before he drove away, he left Cobb with a final threat: Sheriff Beale, a dreaded, violent man, might return soon in his place. Every Black person in the county knew what Beale was capable of.

"He'll come down there and kill the last damn one of you," Logan yelled. "You know how he is…when he comes in he comes in shootin."

"Go ahead and get Mr. Beale, I'll be here when he comes," Cobb replied coolly. "He'd run up against somebody that weren't scared. If they didn't want me to do nothin to em they oughta just stayed away from there or killed me at the start, on first sight, because I was goin to try em, sure as I was alive."

When the sheriff's reinforcements arrived, they did as Logan had promised—and so did Ned Cobb.

"I just stood right on and I was standin alone," he recalled. "I seed there was weak spots in them men and there was bad acts comin up, but I didn't run a step."

The shooting started almost immediately, bullets and shotgun pellets crisscrossing the yard. Ned drew his pistol and fired back at the posse, forcing them to dive for cover. Ned was shot several times in the legs by a deputy's shotgun blasts.

Just then, more men emerged from the woods near the house, their guns raised. But this time, they were union men who had come back to help Ned. He wasn't alone, after all. One of them dropped to his knee and took aim at the deputies' car, shattering its rear window.

At last, the white men retreated, speeding off in the direction they had come from.

Ned saved his neighbor's livestock and livelihood that day, but the confrontation with Beale's men cost him dearly. Ned and his fellow union members were tracked down by a white posse and ended up in a county jail cell. The union sent a white lawyer from New York to represent him, and sent money to support his family. But in the end, Ned was sentenced to twelve years in prison.

———◇———

On his release from prison, Ned returned home, a free man who had weathered the worst days of Jim Crow. He worked the rest of his years as a poor farmer, knowing full well that white men had stolen his chance at a better life.

"I was born and raised here," he reflected, "and I have sowed my labor into the earth and lived to reap only a part of it, not all that was mine by human right."

In his old age, Cobb met a young historian named Theodore Rosengarten, who traveled all the way to rural Alabama from Cambridge, Massachusetts, to learn more about the Alabama Sharecroppers Union. Rosengarten brought a tape recorder and microphone, hoping to capture a few stories about a time that was quickly fading from memory.

Over weeks of interviews, Ned Cobb cracked open an era that had been erased from the history books and brought back to life a time of intense oppression and a story of astonishing bravery.

"The future days follows the present," Cobb said. "And if we didn't do somethin for ourselves today, tomorrow wouldn't be no different."

In his final act of resistance against white supremacy, Ned Cobb made sure that this chapter of American history was rescued. His story was published in a book titled *All God's Dangers*. Over a century after slavery had officially ended, Cobb's electrifying testimony revealed how sharecropping had stalled the hopes and dreams of so many Black people—and explained why so many of them remained poor, in the wealthiest country on earth.

IN THE summertime, the city of Richmond, Virginia, gets hot—sometimes really hot. A record-breaking heat wave in 2019 sent people scurrying into emergency shelters and racing to hospital emergency rooms with life-threatening heat-related illnesses. The temperature that summer reached ninety-nine degrees. Extreme heat killed four people in a single week.

Similar episodes happen all over the United States, as the effects of climate change bear down on America's sweltering cities.

Some neighborhoods in Richmond, however, got much hotter than others. Concrete, asphalt, and other heat-trapping materials concentrate the sun's rays, especially when there are no trees or parks to fend off and dissipate the heat. The number of people who live in a neighborhood can make it hotter, too, especially when houses or apartment buildings are close together.

In the months following Richmond's lethal heat wave, researchers made a startling discovery about the city's hottest neighborhoods: All of them were majority African American. And when they compared these neighborhoods' boundaries to the city's maps from the 1930s, they were precisely the same. Not only did Richmond's Black community live within historically segregated neighborhoods, but these same places were also the least healthy and the most prone to the damaging effects of climate change.

The segregated places where many Black people live can be magnets for pollution and illness. They attract extra attention from the police, regardless of actual crime rates. Home values are often lower, and this results in lower tax revenues that may be spent on schools and basic social services. Long after Jim Crow's credentials were revoked, African American people have felt the burdens of inequality where they live.

Some white people still argue whether Black neighborhoods exist by accident or choice. But history shows that laws, racism, and outright violence created America's racial maps—and its racial walls.

Dr. Ossian Sweet in 1925.

CHAPTER FIVE

★ ★ ★

DR. OSSIAN SWEET
Breaks Through the Color Line to Find a Home in Detroit

In 1925, a young Black doctor named Ossian Sweet purchased a home in a Detroit neighborhood that was, until that moment, 100 percent white.

That Ossian could buy the brick bungalow at 2905 Garland Street was something of an accident. Had his new neighbors, the police, or the Detroit city government known in advance, they would never have allowed it.

Ossian had seen with his own eyes what white people were capable of. As a five-year-old child in East Bartow, Florida, he hid in the tall grass and watched in horror as a group of white men chained sixteen-year-old Fred Rochelle to a tree, doused him in kerosene, and burned him to death while hundreds of white neighbors jeered. The smell and the sights of that nighttime lynching still haunted him.

As a teenager, Ossian studied. He worked. Nights and

weekends, washing dishes and shoveling snow—whatever it took to pay the $118 yearly tuition at Wilberforce University in Ohio, where his parents had sent him as a thirteen-year-old. And then a door opened: Howard University, a prestigious historically Black institution in the nation's capital, offered Ossian a plum spot in its prestigious medical school. He accepted, moved to Washington, and studied even harder.

Four years later, in 1921, Ossian became Dr. Sweet.

Ossian Sweet could have made a comfortable living as the only Black doctor in East Bartow. But he refused to go back to Florida, which was the land of lynchings and Jim Crow.

Instead, Ossian joined the Great Migration of Black people who voted with their feet against white supremacy. They headed to New York, Cleveland, Detroit, and Chicago, cities that seemed to promise a kind of freedom that was unheard of in the Deep South. Freedom to walk down the street, unbothered. Freedom to keep their family secure from poverty. Freedom to make a home.

From 1910 onward, six million African American people left the South, pursuing these freedom dreams.

As he passed through the ornate main hall of Detroit's Michigan Central Station in the summer of 1921, however, Ossian sensed immediately that freedom in the North meant something different for Black people. Suspicious white policemen eyed the new arrivals. The station's visitors' aid desk made sure they got on the right buses and streetcars—the ones leading straight to the city's "colored" neighborhoods. And although jobs were plentiful, Black people always ended up in the lowest-paid positions.

The Motor City welcomed Black people's cheap labor but resented their presence.

Ossian settled in a neighborhood known as Black Bottom, four square miles of narrow streets lined with buildings that looked as if they had not been repaired in decades. White landlords charged sky-high rents for living quarters without running water or indoor bathrooms. Some rooms were rented not by the day but in eight-hour shifts, just long enough for a man to flop down and sleep before heading out again to look for work. Tuberculosis, influenza, and other lethal diseases swept through basements, attics, and sheds jammed with entire families. Forty thousand people called it home.

The young doctor looked around and immediately saw a need that he could fill.

Ossian had arrived in Detroit with only two hundred dollars in his pocket. For a one-hundred-dollar investment, he persuaded the owner of Palace Drug Store to let him set up shop. It was a good bet. Patients soon began streaming into Dr. Sweet's storefront office, and his modest fees slowly filled his bank account.

He earned enough to set aside a little money, and he hoped to start a family of his own. In 1922, he married Gladys Mitchell, the daughter of a respected middle-class Black family. The Sweets even traveled abroad, to Paris, where in 1924 Gladys gave birth to a baby girl named Marguerite Iva.

Just one thing was missing. Outside of Black Bottom, neat rows of houses stretched for miles, evidence that white families were building a future denied to most Black people. Ossian yearned for a clean, respectable house of his own, a safe haven for his family, a property he could pass on to his children someday.

He and Gladys had saved almost $4,000 as a down payment. But from the moment they started looking for a home, they ran into an invisible racial wall.

First, real estate agents simply turned the Sweets away, informing them that no houses were available for sale. In a sense, the agents were telling the truth: The deeds to most homes in Detroit included restrictive "covenants" that forbade owners from selling them to Black people. A typical deed in 1925, for example, proclaimed that "this property shall not be used or occupied by any person or persons except those of the Caucasian race."

Only two decades earlier, local laws had done the work of enforcing housing segregation in American cities. In Baltimore, for example, it was illegal for any Black person to move into a neighborhood where more than half of the residents were white. The Supreme Court declared these laws unconstitutional in 1915; after that, private racial covenants kept segregation alive and well behind the scenes.

More than 80 percent of all homes in Detroit used racial covenants to exclude Black buyers. And the city was in no way unique. All over America in the 1920s, racial covenants made it impossible for Black people to purchase real estate and move up the economic ladder.

As a safeguard in case racial covenants didn't do the job, the city's real estate trade association established the rule that no agent could sell a home in a white neighborhood to an African American.

Black neighborhoods in the North were becoming like prisons—created, walled off, and policed by white people. In a part of Detroit called Eight Mile, one real estate developer in 1941 went so far as to build an actual wall—six feet high and a foot thick—separating Black and white residents.

Ossian had run out of hope when, in the spring of 1925, an opportunity walked through the front door of his office.

One of Ossian's patients, a white woman named Marie Smith, heard that he was shopping for a home. Smith was married to a Black man who passed as white, allowing the couple to live unbothered in their all-white neighborhood. She offered to sell their attractive house to the Sweets in a private deal, so that no real estate agent had to be involved. The Smiths' asking price was quite a bit higher than what a white buyer would pay. What's more, because no bank would lend Ossian and Gladys money to purchase the home, they would have to arrange to make payments directly to the Smiths, with interest far higher than the going rate.

In all, this "racism tax" amounted to over 25 percent of the market value of the bungalow. But Ossian and Gladys knew it might be their only chance. In June of that year, they signed a contract to purchase their piece of the American dream.

———◇———

The streets around Garland Avenue buzzed with gossip well before the Sweets arrived. "Negroes" had been spotted on the porch of the bungalow on Garland Avenue. Had a Black family actually purchased it? Flyers appeared on telephone poles: The newly formed "Waterworks Park Improvement Association" would hold a meeting in the local school to discuss the situation.

"It just isn't right," one neighbor complained of Ossian and Gladys's decision to move in.

Ossian and Gladys weighed the risks of antagonizing their new neighbors. In nearby Lansing, Michigan—just one example of thousands of similar attacks—white men set Earl Little's house ablaze while his wife and four young children slept inside. Earl had purchased the home without realizing that its mortgage contained a racial covenant; his traumatized family escaped with their lives but lost everything else. Earl's four-year-old son, Malcolm, carried the memory of that night with him for the rest of his life.

In Chicago, Illinois, white residents firebombed the homes of Black people *every month* between 1917 and 1921.

White racial resentment reached a boiling point that summer. Ku Klux Klan membership in Detroit spiked to an all-time high as thousands of white people openly signed up for the white supremacist group. The brightly lit red letters

"KKK" shone over its downtown headquarters. In July, more than ten thousand Klansmen rallied in their white robes, cheering as a speaker condemned the "Negro invasion" of the city.

Ossian worried that Klansmen might be lurking among his new neighbors, too.

Still, he refused to be intimidated. "We have decided we are not going to run," he remarked to one of his colleagues.

What Ossian didn't realize was that in the weeks leading up to the Sweets' move, anonymous callers rang Marie Smith's phone at night, threatening to "kill the n——" and dynamite her house. The Waterworks Park Improvement Association even offered to buy the house from Marie Smith directly, but her asking price of $30,000 was more than they could afford.

When the time came to move into their new home, Ossian brought along his two brothers and a half dozen friends to spend the first few nights with him and Gladys, as a precaution. "We're not going to look for any trouble," Ossian said, "but we're going to be prepared to protect ourselves if trouble arises." Along with the furniture they hauled up the stairs on September 8, the men had stashed guns and ammunition.

To everyone's surprise, the first night in their new home passed without incident. Ossian wondered if his worst fears had been overblown.

Garland Street was quiet all afternoon. As dinnertime approached, however, Ossian found Gladys standing motionless at the kitchen sink. He knew right away that something was wrong.

A friend had just rung Gladys on the phone. Earlier that day, she overheard a white woman talking on a streetcar that ran along Charlevoix Street, just around the corner from the house. "Some n——s have moved in and we're going to get rid of them," the woman said. "They stayed there last night but they will be put out tonight."

The quiet outside reminded Ossian of the eerie silence before a lynching in the South. He rushed through the house, pulling down window shades and instructing everyone to prepare for the worst.

As the sun went down, Ossian could hear voices rising and falling through the side streets and alleyways. His brother Henry peered through one of the shades.

"My God," Henry said, "look at the people!"

Neighbors had appeared on their porches and gathered on lawns. An angry crowd formed along Garland Avenue that to Ossian seemed to grow larger and more menacing by the minute.

And then, somewhere in the house, a window shattered, sending the terrified occupants diving for cover. More rocks thudded against the roof and walls. As Ossian and his friends watched through the windows, the angry mob surged toward the house.

From the upper floor of the bungalow, the crack of a rifle cut through the darkness. A former coal miner named Leon Breiner fell on his nearby porch, bleeding to death;

another shot wounded Eric Houghberg in the leg. More bullets whizzed through the darkness. The crowd, enraged and confused, held back. Policemen on the street braced themselves for more violence—which never came.

———◇———

Ossian Sweet feared many possible outcomes when he decided to purchase his new home on Garland Avenue. Waking up in a Detroit jail cell on Thursday, September 10, was not among them. The police charged Ossian Sweet, his wife, his brother, and seven close friends with murder in the first degree. As it turned out, the saga of his home purchase had only just begun.

The national office of the NAACP got wind of Sweet's arrest and sent one of its most senior members to investigate. Walter White—a crusading NAACP journalist who had gone to great lengths to expose lynch mobs across the South—met with Ossian in prison and sent word to the NAACP headquarters that Sweet's case represented a crucial test for equal rights for Black people. In response, NAACP president James Weldon Johnson decided not only to provide Ossian and his codefendants with legal counsel but to hire Clarence Darrow, the most famous trial lawyer in the United States, to defend them.

Were it not for the NAACP, the trial of Ossian Sweet and his codefendants might have gone unnoticed—and all would likely have been convicted and sent to prison. Instead, it made front-page news around the country.

The leaders of the fledgling civil rights movement understood what was at stake in the Sweet case. America was growing into an industrial powerhouse, its cities expanding, drawing in millions of migrants and immigrants from overseas. Would Black people benefit from the promise of upward mobility? Or would their dreams be strangled in racial ghettos and segregated neighborhoods?

Over eight months and two trials, Clarence Darrow made sure that America understood that white racism, not Ossian Sweet, should be on trial in that Michigan court.

In his closing remarks to the jury, Darrow's deep voice echoed through the courtroom. "I insist that there is nothing but prejudice in this case," he declared, adding, "that if it was reversed and eleven white men had shot and killed a black while protecting their home and their lives against a mob of blacks, nobody would have dreamed of having them indicted.... They would have been given medals instead."

Finally, on May 13, 1926, the jury in *The People v. Henry Sweet* issued its verdict: not guilty.

Ossian Sweet's victory was a turning point for the NAACP, as well. Thanks to the publicity surrounding it, the organization was able to raise enough money to establish a legal defense fund for African Americans. The NAACP Legal Defense Fund went on to support the most important legal cases of the civil rights movement, and remains to this day one of the staunchest defenders of equal rights for Black people.

Rather than solving the problem of racial segregation in Detroit, however, the trial only managed to shine a light on how deeply entrenched it had become.

Once the fanfare settled, it became clear that the verdict in *The People v. Henry Sweet* left only the slightest dent on the city's racial walls. As more and more African Americans—including one of the authors' parents—trekked from the Jim Crow South to the Motor City searching for even a half-baked freedom, white Detroiters (and indeed, white Americans everywhere) kept up the fight to keep Black people out of their neighborhoods. They succeeded, for the most part. And when Black Americans moved up the economic ladder, white people fled to the suburbs, where they reestablished the same boundaries that stood for so long inside the city limits. In neighboring Grosse Pointe, real estate agents developed a point system for home buyers, rating them on such categories as religion, accent, and "degree of swarthiness." The point system automatically rejected "Negroes" and "Orientals"; it remained in place until 1960, and to this day, Grosse Pointe is almost 100 percent white.

Detroit itself remains the most segregated city in the United States.

For decades after Ossian Sweet's trial, white America continued the dirty work of forcing Black people into segregated neighborhoods, in places as varied as Boston, Chicago, Seattle, Kansas City, and Los Angeles. The effects of this segregation reverberated through time, as Black buyers were mostly excluded from the benefits of owning homes and prevented from transferring housing wealth from one generation to the next.

Those few Black families who did succeed in buying homes were the exception and not the rule. Their number has increased, especially after the Civil Rights Movement helped outlaw overt housing discrimination. Some areas today, such as Mitchellville, Maryland; Baldwin Hills, California; and Uniondale, New York; have thriving Black communities, and individual Black people and families have integrated some towns and cities across the United States. But the broad pattern of Black places and white places—a direct legacy of Jim Crow—remains etched in the map of America.

———◇———

For Ossian himself, tragedy at home overshadowed acquittal in court. Gladys contracted tuberculosis while in jail and passed it to their baby daughter, who died a short time later. Gladys herself never fully recovered, and passed away from the disease in 1927, at only twenty-seven years of age.

The couple had stayed away from Garland Avenue, and the house at 2905 remained boarded up until Ossian returned there to live alone, following Gladys's death.

In 1958, a tired and aging Dr. Ossian Sweet finally sold his home of thirty-three years, without fanfare. The buyers were migrants from the South, a young Black family seeking a new home away from Jim Crow.

★ ★ ★

KAMALA HARRIS'S mother offered her this advice: "You don't let people tell you who you are. You tell them who you are." It was wise counsel for a young Black girl born in the 1960s, someone who would find herself labeled with false assumptions about her capabilities, how she should act, and how far she could go.

Even after graduating from Howard University, becoming a lawyer, and getting elected to public office in California, other people's doubts piled up around Kamala. "But I didn't listen," Kamala remembered.

Kamala ignored the doubters and set her sights on bigger things. District attorney of San Francisco. Attorney general of California. And finally, in 2016, the United States Senate— the first Indian American, and only the second Black woman ever to hold that post. On January 20, 2021, Kamala Harris, the daughter of Indian and Jamaican immigrants, was sworn in as vice president of the United States.

Kamala Harris always understood that neither race nor gender alone fully explained the hurdles she faced.

"Where there's no name for a problem," the scholar Kimberlé Crenshaw remarked, "you can't see a problem, and when you can't see a problem, you pretty much can't solve it." American history is full of examples of this unnamed problem, which trapped Black women inside a place where race and gender discrimination intersected. Crenshaw decided to name this problem, and its potential resolution, *intersectionality*. Today, many people use this term, and Crenshaw's ideas, to talk about and fight back against the unique forms of systemic inequality faced by women of color.

Throughout American history, Black women have played leading roles in the quest for equality. But their struggles were not always recognized as equal contributions—and their battles were not always the same as those of Black men. The additional barriers they ran into, as women, gave them a deep understanding of how inequality functioned in America, and helped them sharpen the tools to fight against it.

Pauli Murray in 1950.

Note: Pauli Murray used *she/her/hers* pronouns when writing about her life, and we choose to follow her decision here. As many of Pauli's biographers have explored, she grappled with gender identity throughout her life at a time when such questions were banned from public discussion. You can read about Pauli's fascinating and inspiring life in the work of such scholars as Brittney Cooper, Rosalind Rosenberg, Patricia Bell-Scott, and others.

CHAPTER SIX

★ ★ ★

PAULI MURRAY

Discovers the Key to Ending Segregation in Schools

When she was twelve years old, Pauli Murray traveled alone from Durham, North Carolina, to Baltimore, Maryland, to attend her father's funeral.

William Murray's corpse lay in an open casket. Pauli peered in and saw her father's head "split open like a melon and sewed together loosely with jagged stitches." He had been murdered in the basement of the Crownsville Hospital for the Negro Insane, beaten to death with a baseball bat by a white guard.

For the rest of her childhood, Pauli Murray conducted a silent protest against Jim Crow. She would walk rather than ride a segregated train or bus, and go hungry rather than eat at a segregated lunch counter.

The one segregated institution Pauli could not avoid was school. Since the dawn of legal segregation a quarter century earlier, educational progress for Black children had stalled. "Colored" schools in North Carolina were often rickety, drafty buildings where Black teachers were paid half of what white teachers earned. But in a twist of fate, Durham's "colored" public high school had been destroyed by fire when Pauli was beginning the eighth grade. It was rumored among Black people that the only way the conditions of segregated schools improved was when they burned down—and Durham's Black business community in the Hayti neighborhood still had enough clout to demand that the city build a brand-new and spacious building, just in time for Pauli's freshman year.

Hillside High School attracted some of the South's best African American teachers, and unlike most high schools for Black students (which ended at the tenth grade), it went all the way through the twelfth grade. Pauli thrived there, and when she graduated, she wanted more.

She adamantly refused to attend a segregated college. In 1926, that meant heading north to New York City.

Still, getting into and through college wasn't easy. Only a handful of Black women ever made it this far, even in the North.

Her first choice was Columbia, but it was closed to women; nearby Barnard College accepted women but was far too expensive. She settled on Hunter College, but learned that her high school credits weren't sufficient for admission, so she had to spend a year taking classes at Richmond Hill

High School in Queens. There, she was the only African American among more than four thousand students.

Pauli finally entered Hunter just as the Great Depression plunged the nation into a decade of poverty. She worked several low-wage jobs to cover the tuition. To save on rent, she slept on a cot in the laundry room of a hotel where she worked. She later shared a room above a funeral parlor. One year she ate so little that she lost fifteen pounds. A sympathetic administrator at Hunter gave her secondhand clothes.

Through sheer, stubborn effort Pauli eked her way to graduation. She had weathered racism, gender discrimination, and an empty bank account, but in the end, exhausted and exhilarated, Pauli Murray earned a college degree. Now the question was: what next?

———◇———

It had been almost forty years since new laws forced racial segregation onto trains and buses, restaurants and hotels, and above all, schools. But in the early 1930s, lawyers from the NAACP started chipping away at these legal building blocks, hoping that the racial wall could be toppled.

Victory in the Ossian Sweet trial convinced some that the NAACP ought to go after discriminatory housing laws. Others pushed for anti-lynching legislation, to protect Black people from white mobs. But the NAACP's talented new legal adviser, Charles Hamilton Houston, saw opportunity in attacking segregation in schools.

Houston assembled a dream team of Black lawyers, including William Henry Hastie Jr., who would later become the first Black man appointed to the federal bench, and the young Thurgood Marshall, who, after Hastie was passed over by John F. Kennedy in 1962, would be successfully nominated by Lyndon Baines Johnson in 1967 to serve as the first Black justice on the US Supreme Court. They had been children when legal segregation was born, and they aimed to see it end in their own lifetimes.

Houston and Marshall drove thousands of miles through back roads and segregated towns, searching for just the right case to pursue—one they knew they might win. Marshall would steer a "little old beat up '20 Ford," while Houston typed legal documents on the back seat.

Theirs was a perilous mission. The South was hostile territory for anyone talking about civil rights, let alone well-dressed Black lawyers intending to file lawsuits to overturn one of the pillars of white supremacy.

Finally, with the help of local NAACP representatives in St. Louis, they met a Black man named Lloyd Gaines, who had attempted to enroll in the University of Missouri's law school but was rejected because he was Black. Gaines not only had a stellar academic record but also had no other option in his home state because there were no law schools for African Americans in Missouri. If Missouri couldn't provide Gaines with a separate legal education, the NAACP legal team reasoned, then it had to admit Lloyd Gaines to the state's only law school.

Houston and Marshall filed their case and took it all the way to the US Supreme Court. And they won.

Pauli Murray raced through a newspaper article dated December 12, 1938, describing how Black lawyers had breached the wall of segregation for the first time since *Plessy v. Ferguson*.

It was the beginning of the end, Pauli thought.

The *Gaines* victory suddenly cracked open different possibilities for the future. Previously, Black students eager to pursue professional careers had few opportunities, and all of them—for doctors, lawyers, dentists, or professors—were segregated. Now a new world seemed to unfold ahead of them.

Pauli had just applied to study at the graduate school of the University of North Carolina at Chapel Hill. Because the state offered no comparable schools for Black students, the *Gaines* ruling by the Supreme Court offered Pauli an unexpected ray of hope.

Two days after the *Gaines* decision by the Supreme Court, a letter arrived in Pauli's mailbox.

Dear Miss Murray:

I write to state that I am not authorized to grant you admission to our Graduate School. Under the laws of North Carolina, and under the resolutions of the Board of Trustees of the University of North Carolina, members of your race are not admitted to the University. It has long been the social policy of the State to maintain separate schools for the whites and Negroes.

The letter to Pauli might have seemed an accident of bad timing: after all, the admissions office surely hadn't had enough time to learn about the *Gaines* decision. But it signaled that the South wasn't going to let one Supreme Court case clip the wings of Jim Crow overnight. Far from it. News about the *Gaines* decision spread like wildfire across southern colleges and universities, none of which was willing to admit a single Black student. *Gaines*, it turned out, was the beginning—not the end—of the battle to end legal segregation in America.

Pauli Murray would play a key role in this epic, twenty-year-long fight.

Pauli knew that segregationists wielded the law as a weapon of inequality, and she watched in awe as civil rights lawyers reforged it into a tool for positive change. She had wondered about becoming a lawyer herself. But what law school would ever admit a Black woman?

The year after she was refused admission to UNC, Pauli Murray gave an impromptu speech at a church in Virginia, trying to raise money for the legal defense of a sharecropper who had been accused of murder—and who faced an almost certain death sentence. In the audience that day was Leon Ransom, the famed civil rights lawyer and professor at Howard University. Ransom was so impressed with her speech that he invited Pauli to apply to Howard's law school.

In 1941, Pauli Murray traveled to Washington to attend Howard "with the single-minded intention of destroying Jim Crow."

Howard, whose law school served as the unofficial nerve center of the legal campaign to end segregation, was an exhilarating place for an aspiring civil rights lawyer. At a time when the NAACP pursued new cases all over the country, NAACP lawyers would visit the school to test their arguments, inviting law students to challenge and refine their strategies. Pauli had found an intellectual home.

Howard was also where Pauli ran head-on into a new kind of inequality. "Ironically," she said, "if Howard Law School equipped me for effective struggle against Jim Crow, it was also the place where I first became conscious of the twin evil of discriminatory sex bias, which I quickly labeled Jane Crow."

Pauli was the only woman in a classroom full of men, constantly having to prove herself better, smarter, and more able. She endured sexist jokes and social exclusion. Which form of discrimination hurt her more? Pauli wasn't always sure whether her greater enemy was Jim Crow or Jane Crow, or other, sneakier antagonists who sometimes claimed to be her allies in the struggle for equality.

But no one questioned her intelligence, least of all her professors. Pauli ranked first in a class filled with some of the smartest law students of her generation.

In her final year at Howard, Pauli found herself in a heated class discussion, as always, with a room full of men.

Suddenly, in "a flash of poetic insight," Pauli interrupted her classmates with an argument that, although no one could have guessed it on that day in 1944, quietly shifted the course of civil rights history.

The NAACP pushed too hard on the "equal" side of the "separate but equal" doctrine, Pauli proposed to her skeptical classmates.

Fighting to get better facilities for Black people missed the point, she said. It was like trying to fix the effects of segregation without going after the cause. And the cause, she pointed out, was separation itself—the act of segregating African Americans and treating them differently in the first place. Until they fixed this problem, civil rights activists would never achieve true equality for Black people.

"One would have thought I had proposed that we attempt to tear down the Washington Monument or the Statue of Liberty," Pauli recalled. "First astonishment, then hoots of derisive laughter, greeted what seemed to me to be an obvious solution."

Pauli had gotten used to her classmates' reactions by that point, and she dug in. "Opposition to an idea I cared deeply about always aroused my latent mule-headedness," she said.

Separate was never equal, Pauli insisted. Separate, on its face, discriminated against Black people because separate meant that Black people were somehow different. Racism fed off this very idea. In her heart, in her gut, Pauli knew that calling some people "different" was at the root of America's thorniest problems.

Plessy had to go. Black people needed nothing short of full equality, the equality promised to all citizens in the Fourteenth Amendment to the Constitution.

Pauli made a ten-dollar bet that day with her professor, a young legal scholar named Spottswood Robinson. *Plessy v. Ferguson*, she told him, couldn't survive another twenty-five years.

Robinson gladly accepted what he assumed would be an easy wager. Pauli's final paper that semester, her last in law school, explored her arguments in greater detail.

———◇———

Pauli Murray's legal argument turned out to be ahead of its time—a decade, to be exact.

Several years later, a new group of lawyers led by Thurgood Marshall huddled together day after day, preparing their final attack on racial segregation in America. Marshall had recruited Spottswood Robinson of Howard University to join the team that was preparing arguments and evidence in the Supreme Court case of *Brown v. Board of Education of Topeka, Kansas*.

Recalling his ten-dollar bet with Pauli, Robinson managed to locate her final paper in his file cabinet. Pauli Murray's insistence that separate schools are by definition unequal directly shaped the arguments that Marshall, Robinson, and their colleagues would take to the Supreme Court in 1954.

Though it made no mention of her, Pauli Murray's ideas

had found their way into the landmark case that ended legal segregation in America:

> We conclude that, in the field of public education, the doctrine of "separate but equal" has no place. Separate educational facilities are inherently unequal. Therefore, we hold that the plaintiffs...are, by reason of the segregation complained of, deprived of the equal protection of the laws guaranteed by the Fourteenth Amendment.

———◇———

Pauli didn't learn about her direct impact on *Brown v Board of Education* until many years later, long after her career had taken unexpected turns. In her final weeks at Howard, Dean William Henry Hastie Jr. encouraged her to apply to Harvard University for a year of graduate legal study, believing that she could later return to Howard as a professor herself.

Harvard's response to her application echoed earlier disappointments.

"Your picture and the salutation on your college transcript," the letter read, "indicate that you are not of the sex entitled to be admitted to Harvard Law School."

Incensed, Pauli Murray skewered the admissions committee in the letter she sent back several days later.

"Gentlemen," she wrote, "I would gladly change my sex to meet your requirements, but since the way to such change has not been revealed to me, I have no recourse but to appeal to you to change your minds on this subject. Are you to tell me that one is as difficult as the other?"

Pauli stuck to her quest to achieve equality for all people, regardless of race or gender. Her journey took her to Africa, to Yale University, and even to a fateful collaboration with Ruth Bader Ginsburg—the future Supreme Court justice—where the two lawyers forged new arguments about women's equality, based on the experiences of the Black freedom struggle.

In 1964, the same year that Kamala Harris was born in California, Pauli Murray was once again working behind the scenes, shaping the most important law ever passed in support of equal rights for all Americans. Pauli helped make sure that the Civil Rights Act of 1964 included women in its ban on job discrimination, alongside race, color, religion, and national origin. That section of the law, known as Title VII, was the first time that women were taken seriously as victims of discrimination. Ginsburg called Murray "one of the premier legal minds of the 20th century who is often not credited."

Black girls and women today still struggle to overcome the barriers that Pauli Murray faced a century ago. According to the activist and writer Monique W. Morris, Black girls face extra levels of discipline and punishment in schools, where teachers and administrators often try to push them out rather than nurture their futures. Asking too many questions in class can cause a Black girl to be called disruptive—when a white girl would be credited with being curious. Even infractions as simple as dress code violations can invite harsh, sometimes violent responses. "It's not about what they did," Morris says, "but rather, the culture of discipline and punishment that leaves little room for error when one is Black and female." And different, racially motivated treatment can haunt Black girls and women through high school, college, and beyond.

The pioneering work of Black women such as Pauli Murray, Kimberlé Crenshaw, and Monique Morris has kept the struggle for equality alive, in courtrooms, workplaces—and schools. They have given all Americans the tools to cut through the thick woods of discrimination, and to make sure that women like Kamala Harris are the first of many.

IN 1936, a Black woman named Mary Pherribo purchased a house in North Carolina with a $500 down payment. Such a real estate purchase was rare for African Americans in a region—and a country—that conspired to push down Black people at nearly every turn. But Pherribo's small success rippled across the decades. "It's proof that you can change the entire line of your family's story," her granddaughter said, in July of 2020. "My father and my uncle own multiple properties, and pretty much everyone in my family owns a home and has gone to college because of her decision."

Owning a home is how most wealth gets passed from parents to children; it's how the past shapes the future. But for most of the past century, Black people could not purchase real estate, whether they could afford to or not.

From 1930 to 1960, the number of Americans who owned their homes doubled. During that same period—even as the struggle for Black freedom made enormous gains—few Black families could join that giant leap forward in the nation's wealth. The outcome of this history is on display in every city and town in America, even if we may not always recognize it. While almost 75 percent of all white families own their homes, fewer than 45 percent of Black families do.

Racial discrimination blocked people of color from getting home mortgages and accumulating wealth. But this discrimination would never have been possible without the support of laws and government policies. The scholar Ira Katznelson has called this "affirmative action for white people."

Daisy Myers looks out at the crowd gathering in front of her home, August 1957.

CHAPTER SEVEN

★ ★ ★

DAISY MYERS

Integrates the White Suburbs

On the day she moved into her new home, Daisy Myers met the mail carrier, who mistook her for a maid.

"Did you see how he looked?" Daisy remarked to her husband, Bill. "He looked ill."

Upon realizing that a Black family had moved into the tidy little house at 43 Deepgreen Lane in Levittown, Pennsylvania, the shocked mail carrier promptly spread the word to the Myerses' neighbors, all of whom were white. The other homes in Levittown—all 17,500 of them—were owned by white people, most of whom were startled to learn that a Black family had somehow managed to integrate their hometown.

William Myers, Daisy's husband, had met several of his new neighbors before purchasing the property for $12,150 with the help of a sympathetic real estate agent and a homeowner willing to resell his house to a Black family. They seemed to William like nice people.

Levittown was a model suburb, boasting row after row of affordable homes. The town fitted the Myerses' ambitions to a T. "We are church-going, respectable people," William said. "We just want a nice neighborhood in which to raise our family and enjoy life." Daisy taught school nearby, and William, a World War II army veteran, worked as a refrigeration engineer at a company in Trenton, New Jersey. With three young children and middle-class jobs, they were indistinguishable from their new neighbors in most respects. Except that, of course, they were Black.

Trouble arrived on the Myerses' doorstep almost immediately.

On their move-in day, the Myerses' neighbors formed a Levittown Betterment Committee and collected hundreds of signatures on a petition "protesting the mixing of Negroes in our previously all-white community." The local evening newspaper ran the headline, "First Negro Family Moves into Levittown."

By the end of the day, August 13, 1957, white Levittown's protest got louder.

"I expected some trouble, but I never thought it would be so bad," William Myers said. Daisy recalled the scene vividly:

> About 4:30 PM trouble began to brew...small knots
> of people...soon grew into crowds. Traffic increased

and in the next hour automobiles crept bumper to bumper by our house.... Brakes screeched frightfully as drivers stopped suddenly to stare and jammed traffic behind them. Some men stood around passively with their hands in their pockets, but others gestured vigorously as they talked with venomous expressions. As they moved closer and tempers rose, we could hear their rumbling chatter. They were upset and curious, but seemingly reasonable at this stage. Then cars began parking, heavy traffic continued, and the crowd, increasing in size and noise, began to get nasty.

By nightfall, a crowd of people five deep had gathered on the Myerses' front lawn. "They were banging the mailbox," William recalled, "throwing rocks through the windows and lighted cigarettes against the house."

Daisy remembered her shock at the first window shattering in her new home. "The rock, weighing less than an ounce, carried tons of hatred with it," she said.

———◇———

Almost thirty years had passed since an angry mob pelted Ossian Sweet's bungalow in Detroit. For Black people, this ugly scene seemed to repeat itself again and again. Attacks on Black homeowners skyrocketed in the years after World War II—a war fought in part by hundreds of thousands of Black soldiers, to make the world safe for democracy. In 1947 alone, in the city of Chicago, forty-seven Black homes were firebombed when African American families attempted to move into, or even *close* to, white neighborhoods. When a Black bus driver named Harvey Clark tried to rent an apartment in all-white Cicero, for example, a crowd broke in, threw his belongings out the window, and set them on fire. The police stood by, doing nothing. Clark himself was later indicted by a grand jury "for inciting a riot and conspiring to lower property values" in Cicero. His attackers were let off the hook.

For white Americans, in contrast, finding and buying a decent home had become much easier.

A few years into the Great Depression, President Franklin Delano Roosevelt created the Home Owners' Loan Corporation, to help unemployed people struggling to pay their mortgages. HOLC offered homeowners new, low-interest loans that could be paid back over a long period, with low monthly payments. The program saved millions of homeowners from foreclosure.

HOLC created detailed, color-coded maps of every city in the United States. Green areas were low risk, and red areas were high risk. If you lived in a red area, you could not get help from HOLC.

On every single HOLC map, African American neighborhoods were marked as red. "Redlining," as this practice came to be known, excluded Black people from one of the most important financial rescues in all of American history.

The federal government then widened the gap between Black and white even further. In 1934, Roosevelt created the Federal Housing Administration, or FHA, to help *first-time* home buyers. At a time when the vast majority of Americans had no ability to purchase something as expensive as a house, FHA loans were easy to get and required small monthly payments over many years.

For people with modest salaries, an FHA loan was the ticket to the American dream. The FHA had only one requirement: "No loans will be given to colored developments," it declared.

FHA loans would be available only for white borrowers.

A few years later, when World War II ended, these same FHA loans helped fuel the biggest housing boom ever, and with it, a new kind of racial segregation in America. Returning war veterans—including thousands of Black soldiers—came back eager to start new families and new lives. Home builders responded with thousands of new housing developments. The federal government made all of this possible. "By 1948," according to one expert, "most housing nationwide was being constructed with this government financing."

Hundreds of thousands of new, single-family homes sprung up almost overnight, as a nation of cities transformed quickly into a nation of suburbs. And government rules made sure that all these homes were for whites only.

The FHA, moreover, policed its whites-only requirement vigorously. A white man in Berkeley, California, purchased a new home with an FHA loan. When he temporarily rented the house to an African American teacher, the homeowner was investigated by the FBI and permanently ejected from the FHA program. On Long Island, New York, two white renters in FHA-financed homes were evicted for the offense of allowing two Black children to play on their lawn.

Black veterans found themselves systematically excluded from housing benefits.

No house built with US government support, according to the FHA, could be "sold, leased, rented, or occupied by any other than those of the Caucasian race."

FHA loans helped people with modest incomes and little savings make the leap into homeownership. Thanks to the US government, owning a home became a reality for millions of white Americans in the 1940s, '50s, and beyond. The federal government's housing loan program created America's white middle class.

But while construction crews, dump trucks, and excavators transformed huge swaths of open land into leafy suburban towns, redlining ensured that most Black people remained stuck in the same overcrowded and crumbling neighborhoods.

Between 1947 and 1953, in the area around Philadelphia, where the Myerses had lived, developers built 120,000 new homes to keep up with the overwhelming demand. Only 357 of these were made available to Black buyers.

A similar pattern of barring African Americans from purchasing homes repeated itself across all of the United

States. The lack of adequate housing for Black people was becoming a national crisis.

———◆———

The Myers family made it through the first night in their new home unharmed. They got to work cleaning, fixing the windows, and unpacking their moving boxes.

Just to be safe, William drove their three children to stay with their grandparents.

Each day for the next seven days, the crowd outside the Myerses' home grew larger and more menacing. On the fifth night, more than five hundred people gathered outside their home, and a local police officer was knocked unconscious by a rock hurled by one of the white protesters. By the end of the week, several thousand jeering Levittown residents were gathering on Deepgreen Lane each night.

A local political leader called on the Myerses to "go back where you came from," blaming them, not the hostile white mob, for the turmoil.

Police officers stood guard around the clock.

Day after day, newspaper reporters from around the country showed up to tell the story of the northern town that seemed to be behaving very much like one in the segregated strongholds of the Deep South.

Daisy and William had moved to Levittown hoping that it would be a place they could call home. Now, with each passing day, they feared for their personal safety.

But it turned out that not everyone in Levittown objected

to the Myerses' presence. One neighbor, Lewis Wechsler, made a point of visiting the Myerses each night in a show of support. Wechsler's white neighbors rewarded him for his bravery by burning a cross on his front lawn, and painting the letters KKK on the side of his house.

"People brought us food very often," Daisy said. "All kinds of fruit and food and flowers. One woman came from another section of Levittown one day and offered to clean up the house for me." Daisy took calls all day long from supporters around the country, including the novelist Pearl Buck and baseball star Jackie Robinson.

These few supporters helped the Myerses endure constant harassment over the fall of 1957. Their phone would ring again and again, all through the night, but the callers would hang up. A neighbor purchased a new dog and named it N——, shouting its name as he took the pet for walks in front of the Myerses' house. Other neighbors occupied an empty house next door and dubbed it the Dogwood Hollow Social Club, blaring loud music at all hours.

Most surprising of all, perhaps, was the behavior of Daisy and William themselves. They simply stayed put, going about their lives as best they could.

Refusing to be intimidated, William took to weeding the flower beds on the front lawn with his army bayonet.

"Nothing whatever will prevent me from living in the house," William said. "I bought the home and I intend to live there."

Over time, the Myerses' stubborn courage attracted

attention well outside of Levittown itself. At the end of the year, officials from the state of Pennsylvania intervened, issuing an injunction against any Levittown resident harassing the Myers family.

The threat of legal action put an end to the protests, and life for Daisy and William became something like normal.

The calm came in the nick of time. "We were reaching the lowest ebb in our personal determination," Daisy said. "We had tried desperately to maintain a spirit of love for our tormentors. . . . In a way we had succeeded, but we needed the outside stimulus of effective law enforcement."

Others had taken note of the Myers family, too. Soon after the protests had settled down, Daisy and William joined a friend at a dinner in Philadelphia, where an admirer was waiting to meet them. The young Reverend Martin Luther King Jr. had heard all about their struggles and was eager to shake the couple's hands.

Daisy would later be shocked to learn that she earned the nickname "the Rosa Parks of the North", after the NAACP activist in Montgomery, Alabama, whose refusal to give up her bus seat to a white passenger had triggered the Montgomery bus boycott.

Daisy and William never considered themselves activists. "Sooner or later," Daisy concluded, "I know we will be accepted for what we are—for ourselves."

In the long quest for housing equality, individual acts of courage made sure that America couldn't turn away from the shame of segregation in the North. Still, they weren't enough. The full weight of government programs—that allowed so much real estate to be accumulated by whites only—left millions of Black people far behind.

But the Myerses' actions had a ripple effect far beyond Levittown. In January 1966, Martin Luther King Jr. and the Southern Christian Leadership Conference decided to take the Civil Rights Movement north to Chicago, launching what they called the Chicago Freedom Movement. Their goal: to open up the city's rigidly segregated neighborhoods to African American people. King argued that "the moral force of SCLC's nonviolent movement philosophy was needed to help eradicate a vicious system which seeks to further colonize thousands of Negroes within a slum environment."

"If we can break the system in Chicago," King announced, "it can be broken any place in the country."

King and his fellow activists planned demonstrations and marches all through the spring and summer of that year. In July, a huge rally at Soldier Field attracted almost forty thousand people in support of the movement's goals.

But much of the city's large white population remained adamantly opposed to integration, and the tide began to turn against King.

In August, during a march through an all-white neighborhood on Chicago's West Side, white counterdemonstrators hurled bricks and stones at King and his fellow protesters. As King crossed Marquette Park, the crowd chanted, "Kill him!" A rock struck King on the head and knocked him to the ground. "I have seen many demonstrations in the South," King said, "but I can say I have never seen—even in Mississippi and Alabama—mobs as hostile and as hate-filled as I've seen here in Chicago."

By 1967, King acknowledged that his movement had hit a solid wall of resistance in America's third-largest city.

A white assassin murdered King on the balcony of the Lorraine Motel in Memphis, on April 4, 1968. The outrage following the murder helped push Congress to pass the Civil Rights Act of 1968, which is also referred to as the Fair Housing Act. For the first time in the nation's history, this legislation made it illegal for anyone to discriminate against a home buyer or a renter on the basis of race.

The effects of redlining, however, have been difficult to reverse.

"We have created a caste system in this country, with African-Americans kept exploited and geographically separate by racially explicit government policies," writes Richard Rothstein, a journalist and author who exposed the white-washed history of America's racist housing system, in a book titled *The Color of Law.* "Although most of these policies are now off the books, they have never been remedied and their effects endure."

In America today, neighborhoods that were redlined by HOLC in the 1930s remain overwhelmingly African American. Some experts even refer to them as "hypersegregated," because they are *more* segregated by race than they were in the 1930s and '40s.

Near the end of her life, Daisy Myers reflected on what had changed, and what had not. "We had realized years ago, to our sorrow," she said, "that the housing market, above all else, stands as a symbol of racial inequality."

OVER THE COURSE of his life, George Floyd was stopped by the police nineteen times.

George Floyd didn't need statistics to know that to be a Black person in America means living under an intense amount of extra scrutiny by the police. Pulled over, questioned, detained, followed, harassed: Individual stories would fill a library. A Harvard professor arrested on his own front porch, suspected of burglary. A district attorney—whose job it is to prosecute criminals—handcuffed and arrested in Washington, DC, for a crime he didn't commit.

George Floyd experienced the worst of it when he was arrested at gunpoint in Minneapolis on May 25, 2020. His crime? Allegedly passing a counterfeit twenty-dollar bill. The owner of the store where he allegedly passed the fake bill later admitted that most offenders don't even realize they're using counterfeit money. The police officer pushed Floyd to the ground and kneeled on his neck, pressing down hard.

"I can't breathe!" Floyd gasped, again and again. Nine minutes and twenty-nine seconds later, George Floyd was dead.

By the end of the year, police across America had killed 311 Black people. Many thousands more were stopped or arrested on the faintest pretext.

Today's news headlines are the tip of a deep iceberg. A turbulent history of police brutality against Black people roils beneath the surface of the present. And for more than a century, African Americans have been fighting to expose and put an end to it.

Malcolm X speaking at a rally in Harlem,
New York City, June 29, 1963.

CHAPTER EIGHT

★ ★ ★

MALCOLM X
Launches a Struggle
Against Police Brutality

The three white police officers pounded on the Black man, Reece Poe, their nightsticks flailing in the late-afternoon air. It was April 29, 1957, in New York City. The commotion at the corner of Lenox Avenue and 125th Street, the very center of Harlem, attracted three passersby, two of whom were members of the Nation of Islam's Temple No. 7.

"You're not in Alabama," one of the men yelled at the police officers. "This is New York."

For as long as anyone in Harlem could remember, the police had treated Black people as second-class citizens. Attacks and intimidation by police officers were commonplace. According to one Harlem resident, "Police brutality has been the mode in Harlem for years. The nurses and staff at Harlem Hospital see the bloody results daily."

Just a few blocks away from where the police assaulted

Reese Poe, two white policemen had shot and killed an unarmed Korean War veteran named John Derrick several years earlier. Derrick was still wearing his uniform as he lay bleeding on the sidewalk. Adam Clayton Powell, a Black congressman who represented Harlem, said of the shooting: "We don't call them that, but we do have lynchings right here in the North."

On this day, though, some Harlem residents took a stand.

Another man, Hinton Johnson, who called himself Johnson X, stepped forward and asked, "Why don't you carry the man on to jail?"

Outraged, a police officer charged at Johnson and knocked him to the ground in front of a swelling crowd of witnesses.

A young woman who saw the attack rushed to a nearby restaurant to get help. A short time later, Minister Malcolm X of Temple No. 7 arrived at the 28th Precinct House, where the police had dragged the four men, including a badly injured Hinton Johnson.

"I went in," Malcolm X recalled, "as the minister of Temple Seven, and demanded to see our brother."

The police refused at first, not knowing what to make of this demanding minister who spoke with such authority. But as the crowd outside the police station grew, the police finally allowed Malcolm to visit Johnson inside.

"When I saw our Brother Hinton, it was all I could do to contain myself," Malcolm said. "He was only semi-conscious. Blood had bathed his head and face and shoulders." Johnson told Malcolm that after being taken to the precinct, the police officers continued their brutal beating in a cell.

Malcolm X was outraged. "I told the lieutenant in charge, 'That man belongs in the hospital.'"

Born in Omaha, Nebraska, in 1925, Malcolm X—born Malcolm Little—had not yet become a household name in America. His life had taken a bumpy path since the night in 1929 when he witnessed his house set on fire by white men seeking to drive his family out of Lansing, Michigan. He was now a minister in the Nation of Islam, a religious group of Black American Muslims that had established temples wherever large numbers of African Americans made their home. Malcolm had already earned a reputation as an eloquent speaker, someone who understood the struggles of Black people in the North. On that evening, Harlem also learned that Malcolm X could be a fearless leader in the quest for freedom.

Outside of the station house, Malcolm X had been joined by rows and rows of neatly dressed Black Muslims, who stood in silent formation. Their presence was like nothing the residents of Harlem had ever seen. Soon, a crowd of onlookers grew to several thousand people.

"I said that until he was seen, and we were sure he received proper medical attention, the Muslims would remain where they were," Malcolm recalled.

With Malcolm X serving as a negotiator between the angry crowd and the nervous police, an agreement was struck to send Hinton to Harlem Hospital, where he would be treated and then returned to the precinct.

Later that night, Malcom X motioned to the assembled Muslims with a single hand gesture. Moving with military precision, they pivoted and marched away as stunned police commanders looked on.

The next morning's headline in the *Amsterdam News*, a local Black-owned newspaper, proclaimed: "God's Angry Men Tangle with Police."

"Harlem's black people were long since sick and tired of police brutality," Malcolm later wrote. "And they never had seen any organization of black men take a firm stand as we were."

With the help of Temple No. 7, Hinton Johnson filed a lawsuit against the New York Police Department and eventually received a payment of $70,000. It was the largest settlement ever awarded, up to that time, for a police brutality case.

The doctors who treated Hinton Johnson later revealed that he had barely survived, with a fractured skull and a brain hemorrhage. Under normal circumstances—in the United States, in 1957—he should have died. A brutal police attack on a Black man in the largest African American neighborhood in New York City was not unusual. What *was* unusual was that a court of law held them accountable this time.

In the 1950s and '60s, the world's attention focused on the epic battles for civil rights taking place in the South, in places like Birmingham, Alabama, and Nashville, Tennessee. Black people in the North, however, understood that racism and anti-Black violence weren't limited to the former states of the Confederacy. Hinton Johnson's run-in with the police could have happened in Boston, Detroit, Chicago, Seattle, Oakland, or Los Angeles. Sometimes, though, it seemed that the North got a free pass when it came to racial inequality.

"Our war against oppression in the North is often like a battle against evanescent shadows," one Northern civil rights activist remarked. Restaurants and movie theaters in the North didn't post WHITES ONLY signs. Black people could ride public transportation freely and they could vote without being harassed. Instead, racial discrimination happened in ways that attracted less attention outside of Black neighborhoods, from inferior schools and crowded, decrepit housing, to companies that refused to hire or promote African American workers.

The Harlem-born writer James Baldwin, describing the experience of Black migrants to the North, argued that they "do not escape Jim Crow: they merely encounter another, not-less-deadly variety." That "variety" most often took the form of racist policing.

The same year that Hinton Johnson nearly died in police custody, the Detroit Chapter of the NAACP launched an investigation of police brutality in the Motor City. Its findings shocked even those Black Detroiters accustomed to daily harassment by the police.

Black Detroiters described how police would stop them for no reason and go through their pockets, wallets, and purses. Officers would even go inside people's homes without a warrant.

Examining case after case of police-brutality incidents, the NAACP listed the most common complaints leveled against the Detroit Police department:

- "Racial slurs."

- "Assault of friends or relatives who try to protect a person being attacked by police officers."

- "Illegal search and destruction of property in private homes."

- "Abuse of people wrongly arrested inside precinct stations."

- "Accosting black women on the street and accusing them of being prostitutes."

- "Abuse and intimidation of interracial couples."

- "When citizens question the violation of their rights, the officers resort to physical assault, followed by arrest."

This was a different picture of the police than the one seen by most white people. The police did not ensure public safety or "law enforcement" in Black neighborhoods. They acted more like enforcers of an invisible color line: keeping

Black people segregated, fearful, and aware of their unequal status in America.

Reflecting on his experiences with the Detroit Police Department, Joynal Muthleb commented, "I sometimes wonder if a Negro citizen in the city of Detroit can really claim to be a citizen in the full, true sense of the word."

———◇———

By the early 1960s, the Civil Rights Movement in the South put freedom dreams on the front page and in the front of every Black person's mind. On July 2, 1964, President Lyndon B. Johnson signed the epic Civil Rights Act, which outlawed racial discrimination in schools, workplaces, and public accommodations.

If the world reacted with outrage at the dogs and fire hoses unleashed on Birmingham's protesters, then why should the daily police assaults on the Black residents of New York, Detroit, and Los Angeles go unnoticed?

On July 16, 1964, Harlem offered a new answer to this question, when a ninth-grade boy named James Powell was fatally shot by a New York City policeman. After two days of protests, the neighborhood erupted into violent clashes between Harlem residents and police officers in riot gear, many of them on horseback. Police fired live rounds into the protesters. Running battles rocked the city for four days.

The Harlem "riots" were just the beginning. Similar clashes followed in Rochester, New York; Philadelphia,

Pennsylvania; Newark, New Jersey; and other cities all across the North. One year later, during a routine traffic stop, Los Angeles police beat Rena Price and her two sons in front of hundreds of witnesses. As news spread of the incident, the surrounding neighborhood of Watts exploded in fury. Watts residents battled police and national guardsmen for a week, in scenes resembling actual warfare.

But nothing approached the violence or scale of Detroit, in the summer of 1967. On the night of July 23, police raided a "blind pig"—an illegal after-hours bar—on Twelfth Street and arrested eighty Black Detroiters. Outraged at one more example of aggressive policing, the neighborhood erupted. By the next day, 483 fires blazed across the city. Four days of fighting left forty-three souls dead and thousands more injured. The rebellion ended only when tanks rolled into the city and food supplies began to dwindle.

In all, rebellions rocked 250 American cities between 1964 and 1968. Many white leaders, and much of the national media, focused their attention on the destruction of property and on the behavior of looters. To them, this was about a "crime menace," not about how the police menaced Black citizens on a daily basis. California's Governor Pat Brown, who sent in the national guard to put down the uprising in Los Angeles, called it "guerrilla fighting with gangsters." Brown announced publicly that he would "continue to deal forcefully with the terrorists until Los Angeles is safe again."

Black communities, however, clearly understood the massive wave of uprisings as political acts against a society that routinely brought down violence on innocent Black people of all backgrounds.

The playwright Lorraine Hansberry attempted to explain this to a white audience.

"Can't you understand that this is the perspective from which we are now speaking?" she asked. "It isn't as if we got up today and said, you know, 'what can we do to irritate America?' you know. It's because that since 1619, Negroes have tried every method of communication, of transformation of their situation from petition to the vote, everything. We've tried it all. There isn't anything that hasn't been exhausted."

Malcolm X, more than any other American leader, understood how so many Black people could have chosen the path of open rebellion. "Now we have the type of Black man on the scene today," he said to a crowd in Cleveland, in the spring of 1964, "who just doesn't intend to turn the other cheek any longer."

Speaking to an audience in London, England, in February 1965, Malcolm X called out the hypocrisy of the media's coverage of America's urban rebellions. "Actually," he said, "they weren't riots in the first place; they were reactions against police brutality. And when the Afro-Americans reacted against the brutal measures that were executed against them by the police, the press all over the world projected them as rioters. When the store windows were broken in the Black community, immediately it was made to appear that this was being done not by people who were reacting over civil rights violations, but they gave the impression that these were hoodlums, vagrants, criminals....

"And this is what you're trying to make the Black man do," he continued. "You're trying to drive him into a ghetto and make him the victim of every kind of unjust condition imaginable. Then when he explodes, you want him to explode politely!"

Two weeks later, after he had returned home to America, three Nation of Islam gunmen assassinated Malcom X as he began a speech at the Audubon Ballroom in New York City. A number of historians have suspected police involvement in his murder.

In 1967, with the fires in Detroit still smoldering, President Lyndon B. Johnson commissioned a group of experts to investigate the reasons behind the uprisings in America's cities. After exhaustive research and on-the-spot interviews, the National Advisory Commission on Civil Disorders—dubbed the Kerner Commission after its chair Governor Otto Kerner Jr. of Illinois—published a damning report in 1968, drawing conclusions that were not so different from Malcolm X's own.

"What white Americans have never fully understood but what the Negro can never forget," the report declared, "is that white society is deeply implicated in the ghetto. White institutions created it, white institutions maintain it, and white society condones it."

It ended with an ominous warning to all Americans. "This is our basic conclusion: Our nation is moving toward two societies, one black, one white—separate and unequal."

The rebellions in Los Angeles, Newark, New York, Detroit and other cities sent a message to all Americans: The victories against Jim Crow in the South did not end racism in the United States.

Ever since the days of Malcolm X, the struggle to end unequal law enforcement and police brutality has been the longest-running, unresolved battle for equality in America.

AS NEWS SPREAD of George Floyd's murder, LeBron James decided the time had come to make his move. Off the court, the NBA superstar had already devoted time and money to his community, creating new opportunities for young Black people in his home state of Ohio.

Now he wanted to dig deeper—to get at the root of the problem that resulted in police violence, blocked opportunities, and unequal education.

That root was political power.

"I understand how important our vote is," LeBron explained.

Behind the scenes, forces had been gathering for years, determined to suppress the Black vote. In 2016, the percentage of Black people who voted had fallen for the first time in twenty years. This wasn't by choice or accident. In 2020, voting rights were under attack.

Together with a group of his fellow athletes, LeBron released a statement:

> We are not politicians or policy leaders, and we are not trying to be. Our organization is not here

to tell you who to vote for. As individuals, we may choose to talk about specific policies or candidates, but as a team we came together to focus on one issue this year: systemic racism's impact on our right to vote.

LeBron created an organization called More Than a Vote, dedicated to fighting back against voter suppression.

"Yes, we want you to go out and vote, but we're also going to give you the tutorial," LeBron said. "We're going to give you the background of how to vote and what they're trying to do, the other side, to stop you from voting."

For generations, Black people fought and died for the right to cast a ballot.

"Because a lot of us just thought our vote doesn't count," LeBron says. "That's what they've been taught, that's how they've been educated, that's how they've always felt....But I want to give them the right information, I want them to know how important they can be."

Fannie Lou Hamer at the Democratic National Convention in Atlantic City, New Jersey, August 1964.

CHAPTER NINE

★ ★ ★

FANNIE LOU HAMER

Takes Back the
Right to Vote

Fannie Lou Hamer went to work in the cotton fields of Mississippi when she was six years old.

A white man approached her one day as she played alongside a gravel road in her hometown of Ruleville. If she picked thirty pounds of cotton, he told her, she could come to the local commissary and get some treats. After a week in the cotton fields, Hamer returned to the commissary and the man kept his word.

"But what it was doing was actually setting a trap for me," Hamer said. "'Cause the next week it was sixty. The next week it was seventy. And by the time I was thirteen years old I was picking three and four hundred pounds of cotton."

She was the youngest of twenty children in a family with fourteen boys and six girls. The Hamers were desperately poor and rarely had enough food to go around. A chance to work was a chance to eat—but it also meant that Fannie Lou Hamer spent her entire childhood plucking white cotton bolls with her bare hands, dragging a heavy cotton sack behind her.

Fannie Lou attended school, too, when it was open. In Sunflower County, where Ruleville was located, there were just three school buildings for more than eleven thousand Black students. One teacher in the county had nearly eighty children in her classroom.

Black children in Mississippi went to school for four months a year, so their education wouldn't interfere with working in the fields. Their school textbooks didn't teach about democracy, or voting, or the Constitution; Black children were taught to respect the segregation laws and customs of the state of Mississippi. In the 1950s, a children's book was banned in the state because it showed a brown rabbit and a white rabbit getting married, which violated Mississippi's ban on interracial marriage.

"I had never heard, until 1962, that black people could register and vote," Hamer said.

———◇———

Fannie Lou spent most of her adult life toiling on a cotton plantation in Ruleville. The white family who owned it lived in a big house, where even the dog had its own bathroom. The Black sharecroppers like Fannie Lou lived in shacks with no electricity or indoor toilets.

As the years passed, insults and injuries piled up. Fannie Lou was once rushed to the hospital with stomach pains and underwent abdominal surgery. When she recovered, she learned that the white doctor had sterilized her against her will, an experience so common among Black women that it was dubbed a "Mississippi appendectomy." Involuntary sterilizations were a racist practice forced on Black women, to prevent them from having children; it is likely that doctors performed several hundred thousand of these procedures, without the consent of their female patients.

Rumors of Black people "making trouble," standing up for their rights, seeped into Mississippi throughout the 1950s, but nothing seemed to change in Fannie Lou's life, ever.

She was forty-five years old when she heard about a meeting in a local church, William Chapel, on August 27, 1961. Two organizers from a civil rights organization, the Student Nonviolent Coordinating Committee (SNCC), were there to encourage local Black people to register to vote.

Hamer immediately warmed up to the young men, both of whom were only in their twenties. James Forman had grown up in Mississippi, in such poverty that, as a child, he had sometimes eaten dirt to fend off hunger. Robert Moses was from New York City. He had come to Ruleville because he believed that SNCC had "stumbled on the key—the right to vote."

❖

The majority of the people in Sunflower County were Black, but less than 1 percent of Black people were able to vote. Keeping down the Black vote was the glue that held white supremacy together.

A small minority of white voters chose the sheriffs, mayors, congressmen, senators, and other politicians to control the levers of power, at home and in Washington: They controlled how much money was spent on schools, and what students could be taught. They controlled how much the Black workers who picked cotton got paid (around $600 per year, or just over $5,000 in today's dollars). They controlled where Black people could live. They controlled the police officers who enforced the color line.

If the Black majority in the district could vote, the white minority would lose all that control. And, naturally, white voters had no problems registering to vote at all.

The powerful US senator James O. Eastland owned a 5,800-acre plantation in Sunflower County. One of the Senate's most vocal segregationists, Eastland also blocked any effort in Congress to bring democracy to his home state. Eastland regularly preached against "the illegal, immoral and sinful doctrine of school desegregation." He viewed civil rights activism in the South as "subversive activity." As chair of the Senate Judiciary Committee, Eastland went out of his way to keep civil rights bills from seeing the light of day (he sometimes joked that he would keep them buttoned in his pocket—where they would stay).

The Fifteenth Amendment to the US Constitution, passed during Reconstruction, prevented southern states from openly discriminating against Black voters. Instead, beginning in the 1890s, southern lawmakers made it nearly impossible for any Black person to vote. They created poll taxes (charging people money to cast a ballot), which most Black people couldn't afford to pay, because they were so poor. And they established literacy requirements and other written tests a voter had to pass before being allowed to register. Because white people controlled the registrar's offices (having stolen them after Reconstruction) and graded the tests, it was easy for them to block Black voters behind closed doors. And in state after state, that's exactly what they did.

Not that they had to hide their intentions. South Carolina governor Ben Tillman once announced, "The whites have absolute control of the State government, and we intend at any and all hazards to retain it."

Adding insult to injury, Mississippi also required that a Black person who wanted to register to vote had to be accompanied by a white sponsor.

After the *Brown v. Board of Education* decision, Mississippi doubled down on its commitment to white supremacy. In 1954, the state added a "reasonable interpretation" requirement for anyone wanting to register to vote. Eligible voters were required to take a test on the Constitution of the State of Mississippi, and it was up to the white registrar to judge whether they had passed. The registrars made sure that Black people almost never did.

If tricks like this didn't work, white Mississippians were always ready to resort to violence.

In 1955, a Black minister and NAACP supporter named George W. Lee started encouraging his congregation to register, despite the new hurdles set up by the state. Shortly after, Lee was shot to death while driving down a street in Belzoni, Mississippi. No one was arrested for the crime. The next day, the newspaper headline read, "Negro Leader Dies in Odd Accident."

One white planter in Ruleville declared, "If any of my n——s try to register, I'll shoot them down like rabbits."

The message got through. By the end of 1955, the already-small number of Black voters in Mississippi had dropped by half.

However, by the early 1960s, the democracy movement was spreading quietly across the state's Black Belt counties. Aaron Henry, chair of the Clarksdale NAACP chapter, said that, "The vote won't make Mister Charlie love us, but it will stop him from lynching us!"

———◇———

When the meeting ended that night, Forman and Moses asked for volunteers willing to go to the courthouse to register to vote. Fannie Lou Hamer raised her hand "up as high as I could get it."

On the day she attempted to register to vote for the first time in her life, Fannie Lou Hamer packed a bag. "I had a feeling; I don't know why...I said, 'If I'm arrested or anything, I'll have some extra shoes to put on.'"

Hamer joined seventeen other African American volunteers on August 31, for a twenty-five-mile bus ride to Indianola, the county seat. When the bus reached the registrar's office, some of the volunteers grew afraid. But Fannie Lou Hamer, one volunteer recalled, "just stepped off the bus and went right on up to the courthouse and into the circuit clerk's office."

Men with guns stood nearby, menacing the arrivals as they descended from the bus. "I guess if I'd had any sense I'd-a been a little scared," Hamer said.

"What do you want?" the courthouse clerk demanded of Fannie Lou.

"We are here to register," Hamer replied.

The clerk informed them, without explanation, that he would allow only two of the eighteen people to register. Fannie Lou Hamer was one of them.

First, she was required to copy a section from the Constitution of the State of Mississippi , word for word, with no punctuation errors. Then the registrar asked her to provide a "reasonable interpretation" of the section.

"That was impossible," Fannie Lou recalled. "I had tried to give it, but I didn't even know what it meant, much less to interpret it.

"In fact," she said, "the first time I was aware that Mississippi had a constitution was when I tried to register to vote."

Hamer and her traveling partners returned to the bus for the trip back to Ruleville. Not a single person had been allowed to register. But Fannie Lou didn't let the experience break her spirit. "From the back of the bus," one of the SNCC volunteers recalled, "this powerful voice broke out in song. The voice was Mrs. Hamer's. With the power of her voice alone she shored up everybody on the bus."

Fannie Lou soon learned that standing up for herself came at a cost.

Hamer had picked cotton for eighteen years on a plantation owned by W. D. Marlow, a white planter who owned Hamer's house as well. When she returned home, Marlow confronted Fannie Lou.

"You'll have to go down and withdraw your registration," he ordered her, "or you'll have to leave this place."

But Fannie Lou wasn't going to be turned around. "I didn't go down there to register for you," she said. "I went there to register for myself.

"This seemed like it made him madder when I told him that," she later recalled.

Marlow threw Fannie Lou off the plantation—and out of her house—for good. A neighbor, Mrs. Tucker, took Fannie Lou and her family in until they could find a new place to live.

Ten days later, a car passed by the Tuckers' home in the

middle of the night and riddled it with gunshots. No one was injured, but if the attackers intended to scare Fannie Lou off, they had the opposite result.

"There was nothing they could do to me," she reflected. "They couldn't fire me, because I didn't have a job. They couldn't put me out of my house, because I didn't have one. There was nothing they could take from me any longer.

"The only thing they could do to me was to kill me," she said, "and it seemed like they'd been trying to do that a little bit at a time ever since I could remember."

She felt strange—and free.

"Now I can work for my people," Fannie Lou Hamer decided.

Fannie Lou Hamer didn't give up trying to register to vote. She studied the Mississippi Constitution and on December 4 of that year beat the country registrar at his own game—becoming only the fourth Black person in all of Ruleville to register.

Fannie Lou also discovered that her example, and her powerful singing voice, could inspire other people like her to join the new movement for democracy in Mississippi. In no time at all, she become one of its leaders.

"You know the ballot is good," Fannie Lou said to a crowd in Indianola. "If it wasn't good, how come he trying to keep you from it and he still using it?"

In June 1963, sheriff's deputies pulled Hamer from a bus near Winona, Mississippi, as she was traveling home from a voter-education workshop. They tossed her in a dank jail cell. For an entire night, they forced a prisoner to beat her with a blackjack, and abuse her sexually, until she was barely conscious.

Hamer was badly injured but undeterred. "If them crackers in Winona thought they'd discouraged me from fighting," Hamer said, "I guess they found out different. I'm going to stay in Mississippi and if they shoot me down, I'll be buried here."

The more Mississippi's white supremacists tried to take her power, it seemed, the stronger she became.

In 1964, the sharecropper's daughter stood before the Democratic National Convention to demand that it allow representatives from the Mississippi Freedom Democratic Party (which she had cofounded) to help select the next Democratic candidate for president of the United States. Her stirring testimony was broadcast later that night on national television and shone a bright spotlight on Black voters in the South.

Fannie Lou Hamer now had a national stage—and she had helped set into motion a movement that would transform her home state, and the entire South.

Following Hamer's example, SNCC activists and Martin Luther King's Southern Christian Leadership Conference began a massive campaign in Selma, Alabama, to register Black voters. Their grassroots pressure pushed the white power structure to its limits and forced it to reveal to the world the ugly violence that kept white supremacy in place.

During that campaign, in nearby Marion, Alabama, a white police officer murdered voting rights activist Jimmie Lee Jackson, who was trying to shield his mother from a police baton. Outraged at Jackson's murder, SNCC leader John Lewis led a protest march over Edmund Pettus Bridge in Selma on Sunday, March 7. Alabama State policemen brought the march to a halt with a brutal assault on the marchers, earning that day the nickname "Bloody Sunday." (Many years later, as a US congressman, Lewis wrote about these experiences in his three-volume graphic novel, *March*.)

Martin Luther King Jr. organized a new march in Selma two days later and sent a message to clergy from around the nation to join him. James Reeb, a white Unitarian minister from Boston, flew to Selma that very evening and marched with King and hundreds of other protesters on Tuesday. The day after the march, three white men clubbed Reeb to death after he finished dinner at a local restaurant.

Less than a week later, President Lyndon B. Johnson addressed the US Congress, urging it to pass a new Voting Rights Act, which would guarantee voting rights to all citizens. In his speech, Johnson declared that "what happened in Selma is part of a far larger movement which reaches into every section and State of America. It is the effort of American Negroes to secure for themselves the full blessings of American life."

In the space of four years, people like Fannie Lou Hamer

forced the US government to do something it had steadfastly avoided: to extend the right to vote to all Americans.

President Johnson signed the Voting Rights Act into law on August 6, 1965. The law prohibited barriers to voting such as poll taxes and literacy tests, and made it easier for all people to register to vote. In addition, whenever southern states wanted to pass new laws related to voting, they had to apply for "pre-approval" from the US Department of Justice, to ensure that equal voting rights were protected.

The Voting Rights Act did not simply hand Black people the right to vote. In the months and years after its passage, local people fought, voter by voter, county by county, to be represented.

Voting was hard. Voting was dangerous. In a place where white people had spent decades threatening and intimidating Black voters, going to the polls took determination and courage.

But in the face of constant violence, Black people registered to vote by the thousands. In January 1965, no Black person was registered to vote in Lowndes County. By Christmas of that year, *half* of all voters in the county were African American.

A revolution was happening in Lowndes County, in the states of Alabama and Mississippi, and all across the South. The number of Black registered voters in Mississippi increased from 10 percent of the voting age population to 60 percent. In the South, more than a million Black people registered to vote in the years immediately following the Voting Rights Act.

———◇———

White militias stole the vote from Black people in the South after Reconstruction. Almost ninety years later, Black people fought and died to get it back. Over the next decade, they made good on that victory: The number of Black registered voters grew by 1.2 million people, and these voters installed Black people in offices that had been all-white since the nineteenth century, including mayors, sheriffs, school boards, judges, and more. In 1965, in all of the South, there were only 72 Black elected officials; ten years later, there were 1,588.

For the first time since Reconstruction, when Mississippi sent two African American US senators to Washington, African Americans had regained control over their political destinies. They had defeated white supremacy—at least temporarily—and grabbed the reins of American citizenship. It was a defeat white southerners never forgot, and they quickly brushed themselves off and started devising new schemes for keeping the Black vote down.

But for now, at least, time was on the side of democracy.

In December 1964, Hamer spoke at Williams Institutional CME Church in Harlem alongside Malcolm X, almost exactly two months before his death, in February

1965. "And you can always hear this long sob story," she said. "'You know it takes time.' For three hundred years, we've given them time. And I've been tired so long, now I am sick and tired of being sick and tired, and we want a change."

"YOU ONLY GOT in because you're Black."

"She's an upper middle-class white girl from the suburbs. There's no way she'll get accepted."

For Black people, college-admissions talk can seem like a world turned upside down. As spring approaches each year and high school seniors wait for their acceptance letters, a subtle brand of racism seeps into school hallways and social media threads.

The mere presence of Black students in an incoming college class is seen as evidence that something has been denied to white applicants. But here's the truth of the matter: While it's common to hear about Black people having unfair advantages, the reality is that African American students are still catching up, after a long history of total exclusion. Most of the advantages have fallen in the laps of their white classmates.

Until recently, most colleges and universities admitted whites only. Those official barriers fell in the 1960s after generations of struggle, but many informal—and no less real—hurdles keep Black and brown students away. College recruiters focus on the top high schools. Wealthy, mostly white "legacy" applicants (the children of alumni) receive preferential treatment. The courses required for college admissions, and the preparation needed for standardized tests, are often lacking in the high schools where Black students are in the majority.

The idea—the myth—that Black people take spots reserved for whites was born during segregation, when white people fought violently to keep African Americans out.

James Meredith walks to class at the University of Mississippi, accompanied by US Marshals, on October 1, 1962.

CHAPTER TEN

★ ★ ★

JAMES MEREDITH

Integrates the University of Mississippi

"Which one is Meredith?"

Mississippi governor Ross Barnett's voice crackled over the reporters and officials pressed into the tenth-floor lobby of the Woolfolk State Office Building in Jackson. His sly comment was not lost on the crowd. As the onlookers snickered in response, the only Black man in the crowd stood quietly, staring calmly ahead.

James Meredith had come too far to let a racist joke ruffle him. That morning alone, he had flown in a small plane from New Orleans to Jackson, accompanied by a US marshal and a lawyer from the US Department of Justice named John Doar. Planes from the Mississippi Highway Patrol buzzed their flight mid-air, and once they landed, the police carefully tracked their movements; rumors had reached Meredith that the police hoped to arrest him on any false pretext.

A crowd of two thousand jeering anti-integration protesters waited for them outside.

Meredith wasn't a politician, a movie star, or a famous civil rights activist. But he had the full attention of the US president and the governor of Mississippi. He arrived in the state capital that morning in September 1962 to accomplish one simple goal: to register for college.

In the eight years since the Supreme Court declared segregation unconstitutional, southern schools had fought tooth and nail to resist integration. In 1957, President Dwight D. Eisenhower had to send in armed federal troops to protect Black teens as they entered Little Rock Central High School in Arkansas. Two years later, Virginia announced a program of "massive resistance" to integration; in Prince Edward County, the school board refused to give any money at all to public schools that admitted Black children, opting to close the entire school system rather than integrate.

In 1960, having returned home to Mississippi after two tours of duty in the US Air Force, James Meredith decided that he would be the first Black person admitted to Ole Miss, Mississippi's fabled flagship university.

Located just outside of the small city of Oxford, Ole Miss was the pride of white Mississippi. Its bucolic campus, lined with white-columned buildings and manicured grounds, seemed a world away from the Attala County Training School that Meredith had walked miles to attend as a teenager.

Built by the enslaved, and reminiscent of an antebellum plantation, Ole Miss was the training ground for the state's business and political elite. It's where you went to school if you hoped to get ahead in Mississippi, which was precisely James Meredith's plan.

As a public school, Ole Miss was paid for by the state's taxpayers. As it was a segregated institution, 43 percent of those taxpayers couldn't send their children there. The same was true across the South, where only a tiny handful of Black students had managed to force their way through the segregated gates. Meredith, a military veteran who had served his country with distinction, wasn't ready to accept that disparity.

"If America isn't for everybody, it isn't America," James said.

When word leaked out that Meredith had applied to Ole Miss, white Mississippians responded as though one man were threatening their entire civilization.

"Some misguided people ask what difference it makes if only a few Negroes go to a white school," a newspaper article in Meridian, Mississippi, commented. "The difference is that the first Negro is only the opening wedge for a flood in time to come. Massive integration will mean future intermarriage. Intermarriage in the South, where we are so evenly divided white and colored, means the end of both races as such, and the emergence of a tribe of mongrels."

Mississippi's leaders did everything they could to whip

up a political storm around James Meredith, hoping he would simply go away. But something about Meredith's personality seemed perfectly suited to this particular civil rights battle. He was incredibly calm—and he was very, very stubborn.

Predictably, Ole Miss rejected Meredith's application.

With the help of the NAACP, Meredith filed a lawsuit to force the university to admit him. It didn't go well: First, they lost in federal court in Mississippi and then lost their appeal to the US Court of Appeals in New Orleans. But Meredith's lawyers, Constance Baker Motley and Derrick Bell, believed that Mississippi was denying Meredith his fundamental right to equal protection under the law. When they finally took their case to the US Supreme Court, the justices agreed— and, on September 10, 1962, they affirmed his right to attend Ole Miss. Bell, one of the architects of Critical Race Theory more than two decades later, said that he "learned a lot about evasiveness, and how racists could use a system to forestall equality." He also said that he "learned a lot riding those dusty roads and walking into those sullen hostile courts in Jackson, Mississippi. It just seems that unless something's pushed, unless you litigate, nothing happens."

By prevailing in the nation's highest court, Meredith had changed the rules of the game. To refuse him entry to Ole Miss meant defying federal law—which was enforced by the US Justice Department, and ultimately by President John F. Kennedy himself. Kennedy, a Massachusetts-born liberal, had little interest in leading the way in the fight for equality, but he had publicly committed himself to civil rights. Civil rights protesters were making front-page news every week; caving in the face of a cranky, obstructionist governor of a segregated state would ruin the president's image among northern voters.

Neither Governor Barnett nor President Kennedy relished this particular face-off, but thanks to Meredith, they couldn't avoid it. As a result, Meredith now found himself nose to nose with the rabidly segregationist governor of his home state.

Barnett, in the words of *Time* magazine, was "as bitter a racist as inhabits the nation." He wore his trademark black suit and a homburg hat, a look that inspired some critics to compare him to a mortician.

"The good Lord was the original segregationist," Barnett proclaimed. "He made us white, and he intended that we stay that way."

With news cameras whirring and radio stations broadcasting the episode to the crowd below, the governor faced Meredith and read aloud from a prepared document:

> I, Ross R. Barnett, Governor of the State of Mississippi...do hereby finally deny you admission to the University of Mississippi.

"Gentlemen, my conscience is clear," Barnett said.

A defeated Meredith made for the elevators. Policemen

outside had to protect him from the crowd, which was chanting Barnett's name. People danced on the sidewalk.

"We don't want you, n——" someone yelled. On this morning, it seemed that the entire state of Mississippi was bent on stopping one Black man from going to school.

As Meredith's car broke away from the mob, a protester kicked it. A young woman chased after it, screaming.

At that moment, Meredith caught sight of a group of Black women in the distance.

"I waved at them as we pulled away from the light," he later recalled. "They were all common folk, my people, maids still in uniform and common laborers, but the enthusiasm, the friendliness, and above all, the pride that they displayed in contrast to the hostile and painful attitude of the whites,...were overwhelming. This was what I was fighting for, and I had my reward in the brief seconds that I saw my unknown friends on that corner."

Meredith had feared that the day's outcome might go against him. Only three years earlier, a decorated Korean War veteran named Clyde Kennard had attempted to enroll at the University of Southern Mississippi. The police arrested Kennard on trumped-up charges—of stealing chicken feed—and a judge handed him a long sentence at the notorious Parchman Farm prison, built on the grounds of a former slave plantation. The authorities released Kennard when they realized that he had developed cancer while in prison. He died soon afterward. Since then, no Black person had attempted to breach the color line at a Mississippi college.

That night, Meredith received a phone call from Attorney General Robert Kennedy, the brother of the US president.

"It's going to be a long, hard, and difficult struggle," Kennedy told Meredith, "but in the end we're going to be successful."

"I hope so," Meredith replied.

The next day, Meredith and his advisers from the Justice Department decided to try again, this time at the Oxford, Mississippi campus itself. A dozen federal marshals reinforced their number. They would not use violence, but they counted on Mississippi authorities not to risk assaulting any federal officials.

Nobody expected a warm welcome, of course: Students had "lynched" a James Meredith dummy, hanging it from a lamppost with a sign that read HAIL BARNETT. OUR GOVERNOR WILL NOT BETRAY MISSISSIPPI. One man commented to a news reporter, "We got some boys around here that would just love to come in and shoot" Meredith.

Things got off to a bad start. A long line of policemen, standing shoulder to shoulder, blocked the entrance to Ole Miss.

Doar stepped forward and insisted on their right to go ahead. "We want to take Mr. Meredith in under the directions of the federal court and have him registered," he said.

Governor Barnett wasn't present that morning, because his plane had been delayed by fog. In his place, Lieutenant Governor Paul Johnson refused to let Meredith onto the campus. Johnson read aloud from the same prepared document Barnett had read the day before.

Doar grew impatient. "We think we are going in now," he said. He and his men surged forward with Meredith just behind them, pushing into the police, looking for a break in the line. The two groups pushed and pulled, neither backing down but no one wanting to be the first to start a fight.

One of the US marshals squared off with Johnson, the two men shoving and arguing.

"Are these men acting under your authority, physically preventing us from going in?" Doar demanded to know, exasperated.

"They are," Johnson said.

Once more, Mississippi segregationists succeeded in blocking Meredith from integrating Ole Miss. A cheer went up among the policemen and onlookers.

"The state of Mississippi had clearly shown its intention not only to threaten to use violence, but to use it," Meredith later wrote. "In the face of this direct challenge, the federal government had no choice but to act to enforce its authority."

Faced with open rebellion by the state of Mississippi, President John F. Kennedy reluctantly decided that it was time to act—and that more men and more firepower were needed to break the stalemate. Kennedy met with his generals and approved a plan that put thousands of national guard troops and even regular army units within striking distance of Oxford. At one point in the planning, his advisers even discussed sending in an entire Marine Corps division—a force large enough to subdue a small country.

For the first time since the end of Reconstruction in 1877, the federal government aimed to step in, with military force, to enforce the civil rights of a Black citizen.

On September 30, an advance guard of five hundred federal marshals took up positions around the Lyceum in the center of campus. They were an intimidating presence, with riot helmets, tear gas grenades and launchers, and sidearms.

But as the afternoon wore on and evening approached, hundreds and then thousands of angry students and other onlookers started milling about, hurling threats. With night falling, the crowd outnumbered the marshals several times over.

Rocks and bottles pelted the nervous marshals. The mob grew more brazen, lighting fires and shattering windows. The marshals fired tear gas canisters to drive the attackers back, but this just made them more furious.

Inside the Lyceum, US Deputy Attorney General Nicholas Katzenbach learned that because of poor communications, federal reinforcements were several hours away.

And then, as darkness and tear gas enveloped the campus,

the pop of rifles and the boom of shotguns tore through the night. Troopers fell, bloodied; a journalist covering the riot was found dead in the shrubbery, a bullet through his back.

Another reporter described "the cacophony of battle— explosions, shots, crashes, yells—thunders outside. Twelve marshals lie broken and suffering along the blood-spattered corridors inside, nearly obscured now and then in the swirling clouds of tear gas. Others are collapsed, weeping inside their gas masks."

From the roads leading toward Oxford, reports streamed in of armed caravans from Alabama and Louisiana heading toward campus. Segregationists from all over the South were descending on the small city of Oxford, Mississippi, ready to do battle.

Late that night, a deputy informed Katzenbach: "That's not a riot out there anymore. It's an armed insurrection."

The fighting raged all night long.

When hundreds of armed military policemen finally arrived in the wee hours of the morning, the protesters retreated. By daybreak, thousands more rumbled into Oxford on army trucks, fanning out across the campus and the city with fixed bayonets, as helicopters whirred overhead. Eventually, an occupying force of more than twenty thousand troops brought calm to the university.

The rioters never figured out that Meredith had been secreted into his dorm room through a side entrance to the university, flanked by armed guards. He spent the night sleeping, occasionally hearing the popping of gunfire, the chanting of the crowds, and the muffled explosions of tear gas canisters.

At 9:00 the next morning, federal officials and armed guards escorted James Meredith to the university registrar's office to enroll him as a student. They passed shattered windows and bloodstained hallways. Bricks and other debris covered Ole Miss's historic central campus.

When James Meredith stepped into his first classroom that same day—a course on the history of the United States—armed marshals guarded the classroom.

Ole Miss's student body saw to it that he would suffer in other ways. Someone posted flyers around the school that called for completely shunning Meredith. "Let no student speak to him, and let his attempt to 'make friends' fall upon cold, unfriendly faces," it read.

When a group of students decided to join Meredith for dinner, they returned to ransacked rooms that night, with the words N—— LOVER scrawled on the wall in shoe polish.

He couldn't go anywhere without someone calling him n——.

Meredith's seventy-one-year-old father, Moses Meredith, journeyed to Oxford for James's college graduation in August of the following year. Moses's own father had toiled most of his life as an enslaved person in Mississippi, and now Moses's son was earning the state's most prestigious degree.

"I'm proud just to see a man get an education. That's all he ever asked for," Moses said.

It took the full weight of the US military to enroll one Black person at the University of Mississippi.

A statue on the campus of Ole Miss commemorates James Meredith's bravery and his role in opening the campus to a new generation of Black students. Meredith forced open a door, but it never swung open fully.

The battles that followed at colleges and universities across the South were quieter but no less important; each school had its first, followed by small groups of Black students who carved paths for those that followed. Their number grew slowly. White people tried to block their presence on campus from the beginning, their arguments morphing from opposition to integration, to complaints about the supposed unfairness of affirmative action.

But today, it is white students who benefit from affirmative action, through legacy preferences in admission, attending better-resourced high schools, and getting access to financial benefits that make going to college—and staying in college—possible. The myth of racial admissions preferences hides the reality that most Black students still struggle for equal access to higher education. Many are simply left behind.

Anthony Carnevale, an expert who studies higher education, argues that colleges and universities today actually make racial inequality worse, not better. Instead of closing the gap between Black and white people, colleges and universities are actually widening it. Because such a small percentage of Black people attend the best schools, they are "running faster but losing ground."

"We had slavery, Jim Crow, the failure to hand out forty acres and a mule; we had housing policy, veterans' policy, redlining. The new culprit is higher education," he said. "In the end higher education is part of the problem, not part of the solution."

THE LITTLE PROTEST took place on a Monday, outside the state house in Raleigh, North Carolina.

The police arrested seventeen people that morning of April 29, 2013. One of them was the pastor of a church in Goldsboro, in the eastern part of the state. Though tall and strong, Reverend William Barber hunched over and walked slowly, with a cane. A debilitating form of arthritis made it painful for him to move, yet somehow he radiated energy.

Earlier that year, the North Carolina legislature and governor had launched a radical program aimed at changing the way the state government functioned. They cut taxes for the wealthy, reduced programs for the poor, slashed funding for education, threw up hurdles to voting, and even repealed the Racial Justice Act of 2009, which allowed death row inmates to challenge their convictions if they could prove that racial bias was involved.

To Barber, all this was connected: It was part of a plan to roll back the gains of the Civil Rights Movement.

He wasn't surprised at the arrests. "What did surprise me," he recalled, "was the outpouring of support we witnessed as we came out of jail early that next morning. After watching our arrests on the news, hundreds of people called, emailed, and even came down to the jail to ask what they could do to help. It seemed as if our small faith act had sent a spark into a powder keg."

So Reverend Barber scheduled a second protest for the following Monday. And the Monday after that. Several weeks later, more than nine hundred people showed up and were arrested—and more and more arrived each week.

Barber decided to call their weekly protest "Moral Mondays."

Less than a year later, in February 2014, tens of thousands of people gathered in Raleigh, in the largest civil rights protest since the march from Selma to Montgomery in March 1965.

Clayborne Carson, the renowned scholar who is the director of the Martin Luther King Jr. Papers Project, says that "Rev. Barber, of all the contemporary leaders, comes closest to [King's] kind of passion and deep sense of spiritual awareness of the problems of our society. It's almost like [King] is whispering in Reverend Barber's ear."

Martin Luther King Jr. stands with Andrew Young, Ralph Abernathy, and other advisors while being served with a temporary restraining order from a US Marshal, preventing him from leading another march in Memphis. April 3, 1968.

CHAPTER ELEVEN

★ ★ ★

REV. DR. MARTIN LUTHER KING JR. AND MEMPHIS'S SANITATION WORKERS

Protest for Equal Pay

Memphis's dusky skies opened up on February 1, 1968, offering no escape from the downpour. Hoping to stay dry, two garbage collectors jumped into the back of their reeking garbage truck. Segregation was officially over, but the city forbade Black sanitation workers from taking cover under the porches of the nearby white homes.

Memphis provided its largely Black sanitation workforce with nothing more than low, unreliable wages. Garbage collectors in Memphis worked long hours but couldn't even count on their rock-bottom wages—under eight dollars a day in 1968. On days like this one, when it rained hard, many of them were sent home without pay.

Only Black workers were assigned to lift the heavy

garbage bins and hoist their contents into the back of the trucks; city rules reserved the job of drivers and supervisors for whites. Echol Cole and Robert Walker had to buy their own uniforms, gloves, and equipment; they returned home each day filthy and smelling of garbage. On this stormy afternoon, they were exhausted and cold after a grueling day on the job—the last thing they wanted was to get soaked, too.

Their aging truck itself ought to have been replaced years earlier. The new mayor, Henry Loeb, had come into office promising to cut costs, a measure that meant no new equipment and no hopes for a raise for the city's thousands of Black workers.

Ed Gillis was in his seventies and had worked in Memphis as a garbage collector for twenty years, with no hope for a promotion or higher wages. His white supervisors still called him "boy."

"You'd work ten, twelve hours a day," Gillis's coworker James Robinson said. "But you didn't get paid but for eight. You stayed out there until you'd get through. We were out there sometimes till dark. You'd start at seven o'clock in the morning, no extra for overtime."

"There is no worst job," another sanitation worker said. "I would take anything."

The 1,300-man army that moved Memphis's garbage had been recruited from the surrounding cotton fields of the Mississippi River Valley. Beginning in the late 1940s, mechanical cotton harvesters began to replace the sharecroppers and farm workers who had toiled in the South's fields for generations. A single machine worked its way down the cotton rows, picking in one day what it would take eighty people to harvest by hand. For the next twenty years, hundreds of thousands of former sharecroppers and cotton pickers migrated to cities like Memphis in order to survive and feed their families. The Jim Crow wages they now earned just barely enabled them to do that.

By 1968, even the city's skilled Black workers made little more than those at the bottom rung. Nearly two-thirds of Memphis's Black community lived well below the poverty line, making this city of half a million people one of the poorest in the United States.

And Memphis was only one example of what Black workers were facing all over America.

"We didn't have a voice back then," a sanitation worker named J. L. McClain recalled. "You couldn't express yourself. Or if you do, you probably would get fired."

———◇———

The creaky truck rumbled away from the curb as Cole and Walker huddled in the compactor bay at the rear.

Perhaps a shovel fell over and triggered the hydraulic trash compactor, or maybe the decrepit system malfunctioned. But by the time the white driver hit the brakes, it was too late: Both men had been pulled into the maw of the truck.

One of them lurched forward, trying to escape, but his coat got caught and he was yanked backward into the garbage. A bystander reported that "he was standing there on the end of the truck, and suddenly it looked like the big thing just swallowed him."

The force of the truck's powerful compactor jaws crushed Coe and Walker to death in seconds.

By nightfall, word of the accident spread through Memphis's Black neighborhoods as hundreds of sanitation workers returned to their homes. Coe and Walker left behind wives, children, parents, brothers and sisters, all of them in shock at the way the two men had died. Their neighbors and fellow workers, men and women who spent long hours at risky, low-paying jobs, could easily imagine themselves in the victims' places.

But what power did they have to change their own lives?

The next morning, the city's garbage workers bristled with anger over Coe's and Walker's deaths. It didn't help that the funeral home refused to release their bodies until a $500 fee was paid. The money the city offered to the men's families covered this fee and their burial expenses, but nothing else.

"We don't have anything no how," one man said, "and there ain't no need in our standing around 'cause we ain't got anything under the situation we have."

Almost a thousand men and women gathered for a nighttime meeting two days later and wrote up a list of demands for the mayor. The men asked for higher pay, safer working conditions, recognition of their union, and the end to segregated hiring practices. They wanted an end, that is, to Jim Crow jobs. "All we wanted was some decent working conditions, and a decent salary," sanitation worker Taylor Rogers said. "And be treated like men, not like boys."

On February 12, fewer than two hundred garbage collectors showed up for work. Two days later, the city celebrated

Valentine's Day with over ten thousand tons of garbage heaped on its street corners and alleyways.

The city's least powerful workers had brought Memphis to a halt.

The bewildered mayor rejected the strikers' demands out of hand. Loeb assumed the walkout would fizzle in a few days, as the garbagemen and their families grew hungry and desperate. Loeb didn't do much to hide his contempt for Black people; when he met with them in his office, he made it known that he had a loaded shotgun under his desk.

This time, though, he had badly miscalculated. Instead of caving, the striking workers dug in. A city of 500,000 people saw its trash pile up day after day, a crisis measured by the sheer quantity of garbage that sat uncollected.

What Loeb couldn't see was that an entire community, beyond the 1,300 men, stood behind the garbage workers' demands.

Many of the men's wives worked as maids for white families, and now found themselves the sole breadwinners in their households. "It wasn't just men walking out on their jobs," one historian of the strike wrote. "It was entire families putting their livelihood on the line."

On "Black Mondays" students would support the striking sanitation workers by conducting school walkouts. Beverly Turner, the daughter of one of the strikers, recalled that "even the teachers were in support of the sanitation workers, and they were not going to allow those students to fall behind. Everybody in the community played their parts."

On February 23, during a march to pressure Loeb to meet their demands, Memphis police attacked the strikers and their allies with mace and nightsticks. Ed Gillis described the violent scene: "There was about fifteen or twenty police with that mace just gassing us, pushing us over to the wall…and there was nobody cussing, nobody fighting. Just walking down the street."

Eyes and skin burned for days afterward. The mace penetrated deep into the Black community, changing the hearts of ministers, doctors, and teachers—Black professionals who may not have originally sympathized with the strikers' demands but who now realized that this was not simply a fight for wages. The Memphis movement was transforming into a struggle for dignity for all of the city's African American citizens.

Reverend James Lawson, pastor of a local church, one of the foremost theorists and tacticians of nonviolence, and a close friend of Martin Luther King, told a reporter that the mayor "treats the workers as though they are not men.

"That's a racist point of view," Lawson continued, "for at the heart of racism is the idea that a man is not a man, that a person is not a person.

"You are human beings," Lawson preached to the striking workers. "You are men. You deserve dignity."

———◇———

When Martin Luther King Jr. read the headlines from Memphis, he felt the city was rising to the next big challenge of the Civil Rights Movement.

King had just announced what he called a Poor People's Campaign. It was a controversial idea, even among his closest advisers. The idea was that poor people of all backgrounds could join together to demand higher wages and decent jobs for all Americans.

"Now our struggle is for genuine equality, which means economic equality," King said. "For we know that it isn't enough to integrate lunch counters. What does it profit a man to be able to eat at an integrated lunch counter if he doesn't earn enough money to buy a hamburger and a cup of coffee?"

People had fought and died for equality, but poverty was spreading like the weeds that grew in the cracks of Memphis sidewalks.

Two years earlier, King and his close adviser Ralph Abernathy visited a day care center in the tiny town of Marks, Mississippi. Around noon, the teacher took out an apple and started putting small slices on crackers to give to her young students. It became clear to King that this wasn't a snack; it was lunch. These were malnourished children, in the wealthiest country in the world.

That evening, King lay in his motel room, staring at the ceiling. "Ralph, I can't get those children out of my mind," King said.

King decided that the Civil Rights Movement had to enter bolder, more dangerous territory. "It didn't cost the nation one penny to integrate lunch counters," King declared. "It didn't cost the nation one penny to guarantee the right to vote. The problems that we are facing today will cost the nation billions of dollars."

Opinions like this attracted some powerful enemies.

Most people who encountered King personally commented on his inner calm, his generosity, and his uncompromising belief in nonviolence. That month, FBI director J. Edgar Hoover wrote that "this power hungry, evil black devil, posing in a dirty black cloth of Christianity is a bigot, rabble rouser, Communist bedfellow, and an anti-American screwball." In February, right around the time of the sanitation strike, the FBI stepped up its surveillance and harassment of King and his associates.

At Reverend James Lawson's invitation, King flew to Memphis in March to support the strikers. On Monday, March 18—five weeks into the sanitation workers' strike—he addressed a huge audience gathered inside Memphis's historic Pentecostal church, Mason Temple, the largest sanctuary in town.

King's resonant voice soared over the crowd, rising and falling as he implored Memphis's Black citizens to see the connections between the strike and the larger struggle for equality.

"You are reminding, not only Memphis," he intoned, "but you are reminding the nation that it is a crime for people to live in this rich nation and receive starvation wages. And I need not remind you that this is our plight as a people all over America. The vast majority of Negroes in our country are still perishing on a lonely island of poverty in the midst of a vast ocean of material prosperity."

After weeks of protest and marches, and a mayor unwilling to budge, it seemed as if King's inspiring words might push the movement over the finish line to victory.

To force Loeb to the bargaining table, King decided to organize a one-day general strike of all city workers, and a massive march through the city to reveal to Memphis's leaders the power and determination of its Black workers. The date was set for March 28. Organizers fanned out across the city, spreading word. Student leaders attached flyers to school doors, encouraging young people to turn out:

> BE COOL, FOOL,
> Thursday's march is King's thing
> If your school is tops, pops, prove it.
> Be in the know,
> Get on the go,
> Thursday at 10.
> See you then.
> Together we stick,
> Divided we are stuck, Baby.
> C.O.M.E. (Community on the Move for Equality)

By 10:00 AM on the twenty-eighth, thousands of people had already gathered, and the crowds swelled as the day went on. A large group of men wore placards that read I AM A

MAN. A photograph of their solemn march became an indelible image of the Civil Rights Movement.

Soon, however, it became clear that the sheer numbers of people joining the march were overwhelming the planners' expectations. King and his allies became hemmed in by thousands of people pressing into the streets. The Memphis police, no friend to the marchers, grew jittery and aggressive.

No one knew what triggered the chaos. By early afternoon, however, the sound of shop windows shattering sent people running in all directions. The police fired tear gas and attacked the marchers at different points, injuring hundreds.

A Memphis police officer killed sixteen-year-old Larry Payne with a shotgun blast.

By nightfall, Mayor Loeb called in all-white units of the Tennessee National Guard, who patrolled the debris-strewn streets with bayonets and armored vehicles.

Media coverage of the day's events focused on the violence and not on the purpose of the march itself. Mayor Loeb seized on the negative publicity to try to force the strikers back to work without having to make a single concession to their demands. After two months, the garbage worker protest seemed about to collapse.

"At this point," one historian observed, "Memphis looked not like the starting place for the Poor People's Campaign that King had envisioned, but rather like its graveyard."

King refused to be discouraged. Returning to Memphis in early April, he announced a new march through the city.

"There are thirteen hundred of God's children here, suffering," he said. "There is no stopping point short of victory. We aren't going to let any mace stop us."

King hadn't been feeling well that day amid the torrential downpour. He sent his best friend and closest comrade, Ralph Abernathy—accompanied by his aide Jesse Jackson—to Mason Temple that night to speak in his place. When they got to the church, Abernathy phoned King at the Lorraine Motel to say that the huge crowd was hungering for King's prophetic words. No replacement would do.

King got dressed and headed to Mason Temple to deliver arguably the greatest speech of his life. It was a brilliant improvisation on themes he had struck before, but never quite in this way. He spoke of the movement's reach into economic arenas, but he dwelled as well on his own mortality.

True, he didn't speak in quite the eulogistic tone of his February 1968 sermon, "Drum Major Instinct." Delivered at his Atlanta church exactly two months before his assassination, King's homily dwelled extensively on his death and what he'd like said at his funeral. Still, that night in Memphis, premonition hung heavy in the air. After an unusually long and loving introduction by his best friend, King rose to his feet to preach himself from depression to triumph.

He took the audience right along with him. "I may not get there with you," he said, his voice echoing in a rousing crescendo. "But I want you to know tonight that we as a people will get to the Promised Land."

The next day, King huddled in the Lorraine Motel,

making plans with his lieutenants and meeting with local leaders about the march being planned for the following Monday.

At 6:00 PM local, King bantered on the motel balcony with Jesse Jackson, just beneath him in the parking lot. King also requested musician Ben Branch, standing beside Jackson, to play "real pretty" his favorite hymn, "Precious Lord." Just then a rifle crack rang out across the parking lot, and an assassin's bullet severed the leader's necktie at the knot and exploded its message of death inside his jaw.

— ◇ —

After King's murder in 1968, the city finally recognized the sanitation workers' union and met most of its demands. Conditions had improved since the deaths of Robert Walker and Echol Cole, but it was still a struggle to survive.

By 2018, Robert Walker's own son, Jack Walker, had worked for forty-three years in the Memphis sanitation department, loading trucks each day with the city's endless tons of waste.

"It's a dangerous job. You're trying to struggle, and make it out here, making ends meet," Walker's son said.

On April 4, 2018, several hundred of us gathered outside the Lorraine Motel to commemorate Martin Luther King Jr.'s life, cut short on April 4, 1968.

The final speaker that day was Reverend William Barber, who stepped out onto the balcony where King had collapsed fifty years earlier, and gazed out over the crowd, and the city beyond.

In the fifty years since the sanitation strike, Memphis had become a sprawling metropolis that had made huge steps forward in civil rights. Most of its elected officials, including the mayor, were African American, and Black residents had risen to prominent places in business and government across the city. The Lorraine Motel now occupied the grounds of the National Civil Rights Museum, where thousands of Americans explored the history of the long struggle for racial equality.

Memphis was also one of the poorest large cities in America, a place where 80 percent of Black people, including most of the city's children, lived in dire conditions. It was clear that King's hopes for the next phase in the Civil Rights Movement—an end to Black poverty—had not materialized.

"Economic exclusion is exclusion," says Elena Delavega, a professor at the University of Memphis. "It's a sign on the door that says, 'You're not allowed here.' The only thing is, you're saying it with your wallet, not a sign."

"We don't need a commemoration, we need a *reconsecration*," Reverend Barber preached. "The Bible says, 'Woe unto those who love the tombs of the prophets.'"

He called on the crowd to continue King's work rather than simply honor his memory.

"We've got to hold up the banner until every person has health care," Barber said. "We've got to hold it up until every child is lifted in love. We've got to hold it up until every job is a living-wage job, until every person in poverty has guaranteed subsistence."

ON AUGUST 26, 2016, when his teammates on the San Francisco 49ers rose to stand for the national anthem, quarterback Colin Kaepernick stayed put. "I am not going to stand up to show pride in a flag for a country that oppresses Black people and people of color," he explained after the game. "To me, this is bigger than football and it would be selfish on my part to look the other way."

For months, Kaepernick had agonized over the drumbeat of news stories of the killings of unarmed Black people by the police. He knew he had to do something—but as a professional athlete, what difference could he really make?

Kaepernick decided to keep it simple, with a silent protest.

Before the next game, Kaepernick spoke with a US Army veteran about the meaning of his actions and what he wanted them to express. The veteran, Nate Boyer, did some research online and found a photograph of Martin Luther King Jr. kneeling on a sidewalk in Selma, Alabama, at a civil rights protest there in 1965. Boyer suggested to Kaepernick that this would be a better symbolic gesture. So when his teammates stood on September 1 for the anthem, Kaepernick decided to kneel instead.

This time, boos and jeers echoed through the stands.

"I'm not anti-American," Kaepernick explained. "I love America. I love people. That's why I'm doing this. I want to help make America better."

His teammate Eric Reid knelt beside him. Like Kaepernick, Reid had been following news stories about the epidemic of police violence. What pushed him to protest, however, was news of the killing of Alton Sterling in Reid's hometown of Baton Rouge, Louisiana, that same summer.

"This could have happened to any of my family members who still live in the area," Reid said. "I felt furious, hurt, and hopeless. I wanted to do something but didn't know what or how to do it. All I knew for sure is that I wanted it to be as respectful as possible."

Throughout September and October of 2016, more and more players in the National Football League "took a knee" in solidarity with Kaepernick and Reid, and as part of a growing nationwide movement against racism and police brutality.

Kaepernick's "taking a knee" jolted the debate over race in America. He received death threats. One poll voted him the least-liked player in the NFL.

A few months later, Colin Kaepernick discovered what the price would be for speaking up against racism. When the term of his contract with the 49ers was up in March 2017, no team would sign him. He hasn't played professional football since.

Tommie Smith (center) and John Carlos (right) raise their fists on the medal stand at the 1968 Olympics in Mexico City.

CHAPTER TWELVE

★ ★ ★

JOHN CARLOS AND TOMMIE SMITH

Raise a Fist for Black Pride

"When the race popped off, we were all rolling. I have to say, I was flying, man. When that gun went off, I was gone."

The 200-meter dash, one of the premiere events of the 1968 Olympic Games, had the crowd roaring in the stands. John Carlos charged forward, feet pounding, knees cutting through the air in a blur of motion. "You can see as we approach the finish line," Carlos recalled, "I turn one last time over my left shoulder, to see where Tommie is so I'm sure we're both on point for the medal stand."

Carlos had beaten his teammate Tommie Smith in the Olympic trials in Lake Tahoe that year, but officials overruled his win because he was wearing non-regulation shoes.

Carlos planned on clinching victory this time and taking the gold.

But Tommie Smith had other plans: he bounded forward, flying over the finish line and shattering the world speed record for the 200-meter dash.

Now Carlos closed in for second place. "If you notice," Carlos said, referring to film footage of the race, "I don't look over my right shoulder once in the entire race except at that very micro-fraction of a second when we cross the finish line. At that last moment, I saw a white blur and said to myself, 'Oh, shit. It's Peter Norman.'"

Norman, an Australian sprinter, blew past Carlos for the silver medal, and Carlos arrived just behind him, taking the bronze for third place. The unexpected turn of events had the whole stadium crowd on its feet.

A short while later, the three medalists made their way to the platform for the medal ceremony. Nothing seemed out of the ordinary, but keen-eyed observers noted that the two Black American sprinters, Smith and Carlos, carried their shoes and walked in black socks. Each man wore a single, black leather glove. Peter Norman, the white Australian silver medalist, sported a pin with the insignia of the Olympic Committee for Human Rights.

As he climbed the stand, John's mind raced.

> I started reflecting on my dad, the stories he told me about what he endured in the armed forces. I thought about Harlem and the way the integrated community

of my youth became all black, with the money and the opportunity moving away with the white residents. I reflected on the fact that my dad told me with pain in his eyes that I wasn't going to be able to make it to the Olympics in swimming, not because of my abilities, but because of the color of my skin. I pondered what Malcolm always said about being true to yourself even when it hurts. I thought about Dr. King's words about why he had to go back to Memphis even though his life was in jeopardy—because he felt a calling to stand for those people who "couldn't or wouldn't stand for themselves."

The American anthem echoed through the stadium. Smith and Carlos dropped their heads, and each man raised a single, clenched fist.

Another athlete watching from the stands recalled that "there was a gasp...I don't remember booing, but a gasp in the section where I was sitting with a bunch of Americans. All of a sudden around me the atmosphere changed. There were negative comments, racial comments about what they were doing. The atmosphere became explosive."

John Carlos remembered that "those singing the anthem started screaming it out."

Both men held their fists high, standing motionless for the entire ninety-second anthem, while a stunned crowed looked on.

John Carlos's and Tommie Smith's silent gesture was the

loudest act of protest in the entire history of the Olympic Games.

Later, Tommie Smith explained the symbolism of their actions:

> My raised right hand stood for the power in Black America. Carlos' raised left hand stood for the unity of Black America. Together they formed an arch of unity and power. The black scarf around my neck stood for Black pride. The black socks with no shoes stood for Black poverty in racist America. The totality of our effort was the regaining of Black dignity.

Carlos's and Smith's fists were like lightning rods, attracting a bright flash of anger from white America—but also conducting a powerful charge of energy that had been coursing through the Civil Rights Movement for more than two years.

———◇———

On June 5, 1966, James Meredith—having graduated from Ole Miss—began a one-man march through his home state of Mississippi, to make the point that a Black person ought to be able to walk freely through the United States of America. Meredith called it the March Against Fear.

The next day, a white man named Aubrey James Norvell gunned down Meredith as he approached Hernando,

Mississippi, peppering his head and body with three powerful shotgun blasts.

Meredith survived, but word of the attack spread quickly through an outraged Civil Rights Movement. Soon, hundreds of people were converging on Mississippi to take up Meredith's mission. Many of the movement's most important leaders, including Martin Luther King Jr., joined in, vowing to march in defiance of threats to Black lives.

Several days later, on a sweltering evening in Greenwood, SNCC chairman Stokely Carmichael addressed a crowd of more than fifteen hundred marchers.

The words he chose would echo through the decade and for many years after.

"We want Black power!"

Carmichael's words resonated powerfully with Black people. For Carmichael, Black power meant self-determination and self-respect in a nation that seemed to oppose every effort at racial equality.

Thousands of activists and ordinary people adopted the term "Black Power" as their own—and their raised fists became the physical expression of Carmichael's powerful words.

The message of Black power had special meaning for many Black athletes, who had fought for years to break down the barriers of segregation. In 1967, a number of prominent Olympic athletes joined together to form the Olympic Committee for Human Rights to protest racism in sports and, more generally, in the world. The group included John Carlos and Tommie Smith, as well as the college basketball star Lew Alcindor (who eventually converted to Islam and changed his name to Kareem Abdul-Jabbar).

One of the group's central demands was the return of the heavyweight champion title to boxing great Muhammad Ali.

Ali's example of athletic excellence, courage, and defiance had inspired Carlos and Smith in the first place. Born in Louisville, Kentucky, as Cassius Clay, the heavyweight boxer became the youngest champion in the history of the sport when he defeated Sonny Liston for the title in 1964.

The Louisville of Clay's youth was strictly segregated. Early each morning, he would go out for training runs in Chickasaw Park, the only one where African Americans were allowed.

Clay's boxing prowess earned him accolades and prize fights, but his brash, uncompromising rejection of white supremacy electrified Black audiences around the country—and around the globe.

In 1964, Clay shed what he called his "slave name" and took the name Muhammad Ali after joining the Nation of Islam. Ali refused to sign up for the army draft, arguing that he had no personal quarrel with the Viet Cong, the Communist insurgents battling the American-supported government in Vietnam. The US government threatened him with a five-year prison term. He was stripped of his heavyweight title and banned from boxing during the prime of his career.

Ali's skill in the boxing ring and daring political statements made him one of the most famous people in the world—which is exactly why so many white people, particularly powerful white people in professional sports, hated him. By denying him the right to fight, the white men who controlled boxing thought that they could control Ali's political power as well. They were dead wrong. Instead, Ali continued to press for equality and to serve as an example of pride and excellence for all Americans.

"Ali was young, gifted, and black," John Carlos said. "And he was proud of all three of those attributes. He was a gift from God to this society."

He also influenced generations of athletes to stand up for their rights and their political beliefs.

———◇———

The drama of the 1968 Olympic Games played out at a time when America's commitment to civil rights seemed to stall. Ever since Martin Luther King's murder in Memphis six months earlier, a backlash against the quest for racial equality was brewing.

George Wallace, the former governor of Alabama, campaigned for president that year as an independent candidate. Wallace had made headlines in 1963 for trying to physically block the integration of the University of Alabama. In a famous speech, he declared "segregation now, segregation tomorrow, segregation forever!"

In 1968, Wallace's message seemed to appeal to white

people all over the country. After one of his rallies in New York, people streamed out of Madison Square Garden yelling "white supremacy!"

Wallace's Republican opponent Richard Nixon ran a campaign calling loudly for "law and order." For Nixon and his advisers, these were deliberate code words, intended to attract white voters who might be critical of the Civil Rights Movement and hostile toward the goals of the urban rebellions engulfing many of America's cities. One of Nixon's lieutenants said, "The time may have come when the issue of race could benefit from a period of benign neglect."

News coverage of the Olympics was completely dominated by the medal ceremony protest, with most newspapers voicing white America's renewed skepticism about civil rights. A writer in the *Chicago Tribune* called Carlos's and Smith's raised fists "an insult to their countrymen." A *New York Times* editorial expressed the view that the protest was "disgraceful, insulting, and embarrassing." The sportswriter Brent Musburger dubbed the sprinters "a pair of dark-skinned stormtroopers."

The Olympic Committee, and particularly its president, regarded the games as a neutral and fair contest, a place where political statements were inappropriate and unwelcome. That struck many Black athletes as ridiculous. The supposed neutrality of the games seemed more like a smokescreen for covering up the real problems afflicting the athletes' and fans' worlds.

Inside the 1968 Olympic Village, however, the message

had come through loud and clear: no more protests would be tolerated.

"You'd think I committed murder," Smith said to the sportscaster Howard Cosell. "All I did was what I've been doing all along, call the attention of the world to the way Blacks are treated in America."

Caught suddenly in a hail of controversy, Smith's and Carlos's troubles were just beginning.

The International Olympic Committee banned them from the Olympic Village. Despite their victory for the US team—and Smith's world record—the US Olympic Committee ejected both men from the team, forcing them to return home and miss the remainder of the games.

A rumor spread that the International Olympic Committee had even stripped Carlos and Smith of their medals. "Hell no," Carlos said. "I made it very clear to the IOC that they didn't give me this medal, I earned it. They could try to come to Harlem or the Bronx to take it back, but I didn't recommend it."

Back in California, the sprinters found that they had some supporters. The president of their college, San Jose State University, welcomed them back as champions. Baseball legend Jackie Robinson spoke up in their defense.

But the rewards that came with Olympic stardom—highly paid endorsements, job offers, and athletic fame—eluded Carlos and Smith. The controversy over their racial protest clouded their careers, and it seemed as if all that remained of their Olympic triumph was a single black-and-white photograph.

The way he was treated after the Olympic Games confirmed Carlos's worst suspicions about the power of racism in America.

Black athletes had proved themselves in every sport: they had become stars of the court, the field, the gridiron, and the baseball diamond. "I thought about all the greatness that Black people had brought to the table for America," he said, "how we built this country from the sweat of our brows and arches of our backs, and then, in turn, we were always second-class citizens. We could go out and win medals. We could go out and win wars. We could break all the world records, and we could be heroes as long as we stayed in between the lines. But once we got off the field, we were just regular old nothings."

America, his home, was a place "where I was encouraged to run but not to speak," Carlos said.

Carlos was not alone. In every sport, from boxing to baseball, and football to tennis, Black athletes knew that excellence did not translate into independence, let alone power, in the wider world.

Despite the uproar around his Olympics win, John Carlos helped trigger a new wave of activism inside the world of sports, at a time when the nation seemed to be turning against the Civil Rights Movement.

Invitations started to arrive in his mailbox, asking him to speak to college athletes, first in California, and soon all over the United States. Like the Black Panther Party organizing in Lowndes County, Alabama, that same year, John Carlos helped build a new movement from the bottom up. Carlos and Smith traveled to hundreds of college campuses, inspiring the next generation of citizen-athletes.

———◇———

The fire that Carlos and Smith sparked flared again fifty years later, when Colin Kaepernick took a knee.

The impact of Kaepernick's kneeling spread imperceptibly at first. Millions of young people had watched his protests, however, and saw them as an example to follow rather than a cautionary tale.

"Taking a knee" quickly took on a life of its own, ignited protests, hard conversations, and change in high schools, on college campuses, and in cities and towns across the United States.

John Carlos felt a sense of deep connection to the past in this new wave of activism by athletes.

"In life, there's the beginning and the end," he said. "The beginning don't matter. The end don't matter. All that matters is what you do in between—whether you're prepared to do what it takes to make change. When all the dust settles and we're getting ready to play down for the ninth inning, the greatest reward is to know that you did your job when you were here on the planet."

THE SUPERINTENDENT of Howard County, Maryland, could hardly believe what he was hearing. The talk among parents in his school district in 2019 sounded like the arguments of an earlier, segregated era.

"I heard a lot of things said during these meetings," he said, "which sounded almost verbatim like the things that were said in the '50s and '60s and '70s to prevent the integration of schools in Richmond and around the country."

In 2019, parents in Howard County hotly debated the superintendent's plan to reshuffle the student population among different high schools as a way of providing equal opportunities for all kids in the district. Parents of students at the county's mostly white, affluent high school weren't having it.

"When you look at what was said, it's so hurtful," one Black parent said.

The superintendent received death threats. Residents mailed in anonymous letters, including one that said, "Blacks destroy school systems and schools."

By 2020, the plan to integrate Howard County had stalled.

Almost thirty million American kids ride the bus to school every day. For some, especially in rural areas, the ride is long; for others, it can be a couple of miles at most. Riding a school bus is one of the least controversial things about education in the United States—until it comes to racial integration.

When students from different backgrounds attend the same school, grades improve and test scores go up. People become more empathetic. Racial bias tends to decrease.

In the 1970s and '80s, Denver, Colorado, decided to integrate its schools as a way of overcoming decades of racial inequality. For the most part, it succeeded.

"At school," a Black student from Denver said, "I had friends, mostly white or Asian American, who, once they got to know me, pretty much accepted me for who I am. I got a better sense of life's possibilities and was more willing to hang out with different types of people as a result." A white student from the same district recalled that "before integration, Black people were the people who waited on us at the swim club, the guy who cleaned the windows at our house, our cleaning lady, and the crew who mowed our lawn. After integration, Black people were also my friends, the girl who became a doctor, the young man who went to Arizona State University, and so on."

But Denver gave up on its integration plan in the 1990s, and its schools returned to their earlier, segregated ways and outcomes. Most school districts in the United States today are no different.

Ruth Batson, circa 1945.

CHAPTER THIRTEEN

★ ★ ★

RUTH BATSON

Uncovers Segregation in Boston

In the spring of 1933, a high school student named Robert Carter decided to join the swim team at East Orange High School, in New Jersey. Up until that time, no Black student had been allowed on the team; Black children could use the pool only on alternating Fridays, for recreational swimming. As a racist insult, the pool was then washed and disinfected before white students used it again on the following Monday.

Carter read a newspaper article about how the New Jersey Supreme Court had just declared that all schools in the state must provide equal facilities for Black and white students. With a lump in his throat, Carter approached the swim coach and insisted that he had a right to sign up for the team. The coach had no choice but to say yes. However, none of the white boys would get in the pool with Carter, so the following year, East Orange High closed the pool to all students and canceled the swim season altogether.

Twenty years later, Carter sat in the US Supreme Court, one of several NAACP lawyers preparing to argue *Brown v. Board of Education of Topeka, Kansas*, the decision that would permanently bar legal segregation in the United States.

Brown v. Board of Education created a wave of hope that spread across the United States. Black parents all over the country asked hard questions about their children's education. Why shouldn't their kids have the same chances as white students? Why did their school buildings always seem to be crowded and old? And why did Black students always get assigned to all-Black schools when segregation wasn't supposed to exist in the North?

If *Brown v. Board of Education* meant anything at all, it had to apply to the whole country, not simply the South.

———◇———

Ruth Batson would always remember the sight of her mother crossing the stage of the Everett Grammar School on Northampton Street in Boston, to receive her elementary school diploma. A Jamaican immigrant, Ruth's mother had returned to school as an adult to set an example for her children.

"No one can take your education away from you," her mother taught her.

When Ruth had three children of her own, however, she

started to realize just how hard it was for Black Bostonians to get a good education.

At Louisa May Alcott School in the South End, a Black neighborhood, even basic supplies were lacking. "The yellow paper was brown on the edges," a teacher named Jean Maguire reported. "It had been stored and saved and hoarded so there would be enough."

"We didn't have a tape recorder," she added. "We didn't have a music teacher to come in. There were no music lessons....There were no science labs. There was no gymnasium."

At another elementary school, students were found completing assignments on the back of Krueger Beer advertisements.

"The oldest school buildings in Boston were located in the black communities," Batson recalled, "and these buildings were unsafe." In the Roxbury neighborhood, a sickly smell from the aging slate urinals in the Sherwin School wafted out into a neighboring park, which parents would avoid because of the odor.

The inequalities went beyond school supplies and dirty bathrooms. One evening in 1953, Ruth was chatting on the phone with a white friend, who told her about a science project her young son was working on in school.

"When I questioned my daughter about science and about whether this was one of her subjects, she was vague and nonresponsive," Ruth recalled.

There was no science fair in her daughter's all-Black

school, Ruth learned. And no science projects. When she asked the white principal about it (there was not a single Black principal in the entire city), the woman dismissed Ruth's concerns out of hand.

Ruth thought about her mother, about all the opportunities she had lacked, and about the example she had set for Ruth by walking across that stage. Outrage welled up inside her.

She couldn't deny the obvious. "I believed, with all my heart," she said, "that the children in my daughters' schools were receiving an inferior education."

Several hundred miles to the south, NAACP attorneys were meeting day and night, toiling on the case that would thrust the issue of segregated schools onto the front pages of America and supercharge the national movement for civil rights. Many in Boston, the city that launched the American Revolution, and where abolitionists had plotted the overthrow of slavery a century earlier, cheered their efforts. They saw no connection at all between Jim Crow and the harsh reality of Boston's unofficial segregation. Racism, they believed, was a southern problem.

One member of Boston's school committee expressed white Boston's view of the problem with Black schools. "The Negro," he said, "can make their schools the best in the city if they attend schools more often, on time and apply themselves."

Ruth and other Black parents grew outraged at remarks like this, which placed the blame for inequality on the shoulders of children rather than where it belonged: at the feet of the city's all-white leadership, the people who decided where kids went to school and how much money those schools received.

In 1951, with no experience in politics, Ruth decided to run for a seat on the Boston School Committee.

She lost.

Three years later, Ruth was washing the dishes when a friend called with news of the *Brown* decision. She couldn't believe it—the nation's highest court had struck a note for equality for all children.

"Everything was going to be fine now," Ruth reassured herself.

Soon afterward, Ruth saw an announcement in a Black newspaper. The local NAACP office in Boston was encouraging residents to bring in complaints of discrimination. Ruth only had a high school education herself, and she hesitated to step forward. But she knew she had to do something—if her own children were going to have the same chances as their white peers.

It wasn't just that Boston schools were racially segregated; they were becoming *more* segregated each year. Boston's Black population was growing, as more and more southerners joined the Great Migration to the North, and because of the redlining that afflicted all northern cities, African Americans were forced to squeeze into the most overcrowded neighborhoods.

A city that prided itself on neighborhood schools made

sure that better-paid teachers and more modern equipment flowed to white neighborhoods only. The system was set up to deprive Black students of what they needed most, and it did so without anyone uttering the word *segregation*.

The NAACP chapter president listened intently to Ruth's story. The local NAACP, until that moment, had never much considered the problem of unequal schools.

"I left the office angry and utterly disillusioned," Ruth recalled.

But the next day, to her great surprise, the NAACP chapter president called her on the phone. He had just created a new public school committee, and asked Ruth to be in charge of it.

"From that point on, my life changed profoundly," Ruth said. The time had come, she believed, to stir the pot in Boston and to bring America's Civil Rights Movement home.

Black parents and white allies were mobilizing all over the city, pressuring the Boston School Committee to use its powers on behalf of racial equality. It almost seemed as if Boston, with its liberal reputation, might actually lead the way.

But no one had counted on the stubbornness of Boston School Committee member Louise Day Hicks. The only daughter of a state judge, Hicks earned a law degree at a time when few women were practicing lawyers. She still lived in her childhood home, in the white Irish enclave of South Boston, where residents were fiercely loyal to their neighborhood and deeply distrustful of outsiders.

Hicks shared the outlook of her constituents in "Southie." There was no way she would ask them to bus their white children to Roxbury—or to invite Black students from Roxbury into Southie—just to satisfy the NAACP. But she also knew better than to speak the openly racist language of Jim Crow. Instead, Hicks helped develop race-neutral terms such as *forced busing*, *local control*, and *neighborhood schools*, which to this day remain code words for white opposition to school integration.

As the newly elected chairperson of the Boston School Committee, Hicks refused even to discuss inequality in the city's schools; at one meeting, when an NAACP representative merely mentioned the word *segregation*, Hicks gaveled the meeting to a close.

Robert Carter of the NAACP came to Boston to help fight back against Louise Day Hicks's anti-integration movement. To Carter, "separate and unequal were found to go hand in hand, no less in the North than in the South.

"Public schools," according to Carter, "controlled by white middle-class parents and teachers, had become instruments for blocking rather than facilitating the upward mobility of blacks."

In the South, however, segregated schools had been openly created by laws. No one denied they existed. But liberal Boston had a hard time accepting the obvious fact of its intensely segregated system. Why did there need to be integration, many Bostonians asked, when no segregation existed in the first place?

Batson and Carter could easily document that most Black students in Boston attended schools that were either all-Black or nearly so. Exhaustive studies showed conclusively that these schools received much less money and fewer resources than those where white students were in the majority.

Still, common wisdom in Boston (and across the North) held that no one had actually forced Black and white people to live separately. The head of New York City's public schools, for example, had argued that "we did not provide Harlem with segregation. We have natural segregation here—it's accidental."

Louise Day Hicks probably never intended to blow the lid off this common wisdom—or to uncover its thinly veiled bigotry. But along with her vocal and angry supporters, she accidentally revealed to everyone a simple, harsh truth: Many white people simply did not want to send their children to school with Black children. And they were willing to fight—violently, if necessary—to keep things that way.

The battle for educational equality in Boston came to a head when the NAACP filed a federal lawsuit in 1972 to force the city of Boston to eliminate racial segregation in its school system.

In June 1974, Judge Arthur A. Garrity shocked the city when he ruled that Boston had "knowingly carried out a systematic program of segregation affecting all of the city's students, teachers and school faculties and...intentionally brought about and maintained a dual school system.

"Therefore," Garrity declared, "the entire school system of Boston is unconstitutionally segregated." He then ordered that students be moved to different schools to achieve a racial balance throughout the city.

Even for someone as hardened as Ruth Batson to her hometown's brand of racism, white Boston's opposition to Judge Garrity's busing order was breathtaking.

"You would think that aliens were coming," she remarked.

That summer, Hicks and her allies formed a new organization called ROAR (for "Restore Our Alienated Rights") to protest integration.

ROAR became known for its aggressive tactics. Members gathered outside the home of Massachusetts senator Ted Kennedy, who supported Garrity's ruling. "Let your daughter get bused there so she can get raped," they heckled.

Judge Garrity received death threats and had to be guarded around the clock.

When September arrived, the first day of school had to be delayed to allow schools more time to prepare for the exchange of students.

Finally, on the morning of September 12, 1974, Batson watched anxiously as news reporters tracked the first buses to crisscross the city. How would her city respond? Would this experiment in racial equality work?

When a yellow school bus with fifty-three Black high school students pulled up to South Boston High School, stones showered the bus, smashing windows. Terrified Black children huddled inside. A student named Phyllis Ellison recalled "people on the corners holding bananas like we were apes, monkeys. 'Monkeys get out, get them out of our neighborhood. We don't want you in our schools.'"

Teacher Jean McGuire rode the bus to make sure that the Black students got to and from school safely.

"Signs hanging out those buildings, N—— GO HOME," she recalled. "Pictures of monkeys. The words. The spit. People just felt it was all right to attack children."

Seething with anger over being forced to integrate, white Bostonians spilled out into the city's streets and neighborhoods.

In East Boston, Robert "Junior" Lewis watched as a group of white boys gathered in front of his home. One of them lit a homemade firebomb made from rags and a bottle filled with gasoline. As the bottle sailed through the air toward the house, Junior recognized the face of the boy who had thrown it—his lifelong friend, who watched as the bottle exploded into flame on the Lewises' lawn. Junior's family moved out soon after, along with nearly every other Black person in the neighborhood.

That fall, more firebombings forced Black families out of mixed parts of the city and into Black-majority neighborhoods. "I never got over it," said Darneese Carnes, who watched as a firebomb crashed through her window. "It made me hate. I know that I am mean and I'm hard, and I tell people that's just who I am, because of how I grew up."

On April 5, 1976, as the city prepared its celebrations for

the bicentennial of the American Revolution, a twenty-nine-year-old Black lawyer with three degrees from Yale named Ted Landsmark dashed across City Hall Plaza in downtown Boston.

"I had difficulty finding a parking space in downtown Boston," recalled Landsmark. "And I was running a few minutes late for the meeting in city hall. So I was in a hurry and perhaps not paying as much attention as I might have as I approached a corner, where the young demonstrators were coming in the other direction. I did not see them until both they and I were at that corner."

Landsmark had accidentally run head-on into a group of white anti-busing protesters. One of them wielded an American flag like a spear.

"The first person to attack me hit me from behind," Landsmark said, "which knocked off my glasses and ended up breaking my nose. The flag being swung at me came at me just moments after that and missed my face by inches."

A photograph of the exact moment of the attack on equality in schools became the iconic image of America's bicentennial year. Snapped by photojournalist Stanley Forman, the famed photograph, titled *The Soiling of Old Glory*, won Forman the 1977 Pulitzer Prize for Spot News Photography.

———◆———

Judge Garrity lifted his busing order in 1988, not because he had achieved the goal of equality in Boston's schools, but because larger forces had defeated it.

White families were fleeing the city for the more affluent white suburbs and taking their tax dollars with them. Boston's school district—like those in Detroit, Los Angeles, Denver, Seattle, and other cities with large Black populations—had no power to keep them from leaving.

"All of this is very connected," one civil rights activist noted. "The schools. The housing. The government. All of this is a part of the structural racism which is still very much in place."

In Boston, where the vast majority of students are now children of color, the effects are still glaring.

In America today, the promises of *Brown v. Board* have faded in all but a few committed school districts. Most Black and brown students in America attend schools that are majority non-white, and almost 40 percent attend a public school where almost no white students are present at all. (Some schools are so hyper-segregated that education experts refer to them as "apartheid schools"—referring to the extreme system of racial separation in South Africa before 1991.)

Everywhere, school segregation is made worse by the kind of housing segregation experienced by Daisy and William Myers, and by Ossian and Gladys Sweet before them. "Housing segregation is the overriding, number one cause of segregation in schools," argues the law professor John Brittain. And Black parents today find the same inequalities discovered by Ruth Batson in the 1950s: Because most funding for schools in the United States comes from local taxes; wealthier, whiter school districts always spend more on their students than poorer, more diverse ones.

School integration never had a chance to breathe. In New York, Chicago, and elsewhere, segregation in the twenty-first century is a direct result of lost battles in the years following *Brown v. Board.*

———◇———

In the 1970s, America had reached a turning point—where many white people railed against the idea of racial equality and sought to roll back the achievements of Ruth Batson, Robert Carter, and thousands of other freedom fighters.

According to one of our national myths, when the Civil Rights Movement defeated Jim Crow in the South, racism in America came to an end. While individual people might still be racist, the story goes, our society treats all people equally, and the old racial roadblocks—segregated schools, poll taxes, and open displays of bigotry—are a thing of the past.

But the irony is that the successes of the Civil Rights Movement gave some Americans an excuse to say that racism no longer existed—at a time when new kinds of racial inequality were spreading like a virus across the United States. Even as *some* Black people made their way onto college campuses, into white neighborhoods, and into jobs once held exclusively by white people, most others were left behind. Away from the headlines, and long before the days of cell phone cameras, Black communities continued to fall prey to police brutality, racial profiling, housing and school segregation, voter suppression, employment discrimination, and more.

America isn't color-blind. Instead, for the past fifty years, Black people and their allies have been locked in a new struggle with shape-shifting white supremacy.

One of the Black students attending South Boston High School understood exactly what was at stake in her hometown. "If they run us out of that school," she said, "they can run us out of the city. They will be able to stop access wherever they want."

The teacher Jean Maguire couldn't have agreed more. "It isn't the bus you're talking about," she said. "You have to be really honest, [it's] not a thing to do with transportation. Everybody in the suburbs rides a bus to get to school, or driving their cars. It isn't a bus, it's us. It's who you live next to. It's who your kids will marry.

"Part of education isn't just book stuff," Maguire added. "It's how to get along as a city and look out for each other."

★ ★ ★

FOR THE MINISTER, the issue was personal. His own brother had been sent away to federal prison twenty-two years earlier on a nonviolent drug charge.

"He is a veteran of the first Gulf War and has been a model prisoner, no easy feat amid the challenges of prison life, since his incarceration twenty-two years ago," he said. "Yet it is the stigma of color and criminality that makes his story not as uncommon as one might think."

Stigma—the mark of the criminal. It's what kept thousands of men and women in the minister's community from finding work or getting a decent place to live. He knew that the streets of Atlanta were filled with these desperate people, most of them Black, many of them merely charged—not even convicted—of nonviolent crimes.

As pastor of Ebenezer Baptist Church, Reverend Dr. Raphael Warnock had a special connection to the long struggle for equality. After all, Ebenezer was the spiritual home of Martin Luther King Jr. and a home base for the Civil Rights Movement in the 1960s.

Over a half century later, one issue loomed over all others as the civil rights struggle for Warnock's generation: mass incarceration, the system that made America the prison capital of the world, with a higher percentage of its citizens behind bars than any other country. Many of those people are imprisoned for nonviolent crimes, serving long sentences—just like Reverend Warnock's brother.

"Just think about it," he reflected. "The land of the free, the shining city on the hill, shackles more people than anywhere else in the world." That irony was made sharper by the fact that Warnock in 2021 became Georgia's first Black senator and the first Black Democratic senator from the South.

That morning, Warnock's congregation held a "records purging" event, working with local officials in Fulton County to help clear the arrest records of more than a thousand people—people who could now go out into the world and find jobs, or new homes, without being haunted by the ghosts of their pasts. Compared with the scale of the problem, these were small steps, but the Ebenezer congregants had their eyes on a very different future.

"I am clear that fifty years from now," Warnock preached, "our children, our grandchildren are going to ask us, 'What were you doing while this human rights nightmare unfolded on your watch?'"

Michelle Alexander speaking about her book
The New Jim Crow in 2011.

CHAPTER FOURTEEN

★ ★ ★

MICHELLE ALEXANDER
Confronts the New Jim Crow

The uprisings in Harlem, Watts, Detroit, Washington, DC, and other places had something in common. They were all incited by the police threatening, beating, or mistreating Black people. Like Nate Shaw, after years of harassment and intimidation, some people had reached a breaking point.

But other people—in the mayor's offices of major cities, in the White House, and on Capitol Hill—saw the uprisings as evidence of a breakdown of "law and order." These people refused to look outside of America's racial ghettos and ask how they were created in the first place: how laws, government policies, and discrimination created poverty and racial inequality in America. Instead, they pointed the finger at the victims of discrimination themselves, asking what had gone wrong with Black families that so many young "delinquents" roamed the streets.

Law-and-order talk drowned out calls for equal rights. White people found it easier to deny America's three-century history of discrimination and how it still shaped the present.

In the 1970s, America's answer to the problem of poverty and inequality in America was not less poverty and more equality. Its answer was more police—the very thing that had set off the riots in the first place.

Aided by the federal government, cities from Seattle to Cleveland went on spending sprees for their police departments. Millions of tax dollars helped pay for not only more officers and police cars but also military-style weaponry such as helicopters and armored vehicles. And with so many more police on the streets of Black neighborhoods, President Richard Nixon took what he saw as the natural next step. He kicked off the biggest prison-building boom in all of American history.

A nation that only ten years earlier sought to dismantle the segregated world that Jim Crow built now seemed bent on sending more and more Black people to prison.

——◆——

In the mid-1990s, a young lawyer named Michelle Alexander came across an orange flyer taped to a telephone pole near a bus stop advertising a meeting with the headline THE DRUG WAR IS THE NEW JIM CROW. Alexander was skeptical. She had spent much of her career as a lawyer defending young Black clients and trying to keep them out of jail. Yes, she knew that the police had a habit of enforcing the laws unequally, treating white and Black suspects very differently. And, yes, she knew that judges handed down longer sentences when a Black person stood in front of them. In California, where she worked, prisons overflowed with Black and brown inmates.

But to call this "Jim Crow"—a violent, racist system of discrimination that had been defeated by the Civil Rights Movement—wasn't that going a bit too far? After all, many African Americans had achieved dizzying levels of success since the days of the Civil Rights Movement.

"I remember thinking to myself, Yeah, the criminal-justice system is racist in a lot of ways, but it doesn't help to make comparisons to Jim Crow," Alexander recalled. "People will just think you're crazy. And then I hopped on the bus."

Still, something nagged at her, a feeling that the poster's headline might have contained a hidden truth about American society.

The more people Alexander met who had been convicted of crimes, the more she realized that a prison sentence wasn't the end of their story inside the criminal justice system. Rather, a tangled web of laws and rules trapped people for years (sometimes their entire lives) *after* they had been released from prison. This dark reality was hidden from most Americans.

Someone convicted of a felony, such as drug possession,

might be sent to prison as punishment. But the punishment didn't end once the prison sentence ended. Instead, a whole battery of laws prevented them from reentering society on an equal basis.

They couldn't vote.

They couldn't get regular jobs—most employers required applicants to check a box if they had ever been convicted of a crime, and would disqualify a person if the box was checked.

They couldn't get public benefits such as student loans.

They couldn't open bank accounts.

That is, they could be discriminated against—legally. Prison helped create an entire class of American people who no longer had any chance of enjoying the benefits of American citizenship. Most of these people, she learned, were Black.

Finally, as Alexander started to compare the laws that controlled the lives of ex-felons to the segregation laws that defined life under Jim Crow, things started to add up.

"The new Jim Crow" made sense, after all.

Millions of Black people, she realized, had been locked into an invisible cage of racial control—a system that not only seemed like Jim Crow but actually functioned like Jim Crow. The new Jim Crow hid in the shadows, speaking a language of "color-blindness," claiming to be about "law and order" rather than about maintaining racial inequality. But the results spoke for themselves.

Abd'Allah W. Lateef left prison in 2017 after serving thirty-one years, his eyes "brimming with tears of joy and gratitude." But Lateef quickly learned that his parole was a different form of confinement:

> Parole comes with an endless list of prohibitions against the most innocuous human behaviors. There are the frequent, random drug and alcohol tests that I pay for out of pocket, although I haven't used either in over three decades. I have to get permission from my parole agent to change my employment. I also need special permission to travel for work or leisure or to move into a new apartment or house. Wherever I live, I am subject to random, unwarranted searches of my home. And there are restrictions on who I can associate with and the establishments I can patronize. I even have to notify my parole agent of any medications I'm taking, including herbal supplements, allergy pills, and cold medicine.
>
> Does this sound like freedom to you? To me, it sounds like living life as a permanent ward of the state.

America had found a way to force Black people into a permanent second-class status—sometimes referred to as a *caste*—all while professing to be a nation where racial discrimination was in the rearview mirror.

It wasn't simply that many Black people were poor, or attended inferior schools, or lacked the opportunities that many white people enjoyed—though all of these things were true. It was that they were overpoliced, over-arrested, over-convicted, over-incarcerated, and then the law stopped them from joining American society on an equal footing with white people.

How could this have happened, she wondered, in a nation that professed to embrace equality for all? And how had it gone unnoticed for so long?

The answer had everything to do with the War on Drugs, Alexander discovered. Richard Nixon's prison-building spree was only the beginning of what came to be known as America's "mass incarceration" problem.

In 1982, President Ronald Reagan made a fateful decision that would roll back the gains of the Civil Rights Movement for millions of Black Americans. Reagan declared that drug abuse was public enemy number one, even though most Americans did not rank it near the top of the nation's most pressing problems. The president then signed a series of laws that established "mandatory minimum" sentences for even minor drug offenses. These laws took away judges' ability to consider the circumstances of each case and to use their discretion when meting out punishments.

Reagan also gave the police more money and weapons to go after drug users and allowed law enforcement agencies to keep the money and other property they seized during drug raids.

The men who followed Reagan into the Oval Office, first George H. W. Bush and then Bill Clinton, made America's drug laws even harsher. And these laws almost exclusively targeted the residents of the nation's impoverished inner cities. For example, the new drug laws required judges to hand out sentences for the possession of crack cocaine (a cheaper drug found in urban areas) that were *one hundred times longer* than for possession of powdered cocaine (a more expensive drug favored by white people in the suburbs). This 100-to-1 ratio made sure that most of the people in prison for cocaine possession would be Black, not white.

More police on the streets. More surveillance of poor communities and people of color. More judges who sentenced people to be locked up for years for a single, nonviolent offense.

For millions of Black people, the War on Drugs transformed everyday life into something resembling an actual war zone. In poor, mostly Black neighborhoods across the United States, military-style drug raids smashed through front doors and injured innocent bystanders. Young Black men were pulled off the streets by the hundreds of thousands, frisked for drugs, and locked up for minor possession offenses. The sentences they served became longer and longer.

In just under thirty years, the number of Americans in prison went from three hundred thousand to more than two million. Forty percent of these incarcerated people were African Americans, although Blacks represented only 13 percent of the population. Drug convictions were responsible for most of this increase.

In federal prisons today, half of all inmates are serving

sentences related to drugs. And *two-thirds* of prisoners serving drug-related sentences are people of color.

Alexander discovered a shocking fact about the way that police make drug arrests and courts send drug offenders to prison. Even though Black and white Americans committed these offenses at roughly the same rates, Black people were up to *four times* more likely to get arrested and go to jail than white people, *for the same crime*. A white college student caught with marijuana might be fined or given a suspended sentence; a young Black man in the same town would probably find himself in jail—often for a long, long time.

The media made it seem as if the War on Drugs put only hardened criminals behind bars, but the truth was very different.

When she was a nineteen-year-old college student in Virginia, Kemba Smith dated an older man named Peter Hall, who turned out to be a violent and wanted cocaine dealer. As she was drawn into Hall's world, she feared for her life, and he abused her physically and emotionally.

Hall was later murdered. After his death, the government prosecuted Kemba for Hall's drug crimes, claiming she was a willing participant. Despite having no criminal record at all, Kemba was sentenced to almost twenty-five years in prison. She was pregnant on the day she entered prison, and gave birth in jail.

In 1999, Sharanda Jones was sentenced to *life in prison* for conspiring to distribute crack cocaine. She was twenty-three years old. Jones spent seventeen years in prison before her sentence was commuted by President Barack Obama.

By locking up people like Kemba Smith, Sharanda Jones, and hundreds of thousands of others, the War on Drugs didn't make America safer. It didn't reduce the number of people who used drugs or the amount of drugs sold on the streets. The one thing it accomplished was putting an entire generation of Black people under the control of the criminal justice system.

A federal judge named Nancy Gertner had a front-row seat to the devastation, and concluded that what was happening was a war on people, not on drugs. "This is a war that I *saw* destroy lives," Gertner said. "It eliminated a generation of African American men, [and] covered our racism in ostensibly neutral guidelines and mandatory minimums."

The more Michelle Alexander tallied the numbers, the more staggering they became: In our own time, she realized, more Black people are under the control of the criminal justice system *than were enslaved in the years just before the Civil War.* This clearly wasn't a historical footnote or a minor problem. It was a new *system* for oppressing Black people.

Of course, Black people knew the truth about this unequal treatment at the hands of police and courts. But America's leaders weren't listening to the victims of this new war. From the perspective of media, news, politicians, and most white people, the War on Drugs was about law and order and bringing criminals to justice.

Away from the halls of power, a different story was being

written about America's War on Drugs—and on Black people. Hip-hop artists, who came up on the same streets where the drug war claimed most of its victims, were some of the first people to argue that something was very wrong with this new war.

Paul Butler, now a Georgetown law professor and a former federal prosecutor who quit his job to become a critic of the criminal justice system, explained how hip-hop artists were "doing this ground-level reporting on how the criminal justice system really works, and it's [hip-hop] created by the people who know the system best.

"African American young men are the most incarcerated group of people in the history of the world," Butler continued. "So they're telling us how trials work, whether the police are fair, about prosecutors and defense attorneys, and they're doing it in tracks that you can dance to."

In Los Angeles, Tupac Shakur rapped, *"It's war on the streets and a war in the Middle East / Instead of war on poverty / They got a war on drugs so the police can bother me."*

In New York, KRS-One called out the police for hypocrisy: *"There could never really be justice on stolen land / Are you really for peace and equality?"*

Hip-hop's critique of the police and the justice system kept the spark of truth lit, even during the darkest days of the War on Drugs.

Eventually, other voices joined in. In 2010, Michelle Alexander published a book titled *The New Jim Crow*, which told the history of "mass incarceration" and helped explain its connection to the long struggle for equality in America. Her book helped push for fundamental change in the national system of policing and prisons.

"I get my hope," Alexander said, "from this revolutionary idea that doesn't seem to die in the United States. This idea that all people are created equal with certain inalienable rights, including life, liberty, and the pursuit of happiness.

"I think the worst thing we can do," she continued, "is to fall into a sort of cynicism where we imagine nothing can ever be done. You know, these new systems of control just keep being born. This is just part of human nature. Well, it may be part of human nature to fear one another. But there is also a part of human nature I believe that wants to see the equality, even divinity, in each other and to honor it. And that spirit remains alive in the United States today. And if we give up on it, then I think we're giving up on the dream of a truly thriving, equitable multiracial, multiethnic democracy."

IN 1982, state authorities began disposing of thousands of tons of toxic waste into a landfill in Afton, North Carolina. Though a small, rural town, Afton was also home to an African American community that traced its roots all the way back to Reconstruction, and whose members cherished the land they called home. The waste contained polychlorinated biphenyls (PCBs), one of the most poisonous chemicals known to science, so dangerous that their production was completely banned in 1977. PCBs cause cancer and birth defects, and once in the earth, they are difficult to remove.

Local people in Afton and surrounding, majority-Black Warren County were outraged at this dangerous threat to their health. They knew the dumping was wrong, and with the help of a civil rights activist named Ben Chavis and local church groups, they organized to stop it.

For six weeks, hundreds of residents tried to block the poison-laden trucks from reaching the landfill. This wasn't only an environmental issue, they argued. Their community had been targeted. "We were poor, we were Black and we were politically impotent," one protester said.

One day during the protests, a police car pulled Chavis over—for driving too slowly, the officer said. Chavis understood perfectly well, however, that his role in the protests had made him a target.

"This is racism," Chavis yelled, as he was thrown in a local jail. "This is environmental racism."

The Afton protesters failed to stop the landfill. But their actions inspired a new chapter in the movement for racial equality, and Chavis's words—"environmental racism"—have come to define one of the most dire current threats to Black Americans.

For the past forty years, activists have discovered racial inequality in the walls, in the soil, and even in the water.

Catherine Coleman Flowers in Montgomery, Alabama, holding a water testing kit, 2020.

CHAPTER FIFTEEN

★ ★ ★

CATHERINE FLOWERS, DR. MONA HANNA-ATTISHA, AND BARACK OBAMA

Expose America's Crisis of Environmental Racism

When Catherine Flowers hosted special guests in Lowndes County, Alabama, she always took them to see the sewage.

Politicians, journalists, religious leaders, even representatives from the United Nations—Flowers wanted to make sure all of them could see and smell what life was like for poor Black people in Alabama.

Lowndes was one of the poorest counties in the state, and three-quarters of its population was Black. When Flowers was a child, the county was still known as "bloody Lowndes" because of the history of lynching and violent attacks on Black people there.

A lot had changed since then. Black people now served

as school board members, mayors, and even county commissioner. Highway 80, which cuts across the county, had been memorialized as part of the Selma-to-Montgomery heritage trail—one of the most important historical sites of the Civil Rights Movement. So much of the struggle for equality in the 1960s happened in the rural county's small towns and remote crossroads.

One thing remained the same, however. The majority of Lowndes County residents were still very, very poor.

Flowers returned home to Lowndes in 2000 after a long career as a teacher in Washington, DC, and Detroit. Hoping to make a difference, she took a job with the NAACP to continue its work registering Black voters. She soon realized, however, that racial inequality in Lowndes ran much deeper than voting rights.

A childhood neighbor pulled her aside one day. "Things are worse for us than they have ever been," she confided.

Flowers's visitors didn't have to travel far to see the sewage. Homes all over the rural county had failing or clogged septic systems—or lacked them entirely. One resident led Flowers to the back of her house. "Sewage was flowing into a hole in the ground near the back door," she recalled. "Feces, toilet paper, and water were near the top of the hole. Although our visit was in October, the pit was teeming with mosquitoes, some sitting on the raw sewage." It was a sight that could be found all over Lowndes County.

At another home, a white plastic pipe led away from

the house and emptied into a fetid pool. Children's toys lay nearby. In some houses, rain would cause the pipes to back up, flooding bathrooms and even kitchens with raw waste.

The problem was made worse by the region's dense, clay soils, which prevented water and sewage from draining properly. This was not a natural disaster, however—it was a man-made one.

"Why were certain communities impacted and others were not?" Flowers asked. "And why were all of the people impacted generally poor or minorities?"

Even worse, Flowers learned that Lowndes County responded to the sanitation crisis not by helping people but by issuing fines for anyone whose septic systems did not meet local building codes. Some residents were even arrested and jailed for their violations. And it was all because they did not have the money to make improvements.

Until Catherine Flowers started calling attention to the crisis of clean water and sanitation in Alabama, most people didn't know it existed; after all, these were problems that usually plagued the world's poorest, developing countries. The problem of sewage, and of getting people access to functioning septic systems, turned out to be a major public health issue that the government and media had ignored.

Flowers even discovered that hookworm, a parasite that public-health experts assumed had been eradicated decades before, was now plaguing residents all over the county. At first, doctors didn't believe her. "This is not something that we test for in the US because people don't anticipate that we have it," Flowers said. This was the United States of America—the world's richest nation.

Catherine believes that her fight against waste is part of the unfinished business of the Civil Rights Movement. In the 1960s, civil rights activists had fought to bring democracy to Lowndes County, but a half century later, voting rights had not solved many of the area's fundamental problems. Freedom was more than choosing representatives: it was also about access to the basic necessities of life, which for human beings included clean water and adequate sanitation.

Flowers's work took her beyond Lowndes County, her home. She soon learned that the problem of waste in America was national, not just local. "When I began this work more than fifteen years ago," Flowers said, "I thought that it was just in Lowndes County. Now I realize that Lowndes County is symbolic of poor rural communities across the United States that are experiencing the same injustice."

Racial inequality in Alabama, and all over the nation, was making people sick; Flowers called it "America's dirty secret."

——◇——

Dangerous parasites are not the only threat lurking in Black America's water, and rural places such as Lowndes County are not the only places where environmental racism plagues African American communities. Cities, where so many Black people made their homes following the Great Migration of the early twentieth century, have become hot spots for environmental threats to their health and well-being.

Like a magnifying glass that focuses the sun's rays, racism concentrates environmental damage in segregated cities, towns, and neighborhoods.

For the residents of Flint, Michigan, environmental racism isn't an abstract idea; it's a poison that flowed directly into their homes.

———◇———

"It's regular, good, pure drinking water, and it's right in our backyard."ᶜ

Mayor Dayne Walling of Flint, Michigan, was singing the praises of his city's new water source: the Flint River.

For decades, Flint piped its drinking water from nearby Detroit, Michigan's largest city. But by 2014, Flint was facing a financial crisis and was looking to save money on its water bill. A new pipeline was in the works to Lake Huron, but in the meantime, the city would have to rely on a local supply for its 100,000 residents.

Home to General Motors, Flint was once America's industrial powerhouse, known the world over for the cars that rolled off its assembly lines. Now it was a city in decline, where residents struggled to find good jobs.

Despite the city's promises, the new water cost more, too, and the monthly bills ate into the already-tight budgets of Flint's families. Forty percent of them lived below the poverty line; more than half of the city was African American.

But it wasn't the cost of the new water that bothered residents most.

"I don't know how it can be clean if it smells and tastes bad," one resident told a local television reporter.

A local pastor noticed that the fountain in a park near his church spouted brown water. One woman reported that her tap water was foamy and strangely colored; it's "just weird," she said. Children developed rashes after taking baths.

As word spread in the community, Flint residents started stocking up on bottled water. They took showers at friends' and relatives' homes in nearby towns.

Complaints piled up over the months following the switch to the Flint River supply. Residents organized to pressure city hall and lobby the governor in Lansing. But local officials reassured Flint residents, time and time again, that nothing was wrong with the city's water. "It's a quality, safe product," the mayor said that summer. "I think people are wasting their precious money buying bottled water."

Months went by, and then a year. Everyone talked about the water in Flint—and nobody in power did anything about it.

In August 2015, a pediatrician in Flint named Dr. Mona Hanna-Attisha heard a story at a family barbecue. A scientist had tested the water in Flint and found high levels of lead.

"Lead in the water?"

Dr. Mona's mind raced: Few public health risks were more terrifying to a pediatrician. Lead's effect on children—especially babies—could be irreversible. It built up slowly in the body, quietly attacking the brain. Over months and years, children grew tired and unfocused, their grades dropping as their cognitive abilities declined.

"It's really science-fiction comic-book stuff, like the X-Men," she said, "except the victims aren't getting super-powers. Their powers are being taken away."

She started asking questions, but government officials gave evasive, noncommittal answers. Some were even hostile toward her.

Her worst fears came to pass when she began comparing lead levels in the blood of her youngest patients, before and after the city's switch to the Flint River water. There was no longer any question in her mind, and her data supported it: Flint's children were being poisoned by lead. But what could be done about it? Why did the government not seem to care? Frantic, she stopped eating and sleeping as she imagined the toxins seeping into her community.

By September, Dr. Mona knew what she had to do. She met with Mayor Walling, and when he rejected her evidence, she sent it to the news media.

More than eighteen months after poisons started seeping into the city's water, the Flint crisis suddenly ballooned into a national scandal. *How could the people in power have let it go on for so long?* the press wanted to know.

Though she had spent her entire career in Flint, Dr. Mona's campaign against lead took her outside the state, where she started calling attention to how environmental racism damaged cities and communities all around the country, from Newark, New Jersey, to Washington, DC.

Powerful people started paying attention to Dr. Mona's warnings. President Barack Obama declared Flint's water a national emergency. "This was a man-made disaster," he said during a trip to a high school in Flint. "This was avoidable. This was preventable."

———◇———

President Obama would not have been surprised to learn that racism and neglect had polluted Flint. Long before he launched a career in politics, a young Barack Obama had started out as a community organizer—arriving in Chicago in 1985, ready to pick up where the Civil Rights Movement had left off.

Nineteen years before Obama set foot in the city's South Side, Martin Luther King Jr. ran head-on into Chicago's hard wall of white resistance to integration and equality, and his Open Housing Movement was roundly defeated. Now, wherever he looked, Obama could see the wreckage for himself. Black children in the city attending all-Black schools. The city's Black neighborhoods more segregated than ever.

That same year, though, Chicago had also elected its first Black mayor, Harold Washington Jr. Some people saw new opportunities for change: people like Barack Obama. He took a job with the Developing Communities Project, which was run by a group of churches on the city's South Side. His role was to talk to people, knocking on doors and persuading ordinary Black Chicagoans that they could get involved in politics and push the city to make changes. Like Fannie Lou Hamer, Obama strove to convince people who felt powerless that there was power in togetherness.

The residents were skeptical of this handsome, Harvard-educated young man. Obama earned their trust, over weeks and months, by staying in the background—he was just the organizer, he insisted; they were the leaders of their own community.

Together, Obama and his South Side allies improved the area's parks and playgrounds; they created career programs for young people; and they successfully lobbied city hall to increase garbage pickups. These were small dents in a big problem, Obama knew, but they were something. Racial inequality in the nation's third-largest city sometimes seemed to be baked into the pavement and part of the very architecture—and the environment—of Chicago itself.

Nowhere was this truer than in the two thousand apartments that comprised Altgeld Gardens, built during World War II as housing for returning African American veterans. Like most publicly funded housing developments at the time, Altgeld was racially segregated. Many of its new residents went on to work in the factories that lined the nearby Little Calumet River; for the next three decades, Altgeld and its surrounding area became a center of Chicago's African American community on the South Side.

By the 1980s, however, most of the factories had closed down, stranding thousands of unemployed workers and leaving behind a river poisoned with industrial chemicals. A huge landfill separated Altgeld from the rest of the city, and the smell of garbage wafted through apartment windows on hot Chicago days. If that wasn't smelly enough, the city built a sewage treatment plant directly across the street.

Redlining and housing discrimination hemmed in Chicago's Black community, making it all but impossible to avoid the garbage, the odors, and the poisons that surrounded it.

Altgeld's residents felt forgotten and dumped on. "Everything about the Gardens seemed in a perpetual state of disrepair," Obama recalled. "Ceilings crumbled. Pipes burst. Toilets backed up. Muddy tire tracks branded the small, brown lawns strewn with empty flower planters—broken, tilted, half-buried."

Shortly after Obama's arrival, the residents discovered yet another hidden threat to their health. In a routine maintenance announcement, Altgeld's management said that construction workers would be removing asbestos—a dangerous, cancer-causing substance—from its offices.

But if it was in the offices, the residents asked, could asbestos be present all through the development? Did Altgeld have poison in its walls?

Altgeld's buildings manager denied that there was any

risk, but the suspicious residents decided to take their concerns to a higher authority.

Later that week, a fired-up group of Altgeld residents— "Obama's Army," one of them joked—crowded into a city bus to take their protest downtown, to the director of the Chicago Housing Authority.

The director, a startled secretary informed them, wasn't in.

This time, however, word had leaked out about the asbestos at Altgeld, and television reporters pushed their way into the office behind the protesters. Suddenly, it seemed, the Chicago Housing Authority was ready to listen.

Following a public meeting on the South Side, the Chicago Housing Authority agreed to ask the federal government for funds to pay for the emergency removal of asbestos in Altgeld Gardens—and in housing developments all over Chicago. A month later, the cleanup was underway.

A small group of poor, determined Chicagoans had suddenly made the impossible seem possible. And for a brief moment, they revealed to the whole city what its Black residents know to this day, that the desire for healthy homes is inseparable from the broader quest for equality.

———◇———

"Flint and Washington and Newark," Dr. Mona says, "are all viewed as Black cities and have a shared history of segregation, redlining, race riots, white flight, economic decline, violence, a pernicious drug epidemic, and a loss of local control. Newark's water crisis, like Flint's, and even Washington's, is an obvious case of environmental racism, a case of blindness to the people, places, and problems we choose not to see."

In Warren County, North Carolina, Benjamin Chavis discovered how blind most people had been to the environmental threats to African American communities. It was a lesson Catherine Flowers learned many years later, and that most of the country is still only vaguely conscious of today.

Climate change has entered this mix like the hurricanes that are becoming more frequent and more dangerous as the earth's atmosphere warms. Hot summers are getting hotter, and—as Richmond and other segregated cities have seen—the heat beats down unequally on communities of color. Rising seas swamp low-lying flood zones, such as the African American neighborhood of the Ninth Ward in New Orleans, which was demolished in 2005 by Hurricane Katrina. In 2017, Hurricane Harvey battered Texas and Louisiana, wreaking similar destruction.

In Brooklyn, New York, the activist Elizabeth Yeampierre fights for what many are calling "climate justice," part of a movement that seeks to change how racism, environmental destruction, and the warming climate impact communities of color.

"The communities that are most impacted by COVID, or by pollution," Yeampierre says, "it's not surprising that they're the ones that are going to be most impacted by extreme weather events. And it's not surprising that they're the ones that are targeted for racial violence. It's all the same communities, all over the United States. And you can't treat one part of the problem without the other, because it's so systemic."

"WHEN THE POLICE rushed onto our corner," James Forman Jr. recounted, "our students were forced to 'assume the position,' with their legs spread, faces against the wall or squad car, and hands behind their heads. Then they were searched, with the officers feeling every inch of their bodies, turning backpacks and pockets inside out, leaving the sidewalks strewn with notebooks, broken pencils, lipstick, and combs.

"Not once," he added, "over the course of about ten searches, did the police recover anything illegal." Inside the walls of the Maya Angelou Public Charter School in Washington, DC—which Forman had founded in 2000—students worked hard to develop the skills they needed to succeed in America. Outside, they faced daily reminders of how America saw them.

Police departments call these kinds of tactics "stop and frisk."

Forty percent of all police stops in New York City were of young Black and Latino men—a group that is only 5 percent of New York City's population. And the results? More than 80 percent of the time, these young men were totally innocent. White people were actually more likely to be carrying an illegal weapon than were people of color.

Stop and frisk wasn't reducing crime. Instead, it was creating a climate of fear for Black people, in their own home, their own city.

"No one should live in fear of being stopped whenever he leaves his home to go about the activities of daily life," a judge in New York City said. In 2013, she ruled that the police's behavior was unconstitutional.

All over America, Black people are still routinely stopped and searched by police officers, for no reason other than their skin color. "Consider for a moment the kinds of police contact about which Black people have long complained, all with no justification other than our Black bodies," legal expert Devon Carbado writes. "Being watched, approached, questioned, asked for identification, made to feel violent and dangerous, treated as suspect, stopped and frisked, searched and stripped."

For some, an unfair police stop is terrifying or humiliating. For others, the outcome can be fatal.

Yusef Salaam enters the courtroom after being falsely accused
in the Central Park jogger attack, August 18, 1990.

CHAPTER SIXTEEN

★ ★ ★

YUSEF SALAAM

Battles Racial
Profiling

On a spring night in 1989, fifteen-year-old Yusef Salaam joined a group of friends and headed into Central Park in New York City. Kevin Richardson, Korey Wise, Antron McCray, Raymond Santana, and Yusef: five boys, Black and brown, the oldest barely sixteen.

Yusef lived in an apartment with his mother and sisters in Schomburg Plaza, on the northeast corner of the park. Schomburg's two apartment towers were built for middle-class New Yorkers, many of them teachers and other city workers. The Northside Center for Child Development occupied the ground floor; it was founded and run by Kenneth and Mamie Clark, two renowned psychologists who had provided crucial research for the NAACP legal team that argued *Brown v. Board of Education* more than thirty years earlier.

April 19 was an ordinary school night for Yusef, who attended Rice High School, a Catholic school in Harlem. Tall, lean, and gregarious, Yusef prided himself on the friendships he had made all over his neighborhood. "I was a child full of hope, full of dreams, and full of aspirations that hadn't yet been realized," Yusef said.

Several hours later, around 1:00 AM, two construction workers on their way home through the park stumbled across a gruesome sight: a female jogger, brutally beaten, bound and gagged, and a victim of sexual assault. They ran for help. By the time an ambulance arrived at the emergency room, the woman had lost most of her blood, and her body temperature indicated that she was near death. All night long, doctors worked furiously to save the jogger's life.

New York City police detectives moved quickly that night to make arrests, sweeping the park for potential suspects. Yusef and his four friends found themselves caught up in the dragnet.

Before dawn, each boy sat in an interrogation room, police detectives looming over and peppering them with questions and thinly veiled threats. Even though four of the boys were under the age of sixteen and should not have been interrogated alone, the police questioned them without their parents present.

By sunrise, all five boys had confessed to the attack.

Not a single one of them was telling the truth.

———◇———

This was not an unusual outcome: The interrogation tactics used by police often result in false confessions—nearly a third of the time. Over half of all false confessions are made by juvenile suspects, who are more easily threatened and manipulated by adults. Alone, frightened, confused, and disoriented, many if not most young suspects will eventually collapse under hours of harsh questioning—and will say anything to make it stop.

The police looked at the five Black suspects and saw hardened criminals. The American Psychological Association has concluded that "Black boys as young as 10 may not be viewed in the same light of childhood innocence as their white peers, but are instead more likely to be mistaken as older, be perceived as guilty, and face police violence if accused of a crime."

Without waiting for actual evidence, the media pounced. In a firestorm of coverage, newspapers, radio, and television whipped up a story about a white woman being raped by five Black boys—a story that could have been ripped from the pages of a Jim Crow–era newspaper in the Deep South.

Before they had a chance to plead not guilty, the court of public opinion rendered its swift verdict on Yusef Salaam and his four young friends.

A New York real estate tycoon named Donald Trump paid to take out full-page ads in four major newspapers. The headline blared, "Bring Back the Death Penalty." "[T]hey should be forced to suffer and, when they kill, they should be executed for their crimes," Trump wrote.

Using language that Ida B. Wells might have recognized from the previous century, the newspaper columnist Patrick Buchanan declared that if "the eldest of that wolf pack were tried, convicted, and hanged in Central Park, by June 1, and the 13- and 14-year-olds were stripped, horsewhipped, and sent to prison, the park might soon be safe again for women."

Yusef knew that his mother had grown up in the South, under Jim Crow. "But here I was experiencing Jim Crowism in the North," he said. "They were trying to make us modern Emmett Tills, based on Donald Trump's ad."

As they walked into the courthouse for trial, demonstrators crowded the entrance to the building. For the five boys, it was like walking into a nightmare. "Demonstrators, you know people just shouting," Yusef recalled. "'Rapist!' 'You animal!' 'You don't deserve to be alive.'

"It just felt like the whole world hated us," Yusef said.

In the courtroom, Yusef felt powerless as the district attorney laid out her case—which included videotaped confessions of four of the suspects.

"I was a person who thought that I knew how to talk in a way that was compelling," he said, "that could describe things and defend myself. And I realized very quickly that I was in too deep. And by that, I remember going on the witness stand and saying, man, I'm just going to tell them the truth. And my truth wasn't received well. My truth was twisted. My truth was turned against me."

The stories each boy told of that night differed, something that should have caused investigators to question their guilt. They eventually recanted their confessions, and police found no physical evidence linking them to the crime. But Yusef walked into the courtroom with a whole history of presumed guilt weighing on him. The Harvard historian Khalil Gibran Muhammad calls this "the condemnation of blackness."

The jury issued its verdict on Yusef Salaam: guilty. After two separate trials, the five boys all disappeared into the New York State prison system.

Their case cast a long, dark shadow—and the justice system drew all the wrong lessons from it. Over the next decade, the Central Park Five case helped fuel an obsession with teenage criminals. A Princeton University professor conjured a mythological creature known as a "superpredator," which he described as "so impulsive, so remorseless, that [he] can kill, rape, maim, without giving it a second thought." The media amplified worry over these alleged hyper-criminals by treating this description as an indisputable fact of social science. The law wasn't far behind. States passed new laws allowing children as young as thirteen to be tried and sentenced as adults. "In 1998 alone," according to one report, "roughly 200,000 youths were put through the adult court system, and the majority of them were Black."

Through long years in different prisons, the Central Park Five maintained their innocence, even when changing their stories might have persuaded parole boards to release them earlier. Antron, Kevin, Raymond, and Yusef spent the early part of their sentences in juvenile detention facilities, until they reached the age of twenty-one, when they were transferred to adult prisons. "What you see in a youth facility you think is the worst of the worst, until you get to adult prison," Yusef said.

Korey Wise was sixteen when he was sentenced, and was sent immediately to a maximum-security prison in upstate New York. Barely five feet five, with hearing loss from childhood abuse, Korey was thrown in with some of the state's most violent criminals.

"We were in there fighting for our lives," Yusef said.

During his long years behind bars, Korey crossed paths more than once with Matias Reyes, a violent serial rapist who had been arrested in 1989. Reyes heard Korey's story but said nothing.

Many years later, however—whether from guilt or some other motive—Reyes approached prison officials with a startling confession: He was the man who had attacked the Central Park Jogger.

Reyes's confession in May 2002 set investigators scrambling to reexamine old case files and evidence. His account of the attack matched the physical evidence perfectly, in stark contrast to the five boys' forced confessions. Finally, a DNA test conclusively linked Reyes to the victim. There was no longer any question about who had committed this awful crime.

In August 2002, after an exhaustive reinvestigation of the case, the Manhattan district attorney asked the court to overturn the convictions of the Central Park Five. It took until December for their convictions to be vacated and the men to be exonerated.

———◇———

When it was finally over, when the same system that had sent him away for seven years—one-third of his life—decided that he had always been innocent, there was silence.

No flash bulbs, no round-the-clock news coverage.

"We were found innocent," Yusef Salaam said. "There was no tsunami of media that followed in the way that tsunami came out within the first few weeks when they thought we were guilty."

Newspapers had called him and his four innocent friends "mutants" and "animals." None of it was true, but the lies lingered in New York City's memory. And some powerful people, many of them in the police department, still refused to accept the truth. To them, the Central Park Five would always be criminals.

"When I left prison, the officer literally said to me, 'I'll see you later.'"

Yusef had entered prison a boy, but he left a man—and he struggled to turn his ordeal into a positive force. "You can come out better, and not come out bitter," he said.

"Surely, after difficulty, there is relief. There's more to do, in this life."

For Yusef, this meant speaking, writing, and testifying about the false accusations against Black people

Telling his story. This story:

Five innocent boys, swept up by the police and pressured into making false confessions—even as the actual killer still stalked the streets, a free man. How could this have happened? And why did the media swallow the false story so easily and whip up a frenzy to punish them?

The answer to these questions could be found in a long history of false accusations, reaching back a century and more.

All Americans are supposed to be presumed innocent until proven guilty—this idea is the bedrock of our entire legal system. But, according to Khalil Gibran Muhammad, the presumption of *guilt* for Black people "allows law enforcement, just like it did in the 1870s in Alabama, to have the widest berth of discretion to challenge a person, a black male on the streets, to ask them, 'Where are you going? And do you belong here?'"

White America assumes that Black people should be feared and suspected, and that Black neighborhoods need the most policing.

"No white community in America would tolerate this kind of treatment in the name of public safety in its communities, period," Muhammad says.

The Innocence Project, an organization devoted to freeing innocent prisoners convicted on faulty DNA evidence, has found that false accusations are common, even today—and the majority of falsely accused suspects are Black.

According to the Equal Justice Initiative, "there are more innocent people in our jails and prisons today than ever before." A young attorney named Bryan Stevenson founded the Equal Justice Initiative (EJI) in 1989, after Stevenson discovered firsthand how many Black people ended up behind bars on the flimsiest evidence. (Stevenson told his story in a book titled *Just Mercy: A Story of Justice and Redemption*, which was also made into a Hollywood movie.) Researchers at EJI have found that an innocent Black person accused of murder is *seven times more likely* to go to jail than an innocent white person accused of the same crime.

"There is clear evidence of racial bias in the administration of criminal justice in the United States," Stevenson says. "For too many poor citizens and people of color, arrest and imprisonment have become an unavoidable part of the American experience."

In March 1991, a Black man named Rodney King tried to escape from the Los Angeles police. After a high-speed chase on a city freeway and local streets, police officers stopped King and ordered him and his two passengers out of his car. For the next several minutes, while a large group of other officers watched, four policemen beat King brutally. They broke his bones and knocked out his teeth. They fractured his skull. Two 50,000-volt shocks from a Taser stun gun left marks on King's chest. Rodney King crouched low on the asphalt, certain that the officers meant to end his life.

King's attackers intended to claim that he had been injured while resisting arrest. Some made jokes as the beating unfolded; one officer instructed others to "hit his joints, hit the wrists, hit his elbows, hit his knees, hit his ankles." They didn't realize, however, that a bystander across the street was filming the whole attack on a handheld camcorder—the first time in American history that proof of police brutality had been captured on tape.

The bystander mailed a copy of the recording to a local television station. Within a day, footage of Rodney King's ordeal was being broadcast around the world.

Four police officers went to court one year later, charged with assault and excessive force. To most observers, the videotape of the attack made for an airtight case: This was police brutality, pure and simple.

And then, on April 29, 1992, the nearly all-white jury returned its verdict: "Not guilty."

The movie director John Singleton sat in the courtroom audience stunned when the verdict was read. "By having this verdict," he said, "what these people did, they lit the fuse to a bomb."

Within hours, protests and fires broke out in Los Angeles; a day later, the largest insurrection in modern American history engulfed the city—nearly twenty-five years after the Kerner Commission warned America not to repeat the mistakes that had led to the urban uprisings of the 1960s.

Once again, white America was forced to confront the inequality and violence that Black America had lived with for decades. Rodney King—like Emmett Till before him—reminded a new generation that Black people still had far to travel in their quest for genuine freedom.

Ever since slavery, white America has used the police to control the African American community. After emancipation, the Black Codes were a temporary substitute for slavery, until they were struck down by Reconstruction. But in the decades following—all the way to the present day—the nation's police forces have watched, followed, and arrested Black people at far higher rates than white people, with predictably tragic results.

In the late nineteenth century, lynch mobs justified mob violence by conjuring up images of Black rapists; today, white politicians, police, and media routinely overinflate the degree of crime in Black communities (which they usually dub "Black-on-Black crime") to justify excessive policing and police brutality.

One study showed that white people drastically overestimate the degree to which Black people commit crimes—by as much as 30 percent. Police officers have been shown to share these same biases: When asked to describe who looks like a criminal, police in one study most often pointed to a picture of a Black face.

Racist assumptions about Black people and crime lead to the overpolicing of Black drivers, pedestrians, and neighborhoods. Black people are much more likely to be stopped and arrested than white people, despite being no more likely to commit crimes. In Chicago, police department data showed that Black and Latino drivers were pulled over and searched *four times* as often as white drivers—despite the fact that white drivers were *two times more likely* to be carrying contraband such as drugs or weapons.

Racial profiling creates a vicious cycle: Higher arrest rates are cited by police as a justification for treating Black people differently in the first place. The extra scrutiny leads to distrust on both sides. It exposes Black communities to police brutality, even when no crime is involved. Again and again, it leads to the murder of innocent men and women—from Eric Garner to Breonna Taylor and George Floyd—by the same forces that are supposed to protect them.

"To look at America with eyes that can see, with ears that can hear," Yusef Salaam said, "is to look at a place where there are two Americas—divided and unequal."

★ ★ ★

A RECORD NUMBER of African Americans turned out to vote for Barack Obama in the 2008 election, helping to sweep the first Black president into the White House. When Obama was reelected in 2012, the percentage of Black voters was even higher.

The vast majority of Black Americans could not even vote when Obama was born; now their political clout was undeniable. Obama won because Black voters turned out in large numbers—but he also won in spite of a forty-year effort to prevent them from doing so.

Almost as soon as the Voting Rights Act passed in 1965, white people came up with new schemes to limit the impact of Black voting power. Voting rights activists were harassed by government officials, Black voters faced intimidation, and voting districts were "gerrymandered" to reduce the impact of Black voters and enhance the power of white people.

The fight to protect voting rights depended on the bravery of local activists and also on a key provision of the Voting Rights Act of 1965: Section 5, which requires local government officials to prove to the federal government that any changes to their system of voting does not discriminate on the basis of race. From the 1960s until 2012, the federal government blocked 177 proposed changes to the state of Georgia's election system, because they were discriminatory.

Many of the new voter-suppression tactics got a boost in 2013—by none other than the US Supreme Court. In a case called *Shelby County v. Holder*, the nation's highest court decided that because so much time had passed since the era of Jim Crow, the federal government no longer needed to supervise elections in states that had been guilty of discriminating against Black voters.

By invalidating Section 5, the Supreme Court opened the doors to a new era of dirty tricks aimed squarely at African American voters.

In a blistering dissent from the majority's opinion—which she insisted on standing up and reading out loud to the Court—Justice Ruth Bader Ginsburg said that "throwing out [the provision] when it has worked and is continuing to work to stop discriminatory changes is like throwing away your umbrella in a rainstorm because you are not getting wet."

In Georgia, and all over America, the rain is still falling.

Stacey Abrams speaking at a rally on November 5, 2018, in Savannah, Georgia, as she campaigns for governor.

CHAPTER SEVENTEEN

★ ★ ★

STACEY ABRAMS

Leads the Fight Against Voter Suppression

"Georgia's not ready for a Black woman."

In the months since she had decided to run for governor of the state of Georgia, Stacey Abrams heard that sentence more times than she could count. The words weighed on her, pushing down on her hopes. Sometimes, she even believed them. She asked herself whether her dreams were too big or whether her time had not yet come.

Certainly, Georgia's history was not exactly encouraging on this point. In the 1960s, a white restaurant owner in Atlanta named Lester Maddox made headlines when he refused to serve Black customers. His flagrant display of racism made Maddox a hero among white people, and he channeled this support into a political career. Despite having no experience in elected office, he ran for governor in

1967—and won. Maddox once declared that Martin Luther King Jr. was "an enemy of our country."

Georgia had come a long way since then, it was true. John Lewis, beaten and bloodied as a young civil rights activist, now served as a powerful congressman representing Atlanta and its surrounding areas. Stacey Abrams herself had sat in the Georgia House of Representatives for ten years, the last six as minority leader. Abrams earned a reputation among Republicans and Democrats in state government as a smart legislator and an effective dealmaker.

Abrams was ambitious, a trait that some people resented in a Black woman, and she wasn't shy about it. Yet she had built a résumé that qualified her for just about anything. She was the president of her class at Spelman College. She completed graduate degrees at the University of Texas and Yale Law School. She had been a successful lawyer, business owner, and politician. In her many years in the Georgia House of Representatives, she had mastered the intricacies of government.

"People who underestimate her risk complete embarrassment," one Republican legislator commented.

But not *everything* in Georgia had changed since the days of Lester Maddox. No Black person had ever held the governor's office in Georgia; in the 150 years since Reconstruction, only two Black people had served as governor of *any* state. No Black woman had ever been elected governor, anywhere, ever, in the United States of America.

In 2013, the same year that the Supreme Court handed

down its voting rights decision in *Shelby v. Holder*, Abrams founded an organization called the New Georgia Project, dedicated to registering new voters. Abrams learned first-hand about all of the many *new* ways that white political leaders planned to keep Black voters away from the polls.

States have always had the authority to draw the maps of electoral districts. Within these districts, voters cast ballots to send one or more people to represent them in the state or federal government. However, politicians often manipulate the boundaries of electoral districts to give advantages to their own political parties, based on their knowledge of which voters live where. Through skillful line-drawing (known as "gerrymandering") a political party can reduce the voting power of one group and increase the clout of another.

Abrams understood that racial discrimination often factored into these decisions, and that her home state of Georgia had a long history, dating back to the era of the Voting Rights Act, of conniving to reduce the political power of the growing Black electorate. With the stroke of a pen, a majority-Black area could be crisscrossed by new district lines; each piece of the area would then be stitched onto nearby neighborhoods with larger numbers of white voters.

Now, things were even worse. Before *Shelby County v. Holder*, a state like Georgia had to submit its redistricting plans to the US Department of Justice to make sure that the electoral maps had not been drawn with the intent of discriminating against Black people. Now that requirement had been thrown out the window. And in the years since, white political leaders all over the country have scrambled to dampen Black voters' power, reversing decades of gains since the 1960s.

In Georgia, the white political establishment wasn't as enthusiastic as Abrams about increasing the number of voters in the state, let alone making it easier for people of color to vote. In 2014, Georgia Secretary of State Brian Kemp worried that "Democrats are working hard, and all these stories about them, you know, registering all these minority voters that are out there and others that are sitting on the sidelines, if they can do that, they can win these elections in November."

These "voter skeptics" invented and promoted a new reason for challenging the right of Black people to vote: they called it *voter fraud*. Voter fraud happens when someone votes more than once by impersonating someone else or when someone deliberately tampers with an election by illegally increasing the number of votes for a candidate (for example, by creating fake mail-in ballots). Though the idea had been around for some time, its popularity spiked after the 2000 presidential election, when George W. Bush beat Al Gore by a tiny margin of votes. Some people learned from that experience that every vote counts; others concluded that *suppressing* every vote counts, too.

The idea of voter fraud conjured up visions of people voting twice, or of fraudsters registering dead or nonexistent people to vote, or of elections being won with the help of undocumented immigrants or others who could not legally cast a ballot. All over the United States, opponents of voter registration sounded the false alarm.

However, whenever anyone looked closely at supposed voter fraud, the claims seemed to fall apart at the touch. One national study found thirty-one confirmed cases of voter fraud out of one billion votes cast over multiple years and many elections, revealing just how unlikely it is for voter fraud to affect a single election's outcome. Another reported that the likelihood of someone impersonating someone else at the polls is less than the possibility of being struck by lightning. Still other investigations found no examples of voter fraud at all.

David Iglesias, a former US attorney for New Mexico, said that voter fraud is "like the boogeymen parents use to scare their children. It's very frightening, and it doesn't exist."

Voter fraud was a myth, but it served to justify a new wave of efforts to stop people—most of whom were Black—from exercising their right to vote.

Thirty-five US states—including Georgia—have passed what are called voter ID laws. The idea is simple: Voters must bring government-issued photo identification, such as a driver's license, to prove their identity at the polling station, in order to vote. The problem with this requirement is that many people—more than 10 percent of all eligible voters in America—do not have driver's licenses to begin with. More-over, *25 percent* of eligible African American voters lack this identification. Some would-be voters are discouraged by the tangled paperwork requirements of getting a license, especially since many states require birth certificates as proof of identity, which can be impossible for poorer or elderly people to obtain. (In one glaring example of these challenges, voting rights activists found that some Indiana voters needed a birth certificate to obtain a license—but also needed a license to obtain a birth certificate!) Other people simply do not own cars and live in places without public transportation that would allow them to travel to a driver's license office. In Alabama, a state with voter ID requirements, the state closed down thirty-one driver's license offices in mostly-Black counties.

In a 2005 case in Indiana, a federal judge concluded, "Let's not beat around the bush...the Indiana voter photo ID law is a not-too-thinly veiled attempt to discourage election-day turnout by certain folks." Eric Holder, the US attorney general under President Barack Obama, called voter ID laws a new form of the poll tax.

Some states also actively eliminate voter's names from registration lists for minor technical reasons or because someone didn't vote in a previous election, even though voting is not a legal requirement of American citizens. Most of these people have no idea they have been unregistered, and when they turn up to vote on election day, it's too late to fix the problem. Between 2016 and 2018, Georgia purged more than *10 percent* of all voters in the state—more than 1.5

million people—voters that came from more heavily Democratic leaning, African American districts.

Under a new "exact match law" in Georgia and elsewhere, a voter-registration application could be rejected if something as small as a hyphen, period, or capital letter doesn't exactly match the information that a state government already has on file.

Most states have laws that prohibit incarcerated people from voting, and others also prohibit people on parole, probation—or *anyone* with any felony conviction—for the rest of their lives. Since racial profiling and mass incarceration work to ensure many Black people are imprisoned for nonviolent crimes, a large percentage of the more than five million Americans impacted by these laws are Black.

These changes to our system of voting aren't *always* racist on their face, and often their champions will publicly claim that they don't target Black voters. But the same thing happens in every single case: They shrink the number of voters in a state and make sure that more and more of the voting population is white.

In Georgia, the official in charge of the not-so-secret campaign to shrink the size of the electorate was Brian Kemp, the secretary of state.

And in 2018, Kemp decided to run for governor on the Republican ticket—against Stacey Abrams. The very person in charge of the machinery that denied people access to the vote in Georgia was going to try to use that same machinery to win the governor's seat. Not surprisingly, perhaps, many Georgians howled at Kemp's blatant conflict of interest.

In 2018, Stacey Abrams concluded that this was her chance to change the tide of history and to prove the doubters wrong.

Abrams believed that fighting for education, health care, and expanded job opportunities should appeal to ordinary people from all walks of life—and as she traveled the state, she found that she was right. But she also knew that to overcome Georgia's tangled history of racial inequality, she was going to need hundreds of thousands, even millions of new allies.

And Abrams knew exactly where to look: Georgia had just over six million registered voters, and over eight hundred thousand Black people who were not yet registered to vote.

On election day, the Abrams-Kemp race had become a dead heat. Despite all of Kemp's machinations, Abrams's supporters came out in huge numbers to vote for her historic candidacy. At one polling station, a journalist interviewed a ninety-year-old Black woman. "I'm voting because most of my ancestors died for this," she said, "and I'm close to dying myself." Abrams knew that powerful forces were working against her, but she believed that the sheer numbers of voters turning out for her could tilt the election in her favor.

But the system of voter suppression was in full effect that day, with faulty machines, long lines, and essential supplies that simply ran out. Reporters documented lines of voters snaking through Black-majority neighborhoods, where in some cases waits lasted up to five hours. One polling place in central Atlanta had only three voting machines. A sixty-five-year-old Black woman commented, "I haven't had to work so hard to vote ever. It was just a runaround, and I've never experienced anything like this."

By the end of the night, there wasn't a clear winner.

———◇———

"I was numb," Stacey Abrams later recalled. She had just gotten off the phone with her campaign manager, who communicated the final tally of all of the ballots the state had agreed to count. They were short of victory by 17,000 votes.

Over the following days and weeks, the battle between Abrams and Kemp moved to the courts, with Abrams accusing her opponent of outright voter suppression. In particular, she pointed to 53,000 voter registration applications (mostly from Black applicants) that Kemp, as secretary of state, had refused to process.

Abrams used every legal tool at her disposal to challenge Kemp's claims, but in the end she ran out of options. There was no way she could win.

In some ways, Abrams accomplished what she set out to do. Her campaign had electrified Georgians, increasing turnout among African American, white, Latino, and Asian-Pacific Islander voters alike. A new, multiracial and multiethnic majority had pushed back against voter suppression and nearly achieved a historic victory.

Abrams would acknowledge the result of the election and Kemp's victory. But she would not "concede" the election—the traditional term for the way a losing candidate admitted defeat. "Concession means to acknowledge an action is right, true, or proper," Abrams announced in a press conference on November 16. "As a woman of conscience and faith, I cannot concede."

She was making a point that something wrong had happened here. Votes had been stolen, rejected, and suppressed. Black people had been denied their voice in a democratic election.

And then Stacey Abrams got to work. In early 2019, she launched a national voting-rights organization, Fair Fight Action, which continues to fight for all voters' right to have their voices heard.

In 2020, more states passed voter ID laws. A years-long effort to ensure that ex-felons could vote suffered a stinging defeat in court. All over the country, efforts to make voting more difficult for ordinary people gained momentum.

But that fall, all of Abrams's work paid off. For the first time in nearly forty years, Georgia "went blue." A record number of voters picked a Democrat, Joe Biden, for president, and two Democrats for the United States Senate—including Raphael Warnock, pastor of Ebenezer Baptist Church in Atlanta.

Stacey Abrams knew that the battle for the Black vote was not over, that it could never be about a single election. It was about a 150-year fight for voting rights—for the equal right of all people to participate in American democracy.

"Because the title of governor isn't nearly as important as our shared title—voters," she declared. "And that is why we fight on."

MARLOWE STOUDAMIRE WIPED the sweat from his forehead, even though the weather was mild in Detroit that morning. The pancake breakfast on Friday, March 6, drew a crowd, along with more than ninety police officers who had come to eat and chat with members of the local community at the precinct house.

Alarms about the coronavirus were going off around the country, but the pandemic was still a distant rumor in most of America. No one at the breakfast—and nobody anywhere else in Detroit, for that matter—considered wearing masks.

Stoudamire felt healthy and full of energy. He had a reputation as one of the city's heroes, a neighborhood organizer and community leader who had recently helped create an award-winning exhibit at the Detroit Historical Society commemorating the 1967 Detroit uprising. "As a lifelong Detroiter, he had a special skill at telling our stories," one of his colleagues said.

Two weeks later, Marlowe Stoudamire died of COVID-19, the first recorded victim of the new pandemic in the state of Michigan.

By April, the virus's stealth attack on Detroit's Black community broke into the open. The city's police chief tested positive. A popular teacher, only thirty-two years old, died in early April.

"It seems like one after another after another, and it's just hitting close to home," one Detroit man said. "It seems like everybody knows somebody who died."

Cases of the virus multiplied at a terrifying rate, infecting rich and poor alike, but not in equal measure. Like a flood that looks for the path of least resistance, it crept into neighborhoods, workplaces, and homes where the burdens of inequality left some people more exposed than others.

Two months into the worst pandemic in a century, the death rate of Black people was twice as high as that of white people. In a small city in Georgia hit hard by the virus, 99 percent of the victims were African American, although they made up 70 percent of the population.

"It hit like a bomb," the town's coroner said.

Dr. Susan Moore in an undated photograph.

CHAPTER EIGHTEEN

★ ★ ★

DR. SUSAN MOORE

Calls Out America's Unequal Health Care

The terrified patient gripped her cell phone, desperate to get word to someone she knew. She had tested positive for COVID-19 on November 29, and now her condition was getting worse. On December 4, 2020, with a tube in her nose to feed oxygen to her scarred lungs, she posted a short video on Facebook from her hospital bed in Indianapolis.

Her doctor had given her two infusions of remdesivir, an antiviral drug that attacked her COVID symptoms. When it came time for her next dose, however, she found that he had grown skeptical of her claims.

"You don't need it, you're not even short of breath," he said. He was getting ready to send her home.

But how could he have diagnosed her condition properly? "He did not even listen to my lungs," she explained.

"He didn't touch me in any way. He performed no physical exam."

The patient knew that she was ill. She was no stranger to doctors, patients, and hospitals: She was Dr. Susan Moore, an experienced physician herself. Born in Jamaica, Moore studied medicine at the University of Michigan Medical School, one of the top programs in the United States. She had treated patients for nearly twenty years, running her own family and geriatrics practice.

That first week of December, the pandemic in Indiana edged toward a terrifying peak. Ninety-nine people died of COVID-19 on December 4 alone, and nearly eight thousand tested positive for the virus.

COVID-19 infections swept through Black communities in Michigan, New York, Florida, and other virus hot spots. To make matters worse, African Americans were disproportionately among the "essential workers" who could not avoid in-person jobs at factories, warehouses, stores, hospitals, and other workplaces, further exposing them to potential infection. Those who were not "essential workers" met a different fate, as job losses among Black people skyrocketed in the early months of the pandemic. One report declared that "Black workers face two of the most lethal preexisting conditions for coronavirus—racism and economic inequality."

As a Black woman in her fifties with a history of serious illness, Susan Moore understood that the odds of surviving were not in her favor.

She had a nineteen-year-old son and elderly parents who needed someone to care for them. She was desperate to get better, and for that she needed good medical treatment. But now she found herself stuck in a hospital where nobody seemed to believe her.

Like many COVID-19 patients, Moore was also in a great deal of physical pain. Skeptical of her claims, her doctor refused to offer her medicine to treat it.

Moore didn't pretend to be an expert on pain medications, but she understood her own body.

"I told him you cannot tell me how I feel," she said.

As she recorded her Facebook video, Moore's weak voice started to quaver.

"I was in so much pain from my neck. My neck hurt so bad.

"I was crushed.

"He made me feel like a drug addict."

Susan's experience that day could have happened to any Black person. Doubts about her pain. Fears that painkillers might lead to addiction. Researchers have revealed that Black patients are much less likely than white patients to receive the correct dose of pain medicine. They have also found that as many as half of all doctors and nurses hold false, biased beliefs that Black patients have a higher physical tolerance for suffering—even though there is no biological basis for this idea.

Even in cases of serious injury, Black people are much less likely to receive opioids for their pain in emergency rooms. One national study of over a million people showed that Black children recovering from appendicitis were only *one-fifth* as likely to receive proper pain medication as white children.

"You have to show proof that there is something wrong with you in order to get the medicine," Susan said. "I put forth and I maintain that if I was white, I wouldn't have to go through that."

She spoke to a patient advocate at the hospital who told Susan that nothing could be done.

In desperation, Moore contacted the hospital administration. "If they are not going to treat me here properly," she said, "send me to another hospital."

Finally, Susan got word—through a nurse, not her doctor—that the hospital had agreed to treat her pain. Almost three hours passed before anyone arrived to administer pain medication.

Moore was stunned. "Now, that is not how you treat patients, period," she said.

A scan of Susan's lungs revealed the source of her pain: fluid had built up dangerously, and her lymph nodes had swelled. Though confined to a hospital bed and straining to breathe, she managed to get the attention of higher-ups at the hospital, who assured her they would investigate how she had been treated earlier that week.

What she couldn't shake, however, was her rage at the idea that her own doctor was ready to discharge her from the hospital without the proper treatment or medication—in the middle of the worst pandemic in American history. If this was happening to her, what might be happening to Black patients who didn't have the knowledge she had as a physician?

"This is how Black people get killed," Moore said, "when you send them home, and they don't know how to fight for themselves."

Dr. Moore, it turned out, had good reason to be concerned about her lack of care at the hospital. She eventually returned home when her condition stabilized, but only a few hours later her body temperature shot up to 103 degrees and her blood pressure dropped—worrisome signs for a COVID-19 patient. An ambulance came to get her less than a day after her discharge. This time, however, she was admitted to Ascension St. Vincent Carmel, a hospital where she immediately felt better about the care she received for her illness.

Three days later, as her condition worsened, the hospital transferred Dr. Susan Moore into its intensive care unit.

———◇———

Why were Black people the hardest hit by this new disease?

Part of the answer goes back to a time before many of the victims and survivors were born.

On December 1, 1950, a college student named Maltheus Avery was seriously injured in a car accident in rural Alamance County, North Carolina. A veteran of World War II, Avery attended the historically-Black North Carolina A&T

University. (Ten years later, students there would galvanize the Civil Rights Movement with their brave and silent sit-down protests at a local all-white restaurant.)

An ambulance rushed Avery to Duke University hospital in Durham. Duke served both white and Black patients, in segregated wards. When Avery arrived at the emergency room, however, all the "Black beds" were full. The hospital turned him away without treating his injuries.

Maltheus Avery bled to death in the ambulance while the driver raced across town to a Black hospital.

Maddie Gadsen, from Greenville, South Carolina, was luckier. She was taken to Greenville hospital after a car accident and eventually received care.

"There was a separate entrance for blacks," she recalled. "We were sent down to the basement to wait; it looked like a dungeon with pipes and everything. I waited and waited until all the white patients were seen.

"In those days," Maddie said, "you really didn't realize you weren't getting the best of care. Any care was better than none. It was a just a way of life."

Patients like Maddie were fortunate; most Black southerners got no formal medical care at all.

Black doctors couldn't enter white hospitals, even those with segregated wards. The American Medical Association refused to have Black doctors as members, and this limited their professional options.

African American physicians such as Ossian Sweet carried heavy burdens, treating communities that were both excluded and demeaned by white physicians and hospitals, and suspicious of the medical profession as a result.

"I remember when my uncle's friend became Greenville's first black doctor in the 1950s," Maddie Gadsen recalled. "People in the black community flocked to his practice. He did home visits, but I guess he didn't have any hospital privileges, because if you got admitted you had to be seen by a white physician."

In the North, most hospitals were unofficially segregated; in Chicago in the 1950s, Black patients could seek care at Cook County Hospital, which was publicly run, or at one of several Black hospitals. The city's many private hospitals remained off-limits. Black Chicagoans struggled to get adequate medical care for themselves and their families; most of the time, they simply went without.

At a conference in Chicago in 1966, Martin Luther King Jr. declared that "of all the forms of inequality, injustice in health is the most shocking and the most inhumane because it often results in physical death."

In the South, the end of Jim Crow medicine happened without much fanfare. Following the passage of the Civil Rights Act of 1965, the federal government threatened to withhold funding from any hospital that insisted on keeping its facilities segregated. Crusading federal officials worked closely with local Black doctors—and sympathetic white colleagues—to identify and expose hospitals that refused to integrate. In a matter of months, these unlikely activists forced open all of the South's hospitals to Black patients.

The end of segregation, however, did not spell the end of racial inequality in medicine.

———◇———

An early warning about the lingering ghost of Jim Crow sounded only six years later, when in 1972, newspapers broke the story of a little-known medical experiment that had been taking place in Tuskegee, Alabama, for nearly forty years.

In the early 1930s, not far from Ned Cobb's home, fly-ers from the US Public Health Service started appearing on doors and bulletin boards in Black homes, churches, and schools.

> Free Blood Test; Free Treatment, By County Health Department and Government Doctors. YOU MAY FEEL WELL AND STILL HAVE BAD BLOOD. COME AND BRING ALL YOUR FAMILY.

Six hundred men, all of them Black and most of them poor, signed up for the free program. In exchange for donating blood regularly, the researchers gave the men meals and medical checkups and offered them burial insurance—benefits that were unheard of in poor Black communities in the South.

However, the doctor and nurses who organized the study kept its real name a secret from the hundreds of volunteers who signed up: the Tuskegee Study of Untreated Syphilis in the Negro Male.

The initial blood tests revealed that 399 of the men were ill with syphilis, a sexually transmitted disease that can spread throughout the body and damage vital organs, including the heart and brain; 201 additional participants were healthy.

Even after penicillin was discovered as a cure for syphilis in the 1940s, none of the men in the study were given it, told about it, or treated in any way. The men believed they were under the care of doctors who were looking after their health. Instead, the doctors were using them as human guinea pigs, so that medical researchers could observe how this lethal disease would affect their bodies over time. Seven men died directly of their disease, which was left untreated, and more than 150 others died of health complications related to it.

Americans did not learn about the Tuskegee study until six years after legal segregation had ended. But for many Black people, the shocking facts revealed the extent to which racism still stalked the halls of American hospitals and doctors' offices. The experiment's aftereffects afflicted the larger Black community for years, studies have shown, because Black men in particular avoided doctors and hospitals, justifiably suspicious of the treatments they might receive.

In yet another example, the *Boston Globe* reported in 1972 that the surgeons at the city's main hospital were doing tubal ligations or hysterectomies on Black women—procedures that left them unable to have children—at extremely high rates. In New York City, doctors performed similar procedures on Black women without their knowledge or consent. All of these were a form of genocide, aimed specifically at reducing the Black population.

In the decades that followed, as America's health care system grew, many Black people found good medical care out of reach. New hospital centers followed white people into the suburbs, offering spacious offices and the latest treatments for those who could afford them. The best hospitals in America today serve a mostly affluent white clientele.

Once inside a hospital or doctor's office, Black patients still experience racial bias. Treatments and therapies offered to white patients are routinely withheld from Black patients. Black people are challenged and second-guessed about their medical histories and backgrounds. Myths about Black people's pain tolerance run rampant, even among medical professionals. Black patients are much less likely than white patients to be treated adequately for heart disease—even when their symptoms are exactly the same.

In one particularly glaring example of health inequality, Black women nationwide are three to four times more likely to die during childbirth than white women, and in some places—such as New York City—they are *twelve times* more likely to die. The percentage has been growing, not shrinking, in recent years, even as medical technologies improve. And being wealthy or having access to good doctors seems to make little difference for the risks Black women face. In 2017, the tennis superstar Serena Williams experienced a life-threatening complication following the birth of her daughter Alexis Olympia. The doctors and nurses treating Williams initially doubted her when she complained of trouble breathing, and ordered the wrong tests in response—foreshadowing not only Dr. Susan Moore's harrowing experience in 2020 but those of millions of Black women and men caught up in our unequal health care system.

In a nation where only 5 percent of all doctors today are Black, there are few people to stand up for patients like Dr. Susan Moore.

———◇———

In 2020, the new coronavirus fed on old inequalities in Americans' health care.

In a different hospital, and with excellent care, Dr. Susan Moore's condition worsened.

Susan's son Henry was able to speak with her in the hospital. "If you want to fight, now is the time to fight," he said. "But if you need to go, I understand."

Susan Moore died two days later of the effects of COVID-19. Her family and friends, mourning her death, asked whether it could have been prevented.

"Nearly every time she went to the hospital she had to advocate for herself, fight for something in some way, shape, or form, just to get baseline, proper care," her son said.

Black doctors who learned about Susan Moore's story recognized her tragedy as part of a larger problem.

"She is me," said Dr. Alicia Sanders. "She is me and we are her. It could have been any one of us that happened to."

"We all have the stories," Sanders said.

"WHEN I LOOK at George Floyd, I look at my dad," Darnella Frazier said. "I look at my brothers. I look at my cousins, my uncles, because they are all Black. I have a Black father. I have a Black brother. I have Black friends. And I look at that, and I look at how that could have been one of them."

It was an ordinary day when seventeen-year-old Darnella and her young cousin walked to Cup Foods to buy some snacks.

She stumbled onto a distressing scene, as a Minneapolis police officer named Derek Chauvin tackled George Floyd to the ground and placed a knee on his neck. Darnella raised her cell phone and did the only thing she could think of: She recorded a video of the unfolding moments.

Seconds passed, then minutes.

Darnella's nine-year-old cousin watched George Floyd die. "I was sad and kind of mad," the little girl said. "It felt like he was stopping his breathing and it was kind of like hurting him."

Sometimes, memories of that day in May 2020 keep Darnella up at night. She lies awake, she says, "apologizing to George Floyd for not doing more and not physically interacting and not saving his life."

But Darnella had done something momentous. She held steady as she recorded that nearly ten-minute video. She bore witness to a crime and told the world about it. And her witness tilted the course of American history.

Ieshia Evans is arrested on July 9, 2016, while peacefully protesting the killing of Alton Sterling in Baton Rouge, Louisiana.

CHAPTER NINETEEN

★ ★ ★

THE BLACK LIVES MATTER MOVEMENT

Opens the Latest Battle for Racial Equality

On July 13, 2013, when a jury in Florida decided that George Zimmerman was not guilty of murdering Trayvon Martin, a young activist named Alicia Garza poured out her emotions in a series of Facebook posts:

> the sad part is, there's a section of America who is cheering and celebrating right now. and that makes me sick to my stomach. we GOTTA get it together y'all.

> btw stop saying we are not surprised. that's a damn shame in itself. I continue to be surprised at how little

Black lives matter. And I will continue that. stop giving
up on black life.

black people. I love you. I love us. Our lives matter.

That same day, Garza's post inspired her friend Patrisse
Cullors to create a new Twitter hashtag:

#BlackLivesMatter

"Black Lives Matter is our call to action," Cullors
reflected. "It is a tool to reimagine a world where black people are free to exist, free to live. It is a tool for our allies to
show up differently for us."

"I grew up in a neighborhood that was heavily policed,"
she said. "I witnessed my brothers and my siblings continu-
ously stopped and frisked by law enforcement. I remember
my home being raided. And one of my questions as a child
was, why? Why us? Black Lives Matter offers answers to the
why. It offers a new vision for young black girls around the
world that we deserve to be fought for, that we deserve to call
on local governments to show up for us."

Garza explained that #BlackLivesMatter was also a way
of talking about the pride that comes with being Black, even
in a nation that has devalued Black people.

"How do we live in a world that dehumanizes us and still
be human?" Garza asked. "The fight is not just being able to
keep breathing. The fight is actually to be able to walk down
the street with your head held high—and feel like I belong here.

"It's actually OK to be unique and have your own contributions," she added, "to celebrate what it means to be black, how we've survived and thrived through the worst conditions possible.

"We are rooting for us," she said.

With their friend Opal Tometti, Garza and Cullors used the hashtag to bring people together into a new kind of movement. It was even more powerful that three Black women, two of whom are queer, joined ranks to forge a movement that was the very definition of intersectional.

Communicating mainly through Twitter, groups of people around the country formed Black Lives Matter "chapters" in their local communities. Melina Abdullah cofounded one of the first, a gathering of "students, artists, organizers, and mommas" in Los Angeles.

"We knew that it was part of our sacred duty to step up," Abdullah recalled. "And there was an audaciousness that we could transform the world, but we didn't have a plan for it."

Lacking a plan, in this case, proved to be a strength, not a weakness. #BlackLivesMatter was something new in American history—a leaderless movement of thousands of people, organized around a single, powerful declaration. (Some participants liked to call it *leaderfull*.)

Many of the early Black Lives Matter activists found inspiration in the life of Ella Baker, the civil rights activist who worked for decades to build the Black freedom struggle from the ground up. Baker helped grow NAACP chapters in the South in the 1940s; she worked with Martin Luther King to push the Southern Christian Leadership Conference to the forefront of the fight against Jim Crow; and she helped found SNCC, the organization that would take the movement to new places and new victories. Often working behind the scenes, and with a down-to-earth personality that helped bring ordinary people into the movement, Baker believed that people, not leaders, made change happen.

#BlackLivesMatter percolated throughout the fall of 2013 and spring of 2014, channeling energy into a growing number of local chapters.

One year later, on August 9, a high school senior named Michael Brown was walking with a friend down the middle of Canfield Drive in his hometown of Ferguson, Missouri, a suburb of St. Louis.

A police cruiser pulled up behind them and motioned to the boys to move onto the sidewalk. As he drew closer, the officer claimed, he thought he recognized Brown from a description of a robbery suspect that had just been called in to 911; he accelerated and blocked the two boys with his car.

What happened next would be argued over and investigated for months, culminating in a full-scale report by the US Justice Department. But one fact was not in dispute: Within minutes of their first encounter, the officer fired ten shots at Michael Brown, killing him instantly.

The news of Michael Brown's death ricocheted through the streets and apartments that lined Canfield Drive. People who lived near the site of the shooting—many of whom knew or recognized "Mike Mike"—came outside and were shocked to see that his body still lay in the street, in a pool of blood. More people pressed in behind them, until hundreds crowded the area. Hours passed, and no one came to take him away. Where was the ambulance? How could the police treat a human being this way?

"That could be any of us," one man yelled. "That could have been me dead on the street!"

Other voices, outraged and angry, joined in.

A young journalist from St. Louis arrived and began talking to people in the crowd, including Mike Brown's distraught mother. "This was a scene that I had never seen before," the journalist said, "a heartbreak that I had never felt before from the people I was interviewing.

"It just felt different. Something wasn't right. This wasn't the typical police shooting scene."

The protests started that very day, as local people spread the word that another Black person had been shot dead by the police. After a quiet first night, more people came back on August 10. Marchers of all ages joined together that afternoon, chanting "Hands up! Don't shoot!", following a rumor circulating that Mike Brown had uttered these very words before his death.

The police responded with tear gas, officers in full riot gear, and even armored vehicles.

This made the protests grow even larger.

People streamed into Ferguson to join what many were seeing as a new chapter in the Civil Rights Movement, many of them organized by the Black Lives Matter networks around the country. Busloads of "Freedom Riders"—named for the young civil rights activists, including John Lewis, who fought to desegregate the South in 1961—arrived from as far away as Boston.

Throughout the fall of 2014, "Black lives matter" echoed through the streets of Ferguson and focused the nation's attention on police brutality in Black communities.

In November, protests flared again when a grand jury decided not to hand down an indictment of the police officer who shot Michael Brown. Local activists shared their distress in a newsletter circulating among the protesters.

"In Ferguson, a wound bleeds," they wrote. "The results are in. And we still don't have justice."

The movement's work, people came to realize, was only beginning.

Three days before the grand jury announcement in Ferguson, another killing sent shock waves through the nation—jolting a movement still raw with the memory of Michael Brown.

Tamir Rice was twelve years old when a Cleveland police officer shot him dead at a community center playground across from the Marion C. Seltzer Elementary School, where Tamir attended the fifth grade.

A few minutes earlier, one of Tamir's friends lent him a toy airsoft pistol.

Tamir was playing with the plastic gun when a concerned bystander called the police. The caller noted more than once that the gun was "probably fake" and that Tamir and his friend were children. But when two police officers pulled up to the playground, one of them fired his weapon at Tamir within two seconds of arriving on the scene.

Tamir lay on the ground for four minutes before anyone, including the police officers, attempted to save his life. When his fourteen-year-old sister ran screaming toward her younger brother, the policemen tackled her to the ground and handcuffed her; when Tamir's mother arrived moments later, they threatened to arrest her unless she calmed down.

Tamir died the next day at Cleveland's MetroHealth Medical Center.

A grand jury in Cleveland chose not to indict the police officer who killed Tamir Rice. One of the arguments made by the prosecutor was that Tamir looked older than twelve, and that the officer "had reason to fear for his life."

Many Black people drew a different conclusion from Tamir's death: If a police officer could argue that a twelve-year-old child was threatening, then no Black person was safe from the police.

In the months and years that followed, Black people found their suspicions confirmed again and again, as news of one police killing of unarmed African Americans followed another. Black people are *three times* more likely than white people to be shot and killed by police.

————◇————

When the United States Justice Department issued its report on the killing of Michael Brown, its findings went much deeper than explaining why an unarmed teenager had to die.

The *Investigation of the Ferguson Police Department* uncovered a story of ordinary Black citizens getting harassed by police, day in and day out, for years. People stopped on street corners for no reason at all and issued fines for murky or nonexistent violations. Arrests for minor parking offenses. Jail time for late fees on unpaid tickets. Citations given for failing to produce identification—even when nobody had committed a crime. Random, ongoing examples of police brutality, including against Black children.

In just one of thousands of examples, police arrested a Black man for relaxing in his own parked car, because he wasn't wearing a seat belt—and then charged him with providing false information to a police officer, because he gave his name as "Mike" rather than "Michael."

Another man recounted sitting at a bus stop on Canfield Drive, not far from where Michael Brown was killed.

> **Lieutenant:** Get over here.
> **Bus patron:** Me?
> **Lieutenant:** Get the f— over here. Yeah, you.
> **Bus patron:** Why? What did I do?
> **Lieutenant:** Give me your ID.
> **Bus patron:** Why?
> **Lieutenant:** Stop being a smart ass and give me your ID.

According to federal investigators, "[t]he lieutenant ran the man's name for warrants. Finding none, he returned the ID and said, 'get the hell out of my face.'"

Michael Brown, the federal investigators learned, was the tip of the iceberg. The Ferguson report revealed to white America what Ferguson's Black community had known all along: that African American people lived in a very different country, one where white suspicion and harassment were part of daily life.

———◇———

But something was different this time. Over a century earlier, Ida B. Wells and a handful of other brave Black journalists struggled to chronicle the horrors of lynching. The NAACP, embattled and harassed, sought to overturn Jim Crow laws against immense opposition. Early civil rights activists braved hostile crowds to break through the color line.

In the summer of 2020, however, the memories of George Floyd, Breonna Taylor, Ahmaud Arbery and others killed by racist violence stirred the largest mass movement in all of American history.

Darnella Frazier's more than nine-minute video had offered all Americans evidence of things not usually seen. It told a story of unbearable pain and despair. But it also broke open America's decades-long refusal to acknowledge the reality of racial inequality.

Throughout the summer of 2020 and in the months and

years that followed, the new movement found itself confronting older ghosts: the unanswered questions of the Civil Rights Movement and the long struggle for Black freedom that had come before it.

Why are voting rights still under attack, more than fifty years after the Voting Rights Act?

Why are wealth disparities between Black and white families greater than ever?

Why does housing segregation persist?

Why has America abandoned the goal of equal schools for all children?

Why are environmental risks concentrated in communities of color?

Why do so many tax dollars flow to the police, when the police so often target Black people?

For many people, the long story of inequality in America has been an open wound, refusing to heal. But for others, this history is a burning question: *What can we do to make the future different?*

★ ★ ★

Nikole Hannah-Jones.

CHAPTER TWENTY

★ ★ ★

NIKOLE HANNAH-JONES

Taps into the Power of History

On July 6, 2021, Nikole Hannah-Jones announced that she had had enough.

For months, Jones had braved a swirling controversy at the University of North Carolina at Chapel Hill—the Tarheel State's flagship university, where Pauli Murray had unsuccessfully sought admission nearly ninety years earlier.

Earlier that year, the faculty of the journalism school at UNC had voted to offer Hannah-Jones a permanent job as a tenured professor with an endowed chair, only the second such offer of tenure to a Black female journalism professor in the history of the school. But when her job offer went to the university's board of trustees for approval, the decision was mysteriously held up.

Persuading Hannah-Jones to join its faculty should have been a no-brainer for UNC. Among many other accomplishments, Hannah-Jones had created *The 1619 Project* at the *New York Times*—an influential and widely praised effort to examine slavery's central role in American history. Established to correct the still-dominant view of slavery as an important but unfortunate footnote in America's democratic story, *The 1619 Project* showed instead how slavery infected every corner of American life, from the earliest years of European settlement in North America through the Civil War.

It was a correction that needed to be made in 2021. High school history textbooks still have a spotty record when it comes to teaching about slavery and race. One widely used edition still refers to the millions of enslaved Africans brought to America against their will as "immigrants"!

In recognition of *The 1619 Project*, Hannah-Jones had won a Pulitzer Prize, journalism's highest honor. She was one of the most respected journalists of her generation.

But behind the scenes, conservative activists in North Carolina maneuvered to block Hannah-Jones's hiring. Some, like the school's biggest supporter, Walter Hussman Jr. (whose $25 million donation got the journalism school to be renamed in his honor), had ties to the school's board of trustees. Their concerns were not over her skills as a journalist or her ability to teach students. Rather, they objected to the focus of much of Nikole Hannah-Jones's writing: racial inequality in America today.

Why now? Hannah-Jones had been writing for years; her work was well known and highly respected.

Nikole Hannah-Jones wasn't simply the victim of an attack on one high-profile writer. A new movement was forming against the quest for equality in America, and Hannah-Jones (owing to her brilliance and success as a journalist) was one of its earliest targets. In 2021, opponents of racial equality decided to take their fight from the streets and courtrooms and into the nation's classrooms. They gambled that if the facts of history could be hidden from view, the cause of white supremacy might live on, unchallenged by future generations.

This wasn't an argument *about* history; it was an attack on history itself.

———◆———

In the final days of Donald Trump's presidency, his administration released *The 1776 Report*, a set of new guidelines for restricting the teaching of history in schools. For the previous four years, Trump had loudly criticized efforts to teach about racism, and he had gone out of his way to name Nikole Hannah-Jones's work as "unpatriotic." His report called for sidelining discussions of racial inequality in favor of a supposedly more "patriotic" view of America's past. But professional historians, and teachers across the United States, found *The 1776 Report* riddled with mistakes and exaggerations, and it was widely criticized as political propaganda. The incoming administration of Joseph R. Biden shelved the report immediately.

In the early months of Biden's presidency, however,

conservative efforts to censor American history picked up steam in state legislatures across the nation. Throughout that winter and spring, attempts to ban or prohibit teaching about *The 1619 Project*—or even about slavery itself—quickly morphed into a broader and much louder movement, as some conservative writers, media figures, and parent groups added new items to their lists of banned topics.

In particular, they took aim at something called Critical Race Theory.

Critical Race Theory was created by a group of legal scholars who examined laws and court decisions that might be neutral on their face but that actually perpetuated racial inequality. It was developed as a way of looking at American society that helps explain how and why racial inequality has persisted.

Kimberlé Crenshaw, one of Critical Race Theory's most important thinkers, commented that her goal was to "pay attention to what has happened in this country, and how what has happened in this country is continuing to create differential outcomes. Critical Race Theory... is more patriotic than those who are opposed to it because... we believe in the promises of equality. And we know we can't get there if we can't confront and talk honestly about inequality."

To many people watching these new protests from a distance, something seemed not right. For one, few if any public schools were actually teaching about Critical Race Theory, a subject studied mainly in law schools, not high schools. And to the legal scholars who embraced this theory, what the critics were describing bore little resemblance to their work. Critical Race Theory has nothing to do with assigning individual guilt or with making students feel bad about themselves or their country. Rather, it seeks to explain how the same laws affect groups of people differently, and thus help keep racism and inequality alive and well in a nation that had officially banned Jim Crow.

Clearly, these new debates weren't really about Critical Race Theory, which had become a kind of mythical monster to some people. Instead, the new movement against Critical Race Theory and *The 1619 Project* had a much bigger goal. It sought to block students—America's newest generation—from learning the truth of inequality in the United States.

In the spring and summer of 2021, bills were introduced into dozens of state legislatures to ban or limit teaching about slavery, racism, and other "divisive concepts"; in some cases, legislators specifically attempted to outlaw *The 1619 Project* and Critical Race Theory entirely in schools.

A new law in the state of Iowa prohibits teaching "that the United States of America and the state of Iowa are fundamentally or systemically racist or sexist." In Texas, politicians are trying to prevent schools from teaching that the founding of the United States is related to slavery, a fact that historians themselves find uncontroversial. Neither would they be able to declare that the KKK is "morally wrong." In Arkansas, politicians are trying to push through a bill that would ban discussion of social justice for African Americans or other people of color.

Politicians talked openly about children's minds being "poisoned" by "unpatriotic" history lessons. Some claimed that Dr. Martin Luther King Jr. himself, one of America's most important leaders in the struggle for civil rights and racial equality, would be aghast at the idea that children should be taught about America's racist past—and present. The irony is that the same Texas bill would also ban teaching King's words and actions.

King knew firsthand that the long battle for equality in America has also been a battle over the truth. Until the 1960s—and even much later in some parts of the country—it was standard for history textbooks to paint a rosy picture of slavery and even describe the "benefits" of enslavement for African Americans. And those same textbooks didn't say a word about the history of discrimination in America or Jim Crow laws that made Black people second-class citizens.

The historian Timothy Snyder, who had studied the rise of Nazi Germany, pointed out the similarities between these new efforts to regulate how we study the past and similar "memory laws" that have appeared in authoritarian countries seeking to limit public discussion about freedom and democracy.

"In most cases," Snyder observed, "the new American memory laws have been passed by state legislatures that, in the same session, have passed laws designed to make voting more difficult. The memory management enables the voter suppression."

One hundred years earlier, the destruction of Tulsa's

Black community was met with a ninety-year silence, as white supremacists did everything in their power to erase the memory of the massacre. Could something similar happen in our own times?

———◇———

For Nikole Hannah-Jones herself, the efforts to suppress the story she wanted to tell about America only catapulted her to greater fame.

Faculty and students at UNC rallied to her side. Her opponents were forced to recede into the shadows. And in June 2021, the university finally voted to offer her a permanent position.

At that very moment, however, Hannah-Jones decided that the fight for simple recognition had poisoned the well for her at UNC.

"I've spent my entire life proving that I belong in elite white spaces that were not built for Black people," she said in an interview.

"I decided I didn't want to do that anymore."

Instead, Hannah-Jones rejected UNC's offer and decided to join Howard University, the historically Black university based in Washington, DC—the very same institution where so many students and professors had honed their skills for the long fight against racial inequality.

Nikole Hannah-Jones became a target because she tells stories that express something true about America. And like her heroine Ida B. Wells-Barnett, she refused to be silenced.

She intends to continue Wells-Barnett's legacy through the new Center for Journalism and Democracy she has created at Howard University, dedicated to fostering a new generation of Black journalists.

What the attack on *The 1619 Project* revealed, unintentionally perhaps, was the power of words, the importance of reading, and the unbreakable bond between learning and real freedom. Throughout the summer and fall of 2020, millions of Americans turned to books, newspapers, websites, social media, and other sources of information for knowledge about America's past and present, seeking a deeper understanding of the sources of racial inequality. Books like Michelle Alexander's *The New Jim Crow*, Bryan Stevenson's *Just Mercy*, and Ibram X. Kendi's *How to Be an Antiracist* shot to the top of the bestseller lists, as citizens everywhere hungered for ideas and information about fighting white supremacy.

Just as they did 150 years ago, however, the forces of inequality have launched their counterattack—not only with violent assaults on the political institutions of our democracy, but also with a massive campaign of disinformation about the truth of American history. Like their KKK forefathers after Reconstruction, they are hell-bent on seeing history repeat itself. And they know that lies—about voter fraud, about *The 1619 Project*, and about systemic racism—are the surest way to justify a new wave of suppression, and to keep the new Jim Crow alive and well.

Ensuring that white supremacy doesn't succeed will take

a movement that understands and builds on our common history, and that sees and widens the path that leads beyond it. It is up to all of us to study the past, and to marshal and carry forward the freedom dreams of those who have come before us. Maybe yours is the generation that can finally bring about a more equal future.

AFTERWORD

★ ★ ★

THE STORY
OF INEQUALITY
IN AMERICA

The history we learn about in school is a battleground.

The new rules for teaching American history want to limit your knowledge to a few happy tales. They want you to worship the Founding Fathers uncritically and to overlook that many of them owned and mistreated other human beings. They want you to believe that the Civil War, in which hundreds of thousands of Americans died, was not a war over slavery (which is how Americans on both sides of the conflict talked about it at the time) but rather a fight to protect something called "states' rights." (To prove how thin a premise that is, ask yourself what rights the states primarily sought to protect. You got it: the right to enslave human beings.) And they want you to see America as the bastion of freedom and equality, when for many of its citizens, the opposite has been true throughout all of American history.

Opponents of the truth want to close the curtain on the facts.

Fortunately, it's within your power to determine what is true and what is not.

We wrote *Unequal* not as the last word but as an introduction. The first step to changing the world, we think, is to understand what has come before—to see the paths that others have followed, and to choose to go down those paths or to blaze your own. We hope this is only the beginning of your quest, and that the guides listed below (a small sampling of hundreds more) will help you on your way.

—◇—

Alexander, Michelle. *The New Jim Crow: Mass Incarceration in the Age of Colorblindness.* New York: New Press, 2020.

Anderson, Carol with Tanya Bolden. *One Person, No Vote: How Not All Voters Are Treated Equally,* YA edition. New York: Bloomsbury YA, 2019.

Anderson, Carol. *White Rage: The Unspoken Truth of Our Racial Divide.* New York: Bloomsbury, 2016.

Baldwin, James. *The Fire Next Time.* New York: Vintage, 1992.

Baradaran, Mehrsa. *The Color of Money: Black Banks and the Racial Wealth Gap.* Cambridge, MA: Belknap Press, 2019.

Berry, Daina Ramey, and Kali Nicole Gross. *A Black Women's History of the United States*. Boston: Beacon Press, 2021.

Blackmon, Douglas A. *Slavery by Another Name: The Re-enslavement of Black Americans from the Civil War to World War II*. New York: Anchor, 2009.

Blain, Keisha, and Ibram X. Kendi, *Four Hundred Souls: A Community History of African America, 1619–2019*. New York: One World, 2021.

Brown, Austin Channing. *I'm Still Here: Black Dignity in a World Made for Whiteness*. New York: Convergent Books, 2018.

Butler, Paul. *Chokehold: Policing Black Men*. New York: New Press, 2018.

Coates, Ta-Nehisi. *Between the World and Me*. New York: One World, 2015.

Cooper, Brittney. *Eloquent Rage: A Black Feminist Discovers Her Superpower*. New York: Picador, 2019.

DiAngelo, Robin. *White Fragility: Why It's So Hard for White People to Talk About Racism*. Boston: Beacon Press, 2018.

Forman, James, Jr. *Locking Up Our Own: Crime and Punishment in Black America*. New York: Farrar, Straus & Giroux, 2017.

Gates, Henry Louis, Jr. *Stony the Road: Reconstruction, White Supremacy, and the Rise of Jim Crow*. New York: Penguin, 2020.

Glaude, Eddie S. Jr. *Democracy in Black: How Race Still Enslaves the American Soul*. New York: Crown, 2017.

Jewell, Tiffany, and Aurelia Durand (illustrator). *This Book Is Anti-Racist: 20 Lessons on How to Wake Up, Take Action, and Do the Work*. London: Frances Lincoln Children's Books, 2020.

Joseph, Peniel. *Waiting 'Til the Midnight Hour: A Narrative History of Black Power in America*. New York: Henry Holt, 2006.

Kendall, Mikki. *Hood Feminism: Notes from the Women That the Movement Forgot*. New York: Penguin, 2021.

Kendi, Ibram X. *Stamped from the Beginning: The Definitive History of Racist Ideas in America*. New York: Bold Type Books, 2017.

———. *How to Be an Antiracist*. New York: One World, 2019.

Khan-Cullors, Patrisse, and asha bandele. *When They Call You a Terrorist: A Story of Black Lives Matter and the Power to Change the World*, YA edition. New York: Wednesday Books, 2020.

Lewis, John. *March Trilogy*. New York: Top Shelf Productions, 2016.

Loewen, James. *Lies My Teacher Told Me: Everything Your American History Textbook Got Wrong.* New York: New Press, 2018.

———. *Sundown Towns: A Hidden Dimension of American Racism.* New York: New Press, 2018.

Lowery, Wesley. *"They Can't Kill Us All": The Story of the Struggle for Black Lives.* Boston: Back Bay Books, 2017.

Malcolm X and Alex Haley. *The Autobiography of Malcolm X: As Told to Alex Haley.* New York: Ballantine Books, 1992.

Moore, Monique. *Pushout: The Criminalization of Black Girls in School.* New York: New Press, 2019.

Moore, Wes. *The Other Wes Moore: One Name, Two Fates.* New York: One World, 2011.

Oluo, Ijeoma. *So You Want to Talk About Race?* New York: Seal Press, 2019.

Ortiz, Paul. *An African American and Latinx History of the United States.* Boston: Beacon Press, 2018.

Payne, Les, and Tamara Payne. *The Dead Are Arising: The Life of Malcolm X.* New York: Liveright, 2020.

Perry, Imani. *Breathe: A Letter to My Sons.* Boston: Beacon Press, 2019.

Rankine, Claudia. *Citizen: An American Lyric.* Minneapolis: Graywolf Press, 2014.

Reynolds, Jason, and Ibram X. Kendi. *Stamped: Racism, Antiracism, and You.* New York: Little Brown Books for Young Readers, 2020.

Roberts, Dorothy. *Fatal Invention: How Science, Politics, and Big Business Re-Create Race in the 21st Century,* New York: New Press, 2011.

Rothstein, Richard. *The Color of Law: A Forgotten History of How Our Government Segregated America.* New York; London: Liveright, 2017.

Saad, Layla F. *Me and White Supremacy: Combat Racism, Change the World, and Become a Good Ancestor.* Naperville, IL: Sourcebooks, 2020.

Solomon, Akiba, and Kenrya Rankin. *How We Fight White Supremacy: A Field Guide to Black Resistance.* New York: Bold Type, 2019.

Stevenson, Bryan. *Just Mercy: A Story of Justice and Redemption.* New York: Spiegel & Grau, 2015.

Tatum, Beverly Daniel. *Why Are All the Black Kids Sitting Together in the Cafeteria?: And Other Conversations about Race.* New York: Basic Books, 2003.

Wilkerson, Isabel. *Caste: The Origins of Our Discontents.* New York: Random House, 2020.

———. *The Warmth of Other Suns: The Epic Story of America's Great Migration.* New York: Vintage, 2011.

Williams, Chad, Kidada E. Williams, and Keisha N. Blain, eds. *Charleston Syllabus: Readings on Race, Racism, and Racial Violence*. Athens: University of Georgia Press, 2016.

Young, Damon *What Doesn't Kill You Makes You Blacker: A Memoir in Essays*. New York: Ecco, 2020.

Zucchino, David. *Wilmington's Lie: The Murderous Coup of 1898 and the Rise of White Supremacy*. New York: Grove Press, 2021.

ACKNOWLEDGMENTS

★ ★ ★

We are forever indebted to our agent, Tanya McKinnon: matchmaker, instigator, gladiator, and guide.

Lisa Yoskowitz of Little, Brown Books for Young Readers championed this idea from the beginning, shepherded it tirelessly, and shaped it substantively in ways big and small. Lisa's editorial colleague Caitlyn Averett provided expert support throughout. We are also grateful to Mary Auxier, Bill Grace, Jen Graham, Karina Granda, David Koral, Lelia Mander, Amber Mercado, Christie Michel, Marisa Russell, Victoria Stapleton, Sydney Tillman, Megan Tingley, Nyamekye Waliyaya, and everyone else at LBYR for their outstanding contributions to this project on its path from manuscript to book. At a time of soul-searching and change in the book-publishing industry, we hope and pray that Lisa and her colleagues represent the wave of things to come.

As always, Michael's family—Addie Mae, Gregory and Brian, and Marcia, Michael, Maisha, and Mwata—has sustained him, and his colleagues at Vanderbilt, including Tracy Sharpley-Whiting, John Geer, and Emilie Townes, have made his work immensely enjoyable.

Without Patty, Owen, and Emmett Favreau, Marc would lack the inspiration to delve into the past and to imagine a different future. Family and friends on Martha's Vineyard

ACKNOWLEDGMENTS

and in New York, Salem, Kennebunk, Oakland, Washington, Chicagoland, and elsewhere make everything worthwhile. Colleagues at The New Press set the standard for books as tools for social change.

SOURCE NOTES

Chapter One: Mary Church Terrell Fights Back Against Segregation

5   "Instantly I knew this was the Jim Crow coach which I had never seen but about which I had heard": Mary Church Terrell, *A Colored Woman in a White World* (Washington, DC: Ransdell Publishers, 1940), 296.

5   "calculated to freeze the very marrow of my bones": Ibid.

5   "This is first class enough for you, and you stay just where you are": Ibid.

5   "As young as I was": Ibid., 297.

5   "But of the two evils": Ibid.

5   "I am getting off here": Ibid.

6   "You can go into that car if you want to": Ibid., 298.

7   "only effect is to perpetuate the stigma of color": Albion Tourgée, quoted in "Overlooked No More: Homer Plessy, Who Sat on a Train and Stood Up for Civil Rights," *New York Times*, January 31, 2020, https://www.nytimes.com/2020/01/31/obituaries/homer-plessy-overlooked-black-history-month.html.

8   "The Jim Crow law made friends into enemies overnight": Mamie Garvin Fields with Karen Fields, *Lemon Swamp and Other Places* (New York: Free Press, 1983), 47.

8   "When they didn't have sugar, or they didn't have tea or coffee, they'd send over to borrow some": Ibid.

9   "Now here comes Jim Crow": Ibid., 48.

9   "The law made it that we weren't really neighbors anymore": Ibid., 49.

9   "Was it because I showed no submissiveness?": W. E. B. Du Bois, quoted in Leon Litwack, *Trouble in Mind: Black Southerners in the Age of Jim Crow* (New York: Knopf, 1999), 328.

10   "I was never permitted to learn to swim": Dempsey Travis, quoted in "America's Segregated Shores: Beaches' Long History as a Racial Battleground," *Guardian*, June 12, 2018, https://www.theguardian.com/world/2018/jun/12/americas-segregated-shores-beaches-long-history-as-a-racial-battleground.

14   "Why not?": Mary Church Terrell, quoted in Joan Quigley, *Just Another Southern Town: Mary Church Terrell and the Struggle for Racial Justice in the Nation's Capital* (New York: Oxford University Press, 2016), 5.

14   "Because we don't serve colored people here": Thompson's Restaurant manager, quoted in ibid.

Chapter Two: Ida B. Wells Exposes America's Lynching Epidemic

20   "Tell my people to go west. There is no justice for them here": Mia Bay, *To Tell the Truth Freely: The Life of Ida B. Wells* (New York: Hill & Wang, 2009), 85.

22   "our first lesson in white supremacy": Paula Giddings, *Ida: A Sword Among Lions: Ida B. Wells and the Campaign Against Lynching* (New York: HarperCollins, 2008), 188.

22   "an excuse to get rid of Negroes who were acquiring wealth and property": Bay, *To Tell the Truth Freely*, 101.

24   "Well John—This is a token of a great day we had in Dallas March 3rd": David Garland, *Peculiar Institution: America's Death Penalty in an Age of Abolition* (Cambridge, MA: Harvard University Press, 2012), 30.

25   "Nobody in this section of the country believes the threadbare old lie": Bay, *To Tell the Truth Freely*, 103.

25   "slanderous and nasty-minded mulattress": *New York Times* article cited in Richard White, *The Republic for Which It Stands: The United States during Reconstruction and the Gilded Age, 1865–1896* (New York: Oxford University Press, 2017), 746.

28   "We are actually fighting against the same type of tyranny and white supremacy that Ida B. Wells was fighting against all those years ago": Nikole Hannah-Jones, quoted in "Ida B. Wells -Barnett Becomes the First Black Woman to Be Honored in Chicago with a Monument," TheRoot.com, July 2, 2021, https:// www.theroot.com/ida-b-wells-barnett-becomes-first-black -woman-to-be-ho-1847219329.

Chapter Three: Buck Franklin Bears Witness to the Destruction of Black Wall Street

30   "Black families whose heads graduated from college have about 33 percent less wealth than white families whose heads dropped out

of high school": Darrick Hamilton et al., "Umbrellas Don't Make It Rain: Why Studying and Working Hard Isn't Enough for Black Americans," Closing the Racial Wealth Gap Initiative, 3, http:// www.insightcced.org/wp-content/uploads/2015/08/Umbrellas _Dont_Make_It_Rain_Final.pdf.

34   "the richest Negro street in the world": widely used quotation first attributed to John Wesley Dobbs, quoted in Ernie Suggs, "29 Reasons to Celebrate Black History Month: No. 11 Auburn Avenue," *Atlanta Journal -Constitution*, January 4, 2017, https://www.ajc.com/lifestyles /reasons-celebrate-black-history-month-auburn-avenue /TrzGacIFmh9Ktf58xVEGrN.

35   "the freest town for a negro in this country": quoted in David Zucchino, *Wilmington's Lie: The Murderous Coup of 1898 and the Rise of White Supremacy* (New York: Atlantic Monthly Press, 2020), xvii.

36   "It seemed that my world was suddenly crumbling": John Hope Franklin, *Mirror to America: The Autobiography of John Hope Franklin* (New York: Farrar, Straus and Giroux, 2007), 15.

36   "My grandfather often talked about how you could enjoy a full life in Greenwood, that everything you needed or wanted was in Greenwood": Star Williams, quoted in "What the Tulsa Race Massacre Destroyed," *New York Times*, May 24, 2021, https://www .nytimes.com/interactive/2021/05/24/us/tulsa-race-massacre.html.

37   "About midnight, I arose and went to the north porch on the second floor of my hotel": Buck Franklin, "The Tulsa Race Riot and Three of Its Victims," original typescript located at the Smithsonian Institution, National Museum of African American History and Culture, August 22, 1931, 4, https://edan .si.edu/slideshow/viewer/?damspath=/Public_Sets/NMAAHC /NMAAHC_Slideshows/2015_176_1.

38   "For days we did not know if my father was dead, injured, or unharmed": John Hope Franklin, *Mirror to America*, 16.

38   "She was traveling south—hair disentangled and disheveled—in the very path of whizzing bullets": Buck Franklin, "The Tulsa Race Riot and Three of Its Victims," 7.

39   "the ablest Negro surgeon in America": quoted in " 'We Lived Like We Were Wall Street,' " *Washington Post*, October 11, 2018, https://www.washingtonpost.com/history/2018/10/11/we-lived -like-we-were-wall-street.

39   "They took a hatchet to my sisters' piano": Olivia Hooker, quoted in "Eyewitness to the Desolation of 'Black Wall Street,'" *New York Times*, September 13, 2018, https://www.nytimes.com/2018/09/13/opinion/olivia-hooker-tulsa-race-riot.html.

39   "For fully forty-eight hours the fire raged and burned everything in its path and it left nothing but ashes and burned safes and trunks and the like": Buck Franklin, "The Tulsa Race Riot and Three of Its Victims," 9.

41   "The wealth gap is where the injustices sown in the past grow imperceptibly in the present": Mehrsa Baradaran, *The Color of Money: Black Banks and the Racial Wealth Gap* (Cambridge, MA: Harvard University Press), 249.

41   "What if we had been allowed to maintain our family business?": Brenda Nails-Alford, quoted in "What the Tulsa Race Massacre Destroyed," *New York Times*, May 24, 2021, https://www.nytimes.com/interactive/2021/05/24/us/tulsa-race-massacre.html.

42   "My fellow Americans, this was not a riot. This was a massacre, among the worst in our history, but not the only one. And for too long, forgotten by our history": Joseph R. Biden, quoted in "Remarks on Commemorating the 100th Anniversary of the Tulsa Race Massacre in Tulsa, Oklahoma," Gerhard Peters and John T. Woolley, American Presidency Project, https://www.presidency.ucsb.edu/node/350177.

Chapter Four: Ned Cobb Confronts Racial Inequality at Work

47   "He was goin to take what I had if I owed him; if I didn't owe him he was goin to take it," Ned Cobb, quoted in Theodore Rosengarten, *All God's Dangers: The Life of Nate Shaw* (New York: Knopf, 1974), 544. When this book was first published, the editor made the decision to alter Ned Cobb's name to Nate Shaw, to protect his identity while he was still living.

48   "But who's the man ought to decide how much?": Ibid., 108.

52   "We was taught at our meetins that when trouble comes, stand up for one another": Ibid., 304.

52   "Be quiet, whatever we do, let it work in a way of virtue": Ibid., 306.

53   "Mr. Logan, please sir": Ibid.

53   *Somebody got to stand up*: Ibid., 307.

53 "Well, if you take it, I'll be damned if you don't take it over my dead body. Go ahead and take it": Ibid.

53 "Well, if you want to kill me, I'm right before you": Ibid., 308.

54 "I didn't think about gettin shot and I didn't think about not gettin shot: Ibid., 309.

54 "He'll come down there and kill the last damn one of you": Ibid., 308.

54 "Go ahead and get Mr. Beale, I'll be here when he comes": Ibid.

55 "I just stood right on and I was standin alone": Ibid., 309.

56 "I was born and raised here": Ibid., 500.

56 "The future days follows the present": Ibid., 304.

Chapter Five: Dr. Ossian Sweet Breaks Through the Color Line to Find a Home in Detroit

64 "this property shall not be used or occupied by any person or persons except those of the Caucasian race": language from a 1911 restrictive covenant in a St. Louis, Missouri, neighborhood, cited in section 3 of the Supreme Court decision *Shelley v. Kraemer*, May 3, 1948, which held that such covenants violated the equal-protection clause of the Fourteenth Amendment.

66 "It just isn't right": Kevin Boyle, *Arc of Justice: A Saga of Race, Civil Rights, and Murder in the Jazz Age* (New York: Henry Holt, 2001), 147.

67 "We have decided we are not going to run": Ibid., 26.

67 "We're not going to look for any trouble": Ibid.

68 "My God, look at the people!": Ibid., 35.

70 "I insist that there is nothing but prejudice in this case": Edward J. Larson and Jack Marshall, *The Essential Words and Writings of Clarence Darrow* (New York: Modern Library, 2007), 215.

Chapter Six: Pauli Murray Discovers the Key to Ending Segregation in Schools

74 "You don't let people tell you who you are. You tell them who you are": Kamala Harris, quoted in "Kamala Harris Makes Her Case," *New Yorker*, July 15, 2019, https://www.newyorker.com /magazine/2019/07/22/kamala-harris-makes-her-case.

75   "Where there's no name for a problem": Kimberlé Crenshaw, "The Urgency of Intersectionality," TED Talk, October 2016, https://www.ted.com/talks/kimberle_crenshaw_the_urgency_of _intersectionality/transcript.

77   "split open like a melon and sewed together loosely with jagged stitches": Pauli Murray, *Song in a Weary Throat: Memoir of an American Pilgrimage* (New York: Liveright, 2018), 72.

80   "little old beat up '20 Ford": Patricia Sullivan, *Lift Every Voice: The NAACP and the Making of the Civil Rights Movement* (New York: New Press, 2010), 230.

81   "It was the beginning of the end": Pauli Murray, *Song in a Weary Throat*, 148.

81   *"Dear Miss Murray"*: Pauli Murray, *Song in a Weary Throat*, 148.

83   "Ironically, if Howard Law School equipped me for effective struggle against Jim Crow": Ibid., 236.

83   "a flash of poetic insight": Ibid., 285.

84   "One would have thought I had proposed that we attempt to tear down the Washington Monument or the Statue of Liberty": Ibid., 286.

86   "Your picture and the salutation on your college transcript": Ibid., 310.

86   "Gentlemen, I would gladly change my sex to meet your requirements": Ibid., 314.

87   "one of the premier legal minds of the 20th century who is often not credited": Ruth Bader Ginsburg, quoted in a 2017 interview first published in *Time*, October 16, 2020, https://time.com /5896410/ruth-bader-ginsburg-pauli-murray.

88   "It's not about what they did": Monique Morris, quoted in "The Black Girl Pushout," *The Atlantic*, March 15, 2016, https://www.theatlantic.com/education/archive/2016/03/the -criminalization-of-black-girls-in-schools/473718.

Chapter Seven: Daisy Myers Integrates the White Suburbs

89   "affirmative action for white people": See generally, Ira Katznelson, *When Affirmative Action Was White: An Untold History of Racial Inequality in Twentieth Century America* (New York: Norton, 2006).

91   "Did you see how he looked?": Daisy Myers, quoted in David Kushner, *Levittown: Two Families, One Tycoon, and the Fight for*

Civil Rights in America's Legendary Suburb (New York, Walker & Company, 2009), 88.

92   "We are church-going, respectable people": William Myers, quoted in *Gazette and Daily* (York, PA), August 15, 1957.

92   "I expected some trouble, but I never thought it would be so bad": William Myers, quoted in "Embattled Homeowner," *New York Times*, August 22, 1957.

92   "About 4:30 PM trouble began to brew...small knots of people... soon grew into crowds": Daisy Myers and Linda Shopes, "Breaking Down Barriers," *Pennsylvania Heritage*, summer 2002.

93   "They were banging the mailbox": Daisy Myers, quoted in "Trauma of Levittown Integration Remembered," *Baltimore Sun*, August 21, 1997.

93   "The rock, weighing less than an ounce, carried tons of hatred with it": Daisy Myers, quoted in Kushner, *Levittown*, 99.

95   "No loans will be given to colored developments": Richard Rothstein, *The Color of Law: A Forgotten History of How Our Government Segregated America* (New York: Liveright, 2018), 66.

95   "By 1948, most housing nationwide was being constructed with this government financing": Ibid., 71.

96   "sold, leased, rented, or occupied by any other than those of the Caucasian race": Rothstein, *The Color of Law*, 85.

98   "People brought us food very often": Daisy Myers, quoted in "Trauma of Levittown Integration Remembered."

98   "Nothing whatever will prevent me from living in the house": William Myers, quoted in Kushner, *Levittown*, 109.

99   "We were reaching the lowest ebb in our personal determination": Daisy Myers, quoted in Myers and Shopes, "Breaking Down Barriers."

99   "Sooner or later I know we will be accepted for what we are— for ourselves": Daisy Myers, quoted in *Reporting Civil Rights: American Journalism 1941–1963* (New York: Library of America, 2003), 409.

101   "I have seen many demonstrations in the South": Martin Luther King Jr. quoted in Ron Grossman, "50 years ago: MLK's march in Marquette Park turned violent, exposed hate," *Chicago Tribune*, July 28, 2016, https://www.chicagotribune.com/opinion

/commentary/ct-mlk-king-marquette-park-1966-flashback
-perspec-0731-md-20160726-story.html.

101 "We have created a caste system in this country, with African-
Americans kept exploited and geographically separate by racially
explicit government policies": Rothstein, *The Color of Law*, xvii.

102 "We had realized years ago, to our sorrow, that the housing market,
above all else, stands as a symbol of racial inequality": Daisy Myers,
quoted in Myers and Shopes, "Breaking Down Barriers."

Chapter Eight: Malcolm X Launches a Struggle Against Police Brutality

105 "You're not in Alabama": Lee Potts and Johnson Hinton, quoted
in Manning Marable, *Malcolm X: A Life of Reinvention* (New York,
Penguin Press, 2011), 127.

105 "Police brutality has been the mode in Harlem for years. The
nurses and staff at Harlem Hospital see the bloody results
daily": Hubert Delaney, quoted in Michael Flamm, *In the Heat
of the Summer: The New York Riots of 1964 and the War on Crime*
(Philadelphia: University of Pennsylvania Press), 61.

106 "We don't call them that, but we do have lynchings right here in
the North": Congressman Adam Clayton Powell, quoted in Martha
Biondi, *To Stand and Fight: The Struggle for Civil Rights in Postwar New
York City* (Cambridge, MA: Harvard University Press, 2006), 193.

106 "Why don't you carry the man on to jail?": Johnson Hinton,
quoted in Peniel Joseph, *Waiting 'Til the Midnight Hour: A
Narrative History of Black Power in America* (New York: Henry
Holt, 2006), 9.

106 "I went in as the minister of Temple Seven, and demanded to see
our brother": Malcolm X, *The Autobiography of Malcolm X: As Told
to Alex Haley* (New York: Ballantine Books, 1992), 269.

106 "When I saw our Brother Hinton, it was all I could do to contain
myself": Ibid., 269.

107 "I told the lieutenant in charge, 'That man belongs in the
hospital'": Ibid., 269.

108 "God's Angry Men Tangle with Police": *Amsterdam News*
headline quoted in Joseph, *Waiting 'Til the Midnight Hour*, 10.

108 "Harlem's black people were long since sick and tired of police
brutality": Malcolm X, *The Autobiography of Malcolm X*, 269.

109   "Our war against oppression in the North is often like a battle against evanescent shadows": Richard Henry quoted in Joseph, *Waiting 'Til the Midnight Hour*, 51.

109   "do not escape Jim Crow: they merely encounter another, not-less-deadly variety": James Baldwin, "Fifth Avenue, Uptown," *Esquire*, July 1960.

110   "Racial slurs.": All quotations from the NAACP Detroit branch report on police brutality, 1958, https://policing.umhistorylabs .lsa.umich.edu/files/original/6a268d045c0e4e706f185209f8d2267 87dda8086.pdf.

110–111   "I sometimes wonder if a Negro citizen in the city of Detroit can really claim to be a citizen in the full, true sense of the word": Joynal Muthleb, former Detroit police officer, testifying in the hearings before the United States Commission on Civil Rights, Detroit, Michigan, December 14, 1960, 323.

112   "guerrilla fighting with gangsters" California governor Edmund Brown, quoted in Elizabeth Hinton, *From the War on Poverty to the War on Crime: The Making of Mass Incarceration in America* (Cambridge, MA: Harvard University Press, 2016), 69.

112–113   "Can't you understand that this is the perspective from which we are now speaking?": Lorraine Hansberry, speaking at "The Black Revolution and the White Backlash" Forum (Town Hall, New York City, sponsored by the Association of Artists for Freedom, June 15, 1964), http://americanradioworks.publicradio .org/features/blackspeech/lhansberry.html.

113   Actually, they weren't riots in the first place; they were reactions against police brutality": Malcolm X, speech at the London School of Economics (February 11, 1965, to a meeting sponsored by the school's Africa Society), http://www.hartford-hwp.com /archives/45a/461.html.

Chapter Nine: Fannie Lou Hamer Takes Back the Right to Vote

116   "I understand how important our vote is": LeBron James, quoted in "LeBron James on Black Voter Participation, Misinformation and Trump," *New York Times*, December 3, 2020, https://www .nytimes.com/2020/10/21/us/politics/lebron-james-trump-black -voters.html.

117   "Yes, we want you to go out and vote, but we're also going to give you the tutorial": LeBron James, quoted in "LeBron James

and Other Stars Form a Voting Rights Group," *New York Times,* June 10, 2020, https://www.nytimes.com/2020/06/10/us/politics/lebron-james-voting-rights.html.

117 "Because a lot of us just thought our vote doesn't count": LeBron James, quoted in "LeBron James on Black Voter Participation, Misinformation and Trump."

119 "But what it was doing was actually setting a trap for me": Fannie Lou Hamer, interview with Neil McMillen, Civil Rights in Mississippi Digital Archive, McCain Library and Archive, University of Southern Mississippi. From interviews conducted on April 14, 1972, and January 25, 1973, at Fannie Lou Hamer's home in Ruleville, Mississippi.

120 "I had never heard, until 1962, that black people could register and vote": Hamer, interview.

121 "stumbled on the key—the right to vote": Robert Moses, quoted in Charles M. Payne, *I've Got the Light of Freedom: The Organizing Tradition and the Mississippi Freedom Struggle* (Berkeley: University of California Press, 2007), 106.

123 "The whites have absolute control": South Carolina governor Ben Tillman quoted in Heather Cox Richardson, *West from Appomattox: The Reconstruction of America After the Civil War* (New Haven: Yale University Press, 2007), 245.

124 "If any of my n——s try to register, I'll shoot them down like rabbits": Ruleville, Mississippi, planter quoted in Chris Myers Asch, *The Senator and the Sharecropper: The Freedom Struggles of James O. Eastland and Fannie Lou Hamer* (New York: New Press, 2008), 171.

124 "The vote won't make Mister Charlie love us, but it will stop him from lynching us!" Civil rights activist Aaron Henry, quoted in ibid., 175.

124 "up as high as I could get it": Hamer, interview.

125 "I had a feeling; I don't know why...I said, 'If I'm arrested or anything, I'll have some extra shoes to put on'": Ibid.

125 "just stepped off the bus and went right on up to the courthouse and into the circuit clerk's office": voting rights activist, quoted in Kay Mills, *This Little Light of Mine: The Life of Fannie Lou Hamer* (Louisville: University Press of Kentucky, 2007), 36.

125 "I guess if I'd had any sense I'd-a been a little scared": Hamer, quoted in Asch, *The Senator and the Sharecropper*, 177.

125 "That was impossible. I had tried to give it, but I didn't even know what it meant, much less to interpret it": Hamer, interview.

126 "In fact, the first time I was aware that Mississippi had a constitution was when I tried to register to vote": Ibid.

126 "From the back of the bus": voting rights volunteer, quoted in Maegan Parker Brooks, *Fannie Lou Hamer: America's Freedom Fighting Woman* (New York: Rowman and Littlefield Publishers, 2020), 41.

126 "You'll have to go down and withdraw your registration": Hamer, interview.

126 "This seemed like it made him madder when I told him that": Ibid.

127 "There was nothing they could do to me": Hamer, quoted in Asch, *The Senator and the Sharecropper*, 178.

127 "Now I can work for my people": Ibid.

127 "You know the ballot is good": Fannie Lou Hamer, quoted in Meaghan Parker Brooks and Davis Houck, *The Speeches of Fannie Lou Hamer: To Tell It Like It Is* (Oxford: University Press of Mississippi, 2011), 5.

128 "If them crackers in Winona thought they'd discouraged me from fighting": Hamer, quoted in Brooks, *Fannie Lou Hamer*, 60.

129 "what happened in Selma is part of a far larger movement": President Lyndon Baines Johnson, Special Message to Congress, March 15, 1965, http://www.lbjlibrary.org/lyndon-baines-johnson /speeches-films/president-johnsons-special-message-to-the -congress-the-american-promise.

Chapter Ten: James Meredith Integrates the University of Mississippi

135 "Which one is Meredith?": Mississippi governor Ross Barnett quoted in James Meredith, *Three Years in Mississippi* (Oxford: University Press of Mississippi, 2019), 186.

137 "If America isn't for everybody, it isn't America": Ibid., 208.

137 "Some misguided people ask what difference it makes if only a few Negroes go to a white school": Ibid., 102.

138 "learned a lot about evasiveness, and how racists could use a system to forestall equality": Derrick Bell, quoted in *Boston Globe*, March 25, 1992.

139 "The good Lord was the original segregationist": Mississippi governor Ross Barnett, quoted in Charles W. Eagles, *The Price of Defiance: James Meredith and the Integration of Ole Miss* (Chapel Hill: University of North Carolina Press, 2009), 282.

139 "Gentlemen, my conscience is clear": Ibid., 317.

140 "We don't want you, n——": white protester, quoted in ibid., 317.

140 "I waved at them as we pulled away from the light": Meredith, *Three Years in Mississippi*, 187.

141 "It's going to be a long, hard, and difficult struggle": Robert Kennedy, quoted in William Doyle, *An American Insurrection: James Meredith and the Battle of Oxford, Mississippi, 1962* (New York: Anchor Books, 2003), 84.

141 HAIL BARNETT. OUR GOVERNOR WILL NOT BETRAY MISSISSIPPI: Eagles, *The Price of Defiance*, 284.

142 We think we are going in now": Ibid., 322.

142 "The state of Mississippi had clearly shown its intention not only to threaten to use violence, but to use it": Meredith, *Three Years in Mississippi*, 197.

144 "That's not a riot out there anymore. It's an armed insurrection": deputy marshal, quoted in Doyle, *An American Insurrection*, 186.

145 "I'm proud just to see a man get an education. That's all he ever asked for": Moses Meredith, quoted in ibid., 198.

147 "running faster but losing ground": Anthony Carnevale, quoted in "Racial Inequality, At College and in the Workplace," *Inside Higher Ed*, October 18, 2019, https://www.insidehighered.com /news/2019/10/18/racial-inequality-college-and-workplace.

147 "We had slavery, Jim Crow, the failure to hand out forty acres and a mule; we had housing policy, veterans' policy, redlining": Ibid.

Chapter Eleven: Rev. Dr. Martin Luther King Jr. and Memphis's Sanitation Workers Protest for Equal Pay

148–149 "What did surprise me was the outpouring of support": The Reverend Dr. William J. Barber II, *The Third Reconstruction: How a Moral Movement Is Overcoming the Politics of Division and Fear* (Boston: Beacon Press, 2016), 101.

149   "Rev. Barber, of all the contemporary leaders": Clayborne Carson, quoted in "Walking in the Footsteps of MLK, Rev. William Barber Brings Stanford Audience to Its Feet," *KQED*, January 20, 2019, https://www.kqed.org/news/11719472/walking-in-the -footsteps-of-mlk-reverend-william-barber-brings-a-stanford -audience-to-its-feet.

152   "You'd work ten, twelve hours a day": James Robinson, quoted in Michael K. Honey, *Going Down Jericho Road: The Memphis Strike, Martin Luther King's Last Campaign* (New York: Norton, 2008), 111.

152   "There is no worst job": sanitation worker, quoted in ibid., 109.

153   "We didn't have a voice back then": sanitation worker J. L. McClain, quoted in https://strikingvoices.com.

154   "We don't have anything no how": Honey, *Going Down Jericho Road*, 161.

154   "All we wanted was some decent working conditions": sanitation worker Taylor Rogers, quoted in ibid., 281.

155   "It wasn't just men walking out on their jobs": Emily Yellin, quoted in "How Women Shaped the Sanitation Workers' Strike in Memphis, Tennessee," National Trust for Historic Preservation article, March 13, 2018, https://savingplaces .org/stories/how-women-shaped-the-sanitation-workers -strike-in-memphis-tennessee#.YR-Q2MYpBaI.

156   "That's a racist point of view": Reverend James Lawson, quoted in Honey, *Going Down Jericho Road*, 281.

156   "You are human beings": Ibid.

157   "Now our struggle is for genuine equality, which means economic equality": Ibid., 379.

157   "Ralph, I can't get those children out of my mind": Martin Luther King Jr., quoted in "The Last March of Martin Luther King," *The Atlantic*, April 4, 2018, https://www.theatlantic.com/politics /archive/2018/04/mlk-last-march/555953.

157–158   "It didn't cost the nation one penny to integrate lunch counters," "New Front in the Fight for Freedom," APM Reports, https://features.apmreports.org/arw/king/b1.html.

158   "this power hungry, evil black devil": Honey, J. Edgar Hoover, quoted in Honey, *Going Down Jericho Road*, 247.

158 "You are reminding, not only Memphis": Martin Luther King Jr., quoted in ibid., 365.

159 "Be cool, fool, Thursday's march is King's thing": Ibid., 416.

160 "At this point, Memphis looked not like the starting place for the Poor People's Campaign that King had envisioned, but rather like its graveyard": Ibid., 506–7.

161 "There are thirteen hundred of God's children here, suffering": Ibid., 510.

161 "I may not get there with you": Ibid., 516.

162 "It's a dangerous job. You're trying to struggle, and make it out here, making ends meet": Jack Walker quoted, in *1300 Men: Memphis Strike, '68*, episode 2: "The Tragic Deaths of Robert Walker and Echol Cole Sparked 1968 Memphis Sanitation Strike," https://www.theroot.com/watch-the-tragic -deaths-of-robert-walker-and-echol-col-1822619781.

163 "Economic exclusion is exclusion": Elena Delavega, quoted in Chris Davis, "There Are No Bootstraps," *Memphis Flyer*, April 27, 2018, https://www.memphisflyer.com/there -are-no-bootstraps-qa-with-memphis-poverty-report-author -elena-delavega.

163 "We don't need a commemoration, we need a *reconsecration*": Reverend William Barber, quoted in "William Barber Takes on Poverty and Race in the Age of Trump," *New Yorker*, May 14, 2018, https://www.newyorker.com/magazine/2018/05/14/william -barber-takes-on-poverty-and-race-in-the-age-of-trump.

Chapter Twelve: John Carlos and Tommie Smith Raise a Fist for Black Pride

164 "I am not going to stand up to show pride in a flag for a country that oppresses Black people and people of color": Steve Wyche, "Colin Kaepernick Explains Why He Sat During National Anthem," *NFL Media*, August 26, 2016, https://www.nfl.com /news/colin-kaepernick-explains-why-he-sat-during-national -anthem-0ap3000000691077.

164 "I'm not anti-American": Transcript of Colin Kaepernick's comments after preseason finale, *ESPN*, September 2, 2016, https://www.espn .com/blog/san-francisco-49ers/post/_/id/19126/transcript-of-colin -kaepernicks-comments-after-preseason-finale.

165   "This could have happened to any of my family members who still live in the area": Eric Reid, "Why Colin Kaepernick and I Decided to Take a Knee," *New York Times*, September 25, 2017, https://www.nytimes.com/2017/09/25/opinion/colin-kaepernick -football-protests.html?mcubz=0.

167   "When the race popped off, we were all rolling. I have to say, I was flying, man. When that gun went off, I was gone": John Carlos with Dave Zirin, *The John Carlos Story: The Sports Moment That Changed the World* (Chicago: Haymarket Books, 2011), 116.

167   "You can see as we approach the finish line": Ibid., page 116.

168   "If you notice": Ibid., 116.

168–169   "I started reflecting on my dad": Ibid., 119.

169   "those singing the anthem started screaming it out": Douglas Hartmann, *Race, Culture, and the Revolt of the Black Athlete: The 1968 Olympic Protests and Their Aftermath* (Chicago: University of Chicago Press, 2003), 158.

170   My raised right hand stood for the power in Black America: Mike Marqusee, *Redemption Song: Muhammad Ali and the Spirit of the Sixties* (New York: Verso, 1999), 244.

171   "We want Black power!": Stokely Carmichael, quoted in Hasan Kwame Jeffries, *Bloody Lowndes: Civil Rights and Black Power in Alabama's Black Belt* (New York: NYU Press, 2010), 187.

173   "segregation now, segregation tomorrow, segregation forever!": Inaugural Address of Alabama governor George Wallace, January 14, 1963, https://digital.archives.alabama.gov /digital/collection/voices/id/2952.

174   "white supremacy!": "Lessons from the Election of 1968," *New Yorker*, January 1, 2018, https://www.newyorker.com/magazine /2018/01/08/lessons-from-the-election-of-1968.

174   "The time may have come when the issue of race could benefit from a period of benign neglect": Daniel Patrick Moynihan, quoted in "The Moynihan Report at Fifty," *Boston Review*, June 24, 2015, https://bostonreview.net/us /stephen-steinberg-moynihan-report-black-families-nathan -glazer.

174   "an insult to their countrymen"; "disgraceful, insulting, and embarrassing"; "a pair of dark-skinned stormtroopers": all

quoted in Hartman, *Race, Culture, and the Revolt of the Black Athlete*, 11.

175 "You'd think I committed murder": Ibid., 153.

175 "Hell no, I made it very clear to the IOC that they didn't give me this medal, I earned it": Carlos and Zirin, *The John Carlos Story*, 129.

176 "where I was encouraged to run but not to speak": Ibid., 111.

177 "In life, there's the beginning and the end": John Carlos, quoted in "The Man Who Raised a Black Power Salute at the 1968 Olympic Games," *The Guardian*, March 30, 2012, https://www.theguardian .com/world/2012/mar/30/black-power-salute-1968-olympics.

Chapter Thirteen: Ruth Batson Uncovers Segregation in Boston

178 "I heard a lot of things said during these meetings": Jason Kamras, quoted in "Parent Resistance Thwarts Local School Desegregation Efforts," CBS Baltimore, January 29, 2020, https://baltimore.cbslocal.com/2020/01/29/parent-resistance -thwarts-local-school-desegregation-efforts.

178 "When you look at what was said, it's so hurtful": Ibid.

178 "Blacks destroy school systems and schools": "Where Civility Is a Motto, School Desegregation Fight Turns Bitter," *New York Times*, November 12, 2019, https://www.nytimes.com/2019/11/12 /us/howard-county-school-redistricting.html.

179 "At school, I had friends, mostly white or Asian American": Reggie E. Scott, quoted in "Decades of Desegregation: Denver Readers Recall Their Own Stories of 'Busing,'" *Chalkbeat Colorado*, July 24, 2019, https://co.chalkbeat.org/2019/7/24 /21108576/decades-of-desegregation-denver-readers-recall-their -own-stories-of-busing.

182 "No one can take your education away from you": Ruth Batson, *The Black Educational Movement in Boston: A Sequence of Historical Events, A Chronology* (Boston: Northeastern University Faculty Publications, 2001), 2.

183 "We didn't have a tape recorder": Rucker C. Johnson, *Children of the Dream: Why School Integration Works* (New York: Basic Books, 2019), 145.

183 "The oldest school buildings in Boston were located in the black communities": Jeanne Theoharis and Komozi Woodard, eds.,

Groundwork: Local Black Freedom Movements in America (New York: NYU Press, 2005), 20.

184 "I believed, with all my heart": Batson, *The Black Educational Movement in Boston*, 7.

184 "The Negro can make their schools the best in the city": Theoharis and Woodard, eds., *Groundwork*, 26.

185 "Everything was going to be fine now": Batson, *The Black Educational Movement in Boston*, 47.

186 "I left the office angry and utterly disillusioned": Ibid., 8.

187 "separate and unequal were found to go hand in hand, no less in the North than in the South": Robert Carter, *A Matter of Law: A Memoir of Struggle in the Cause of Equal Rights* (New York: New Press, 2005), 172.

187 "Public schools, controlled by white middle-class parents and teachers": Ibid., 191.

188 "we did not provide Harlem with segregation": Jeanne Theoharis, *A More Beautiful and Terrible History: The Uses and Misuses of Civil Rights History* (Boston: Beacon Press, 2018), 38.

188 "knowingly carried out a systematic program of segregation affecting all of the city's students": Johnson, *Children of the Dream*, 146.

189 "You would think that aliens were coming": Theoharis and Woodard, eds., *Groundwork*, 92.

189 "Let your daughter get bused there": Johnson, *Children of the Dream*, 162.

190 "people on the corners holding bananas like we were apes, monkeys": Phyllis Ellison, quoted in Henry Hampton and Steve Fayer, *Voices of Freedom: An Oral History of the Civil Rights Movement from the 1950s Through the 1980s* (New York: Bantam Books, 1990), 610.

190 "Signs hanging out those buildings": Johnson, *Children of the Dream*, 162.

190 "I never got over it": Darneese Carnes, quoted in "Did Busing Slow Boston's Desegregation?" *Boston Globe*, August 9, 2015, https://www.bostonglobe.com/opinion/2015/08/08/did-busing-slow-boston-desegregation/5HXQbNFyuvD0SV4UdhNgAL/story.html.

191   "I had difficulty finding a parking space in downtown Boston":
      Ted Landsmark, quoted in "Life After Iconic 1976 Photo: The
      American Flag's Role in Racial Protest," September 18, 2016,
      https://www.npr.org/2016/09/18/494442131/life-after-iconic
      -photo-todays-parallels-of-american-flags-role-in-racial-protes.

192   "All of this is very connected": Elaine Gross, quoted in "This
      Supreme Court Case Made School District Lines a Tool for
      Segregation," NPR, July 25, 2019, https://www.npr.org/2019/07
      /25/739493839/this-supreme-court-case-made-school-district
      -lines-a-tool-for-segregation.

192   "Housing segregation is the overriding, number one cause of
      segregation in schools": John Brittain, quoted in "Breaking a
      'Steady Habit' of Inequitable Housing, Education," Brandeis
      Heller School for Social Policy and Management, July 13, 2021,
      https://heller.brandeis.edu/news/items/releases/2021/steady-habit
      -segregation-ct.html.

194   "If they run us out of that school": Theoharis and Woodard, eds.,
      Groundwork, 38.

194   "It isn't the bus you're talking about": Jean Maguire, quoted in
      "How the Boston Busing Decision Still Affects City Schools 40
      Years Later," WBUR, December 19, 2014, https://www.wbur.org
      /news/2014/06/20/boston-busing-ruling-anniversary.

Chapter Fourteen: Michelle Alexander Confronts the New Jim Crow

196   "He is a veteran of the first Gulf War": Raphael Warnock,
      quoted in "Reforming the Criminal Justice System," *Harvard
      Gazette*, October 16, 2019, https://news.harvard.edu/gazette/story
      /2019/10/the-rev-raphael-g-warnock-takes-aim-at-nations-prisons.

197   "Just think about it": Raphael Warnock, quoted in
      "Ebenezer Pastor: Mass Incarceration is a Scar on the
      Soul of America," *Atlanta Journal-Constitution*, June
      18, 2019, https://www.ajc.com/news/local/ebenezer
      -pastor-mass-incarceration-scar-the-soul-america
      /yETI5Xo57X3uMZED0JB6WP.

197   "I am clear that fifty years from now": Raphael Warnock quoted
      in "Reforming the Criminal Justice System," *Harvard Gazette*.

201   "I remember thinking to myself, Yeah, the criminal-justice
      system is racist in a lot of ways": Michelle Alexander, quoted in
      "Ten Years After 'The New Jim Crow,'" *New Yorker*, January

17, 2020, https://www.newyorker.com/news/the-new-yorker
-interview/ten-years-after-the-new-jim-crow.

202–203   "brimming with tears of joy and gratitude": Abd'Allah Latif,
"Parole Is Better Than Prison. But That Doesn't Mean I'm Free,"
Marshall Project, May 13, 2021, https://www.themarshallproject
.org/2021/05/13/parole-is-better-than-prison-but-that
-doesn-t-mean-i-m-free.

207   "This is a war that I *saw* destroy lives": Judge Nancy Gertner,
quoted in "Federal Judge: My Drug War Sentences Were 'Unfair
and Disproportionate,'" *The Atlantic*, June 29, 2015, https://www
.theatlantic.com/politics/archive/2015/06/federal-judge-my-drug
-war-sentences-were-unfair-and-disproportionate/397130.

208   "African American young men are the most incarcerated group
of people in the history of the world": Paul Butler, quoted in
"Former Prosecutor Pens a Hip-Hop Theory of Justice," *NPR*,
November 19, 2009, https://www.npr.org/templates/story/story
.php?storyId=120567780.

209   "I get my hope from this revolutionary idea that doesn't seem
to die in the United States": Michelle Alexander, quoted
in "Michelle Alexander on Bill Moyers: Locked Out of the
American Dream," December 20, 2013, https://billmoyers.com
/segment/michelle-alexander-locked-out-of-the-american-dream.

Chapter Fifteen: Catherine Flowers, Dr. Mona Hanna-Attisha, and Barack Obama Expose America's Crisis of Environmental Racism

211   "We were poor, we were Black and we were politically impotent":
Ben Chavis, quoted in "'This is Environmental Racism': How a
Protest in a North Carolina Farming Town Sparked a National
Movement," *Washington Post*, April 6, 2021, https://www
.washingtonpost.com/climate-environment/interactive/2021
/environmental-justice-race.

211   "This is environmental racism": Ibid.

214   "Things are worse for us than they have ever been": Catherine
Coleman Flowers, *Waste: One Woman's Fight Against America's
Dirty Secret* (New York: New Press, 2020), 98.

214   "Sewage was flowing into a hole in the ground near the back
door": Ibid., 128.

215   "Why were certain communities impacted and others were not?":
Catherine Coleman Flowers, interviewed in "From Lowndes

County, a Connection Between Environmental Activism and Civil Rights," Duke Today, March 22, 2017, https://today .duke.edu/2017/03/lowndes-county-connection-between -environmental-activism-and-civil-rights.

215–216 "This is not something that we test for in the US": Catherine Coleman Flowers, interviewed in "'Waste' Activist Digs into the Sanitation Crisis Affecting the Rural Poor," NPR, November 23, 2020, https://www.npr.org/sections/health-shots/2020/11 /23/937945160/waste-activist-digs-into-the-sanitation-crisis -affecting-the-rural-poor.

216 "When I began this work more than 15 years ago": Catherine Coleman Flowers, interviewed in "From Lowndes County, a Connection Between Environmental Activism and Civil Rights."

217 "It's regular, good, pure drinking water, and it's right in our backyard": Flint mayor Dayne Walling, quoted in "What Went Wrong in Flint," *New York Times*, March 3, 2016, https://www .nytimes.com/interactive/2016/03/04/us/04flint-mistakes.html.

218 I don't know how it can be clean if it smells and tastes bad": Flint resident, quoted in "'Nothing to Worry About, the Water is Fine: How Flint Poisoned Its People," *The Guardian*, July 3, 2018, https://www.theguardian.com/news/2018/jul/03 /nothing-to-worry-about-the-water-is-fine-how-flint-michigan -poisoned-its-people.

218 "It's a quality, safe product": "What Went Wrong in Flint," *New York Times*.

218 *"Lead in the water?"*: Dr. Mona, *What the Eyes Don't See: A Story of Crisis, Resistance, and Hope in an American City* (New York: One World, 2018), 39.

220 "This was a man-made disaster": President Barack Obama, quoted in "Obama Sips Flint Water, Urges Residents to Be Tested for Lead," Reuters, May 4, 2016, https://www.reuters.com/article /us-michigan-water-obama/obama-sips-flint-water-urges -children-be-tested-for-lead-idUSKCN0XV0YT.

222 "Everything about the Gardens seemed in a perpetual state of disrepair": Barack Obama, *Dreams of My Father: A Story of Race and Inheritance* (New York: Crown, 1995), 165.

223 "Flint and Washington and Newark": Dr. Mona, "I Helped Expose the Lead Crisis in Flint," *New York Times*, August 27,

2019, https://www.nytimes.com/2019/08/27/opinion/lead-water
-flint.html.

224 "The communities that are most impacted by COVID, or by
pollution": Elizabeth Yeampierre interviewed in "Unequal
Impact: the Deep Links Between Racism and Climate Change,"
Yale Environment 360, June 9, 2020, https://e360.yale.edu/features
/unequal-impact-the-deep-links-between-inequality-and-climate
-change.

Chapter Sixteen: Yusef Salaam Battles Racial Profiling

226 "When the police rushed onto our corner": James Forman Jr.,
Locking Up Our Own: Crime and Punishment in Black America
(New York: Farrar, Straus and Giroux, 2017), 153.

226 "Not once, over the course of about ten searches, did the police
recover anything illegal": Ibid., 154.

227 "No one should live in fear of being stopped whenever he leaves
his home to go about the activities of daily life:" Judge Shira
Scheindlin, quoted in "Judge Rejects New York's Stop and Frisk
Policy," *New York Times*, August 12, 2013, https://www.nytimes
.com/2013/08/13/nyregion/stop-and-frisk-practice-violated
-rights-judge-rules.html.

227 "Consider for a moment the kinds of police contact about
which Black people have long complained": Devon Carbado,
Unreasonable: Black Lives, Police Power, and the Fourth Amendment
(New York: New Press, 2022), page 18.

230 "I was a child full of hope, full of dreams, and full of aspirations
that hadn't yet been realized": " 'You Have A Hole That Can't Be
Filled': Yusef Salaam Reveals Pain After Going From 'Central
Park Five' To 'Exonerated Five,' " CBS New York, April 16, 2020,
https://newyork.cbslocal.com/2020/04/16/yusef-salaam-central
-park-jogging-case-exonerated-five-interview.

231 "Black boys as young as 10 may not be viewed in the same
light of childhood innocence as their white peers": American
Psychological Association report, "The Essence of Innocence,"
2014, https://www.apa.org/news/press/releases/2014/03/black
-boys-older.

231 "[T]hey should be forced to suffer and, when they kill, they
should be executed for their crimes": Donald Trump, quoted in
Matt Ford, "Donald Trump's Racially Charged Advocacy of the

Death Penalty," *The Atlantic*, December 18, 2015, https://www
.theatlantic.com/politics/archive/2015/12/donald-trump-death
-penalty/420069.

232   "the eldest of that wolf pack were tried, convicted and hanged in
Central Park": "One of the Falsely Accused Central Park Five
Tells His Story In 'Better, Not Bitter,'" NPR, May 18, 2021,
https://www.npr.org/2021/05/18/997792060/in-better-not-bitter
-one-of-the-central-park-five-tells-his-own-story.

232   "But here I was experiencing Jim Crowism in the North":
Yusef Salaam, interviewed in "Defying Trump's Racist Death
Sentence," *Jacobin Magazine*, October 31, 2016, https://www
.jacobinmag.com/2016/10/trump-central-park-five-jogger
-wrongful-conviction.

232   "Demonstrators, you know people just shouting": Antron
McCray, quoted in "The True Story of How a City in Fear
Brutalized the Central Park Five," *New York Times*, May 30, 2019,
https://www.nytimes.com/2019/05/30/arts/television/when-they
-see-us-real-story.html.

232   "It just felt like the whole world hated us": Ibid.

232   "I was a person who thought that I knew how to talk in a way that
was compelling": Yusef Salaam, interviewed in *Frontline*, June
30, 2020, https://www.pbs.org/wgbh/frontline/interview/yusef
-salaam.

233   "the condemnation of blackness": See generally, Khalil Gibran
Muhammad, *The Condemnation of Blackness: Race, Crime, and the
Making of Modern Urban America* (Cambridge, MA: Harvard
University Press, 2019).

233   "so impulsive, so remorseless, that [he] can kill, rape, maim,
without giving it a second thought": "How the 'Central Park
Five' Changed the History of American Law," *The Atlantic*,
June 2, 2019, https://www.theatlantic.com/entertainment/archive
/2019/06/when-they-see-us-shows-cases-impact-us-policy
/590779.

233   "In 1998 alone, roughly 200,000 youths were put through the
adult court system, and the majority of them were Black": Ibid.

234   "What you see in a youth facility, you think is the worst of the
worst, until you get to adult prison": Yusef Salaam, quoted in
Sarah Burns, *The Central Park Five: The Untold Story Behind One*

of New York City's Most Infamous Crimes (New York: Hodder and Stoughton, 2019), 180.

234 "We were in there fighting for our lives" Yusef Salaam, quoted in "The Spectrum's exclusive interview with Yusef Salaam of the 'Exonerated 5,'" *Spectrum*, February 26, 2020, https://www .ubspectrum.com/article/2020/02/the-spectrums-exclusive -interview-with-yusef-salaam-of-the-exonerated-5.

235 "We were found innocent": Yusef Salaam, quoted in "The Central Park Five: 'We Were Just Baby Boys,'" *New York Times*, May 13, 2019, https://www.nytimes.com/2019/05/30/arts/television/when -they-see-us.html.

235 "When I left prison, the officer literally said to me, 'I'll see you later'": Yusef Salaam, quoted in "Yusef Salaam of the 'Exonerated Five' Gives Talk on Injustice in America," *The Bottom Line*, February 2020, https://thebottomline.as.ucsb.edu/2020/02/from -the-central-park-five-to-the-exonerated-five-yusef-salaam-talk -copy.

235 "Surely, after difficulty, there is relief. There's more to do, in this life": Yusef Salaam, quoted in "Salaam Promotes Value of Resilience, Faith in MLK Lecture," *Cornell Chronicle*, February 19, 2020, https://news.cornell.edu/stories/2020/02/salaam -promotes-value-resilience-faith-mlk-lecture.

236 "allows law enforcement, just like it did in the 1870s in Alabama, to have the widest berth of discretion to challenge a person, a black male on the streets": "Khalil Muhammad on Facing Our Racial Past," *Moyers*, June 29, 2012, https://billmoyers.com /segment/khalil-muhammad-on-facing-our-racial-past.

236 "No white community in America would tolerate this kind of treatment in the name of public safety in its communities, period": Ibid.

236–237 "there are more innocent people in our jails and prisons today than ever before": Equal Justice Initiative, "Wrongful Convictions," https://eji.org/issues/wrongful-convictions.

237 "There is clear evidence of racial bias in the administration of criminal justice in the United States": Bryan Stevenson, "Testimony on Criminal Justice for the United National Special Rapporteur on Racism," May 26, 2008, https://eji.org/files/bryan -stevenson-testimony-united-nations-special-rapporteur-racism -2008.pdf.

238 "By having this verdict, what these people did, they lit the fuse to a bomb": John Singleton, quoted in "Race+Rage: The Beating of Rodney King," CNN documentary, March 5, 2011, https://transcripts.cnn.com/show/cp/date/2012-04-29/segment/01.

239 white people drastically overestimate the degree to which Black people commit crimes: Elizabeth Hinton, "An Unjust Burden: The Disparate Treatment of Black Americans in the Criminal Justice System," *Vera Institute of Justice Evidence Brief*, May 20, 2018, https://www.vera.org/downloads/publications/for-the-record-unjust-burden-racial-disparities.pdf.

239 In Chicago, police department data showed that Black and Latino drivers were pulled over and searched *four times* as often as white drivers: Ibid.

240 "To look at America with eyes that can see, with ears that can hear": Yusef Salaam, quoted in "Salaam, One of the Central Park Five, Shares Story of Exoneration and Faith, *Princeton Alumni Weekly*, November 21, 2019, https://paw.princeton.edu/article/salaam-one-central-park-five-shares-story-exoneration-and-faith.

Chapter Seventeen: Stacey Abrams Leads the Fight Against Voter Suppression

243 "throwing out [the provision] when it has worked and is continuing to work to stop discriminatory changes is like throwing away your umbrella in a rainstorm because you are not getting wet": Justice Ruth Bader Ginsburg, dissent in *Shelby County v. Holder*, https://www.supremecourt.gov/opinions/12pdf/12-96_6k47.pdf.

245 "Georgia's not ready for a Black woman": Stacey Abrams, *Lead From the Outside: How to Build Your Future and Make Real Change* (New York: Picador, 2019), 31.

246 "an enemy of our country": Lester Maddox, quoted in "Lester Maddox: His Diner Became a Race Flashpoint," *The Guardian*, June 25, 2003, https://www.theguardian.com/news/2003/jun/26/guardianobituaries.

246 "People who underestimate her risk complete embarrassment": Georgia state representative Allen Peake, quoted in "Abrams Ensures Dems Get Heard," *Atlanta Journal-Constitution*, March 27, 2011, https://www.ajc.com/news/local-govt--politics/abrams-ensures-dems-get-heard/Oa09YGPiNmBA2byID9vdPJ.

248 "Democrats are working hard, and all these stories about them": Brian Kemp, quoted in Carol Anderson, "Brian Kemp's Lead in Georgia Needs an Asterisk," *The Atlantic*, November 7, 2018, https://www.theatlantic.com/ideas/archive/2018/11/georgia-governor-kemp-abrams/575095.

249–250 More than 10 percent of all eligible voters in America—do not have drivers licenses to begin with. Moreover, *25 percent* of eligible African American voters lack this identification: Data cited in Keesha Gaskins and Sundeep Iyer, "The Challenge of Obtaining Voter Identification," Brennan Center For Justice Report, July 18, 2012, https://www.brennancenter.org/our-work/research-reports/challenge-obtaining-voter-identification.

250 "Let's not beat around the bush...the Indiana voter photo ID law is a not-too-thinly veiled attempt to discourage election-day turnout by certain folks": Judge Terrence T. Evans, quoted in Herma Percy, *Will Your Vote Count?: Fixing America's Broken Election System* (Westport, CT: Praeger, 2009), 72.

250 Between 2016 and 2018, Georgia purged more than *10 percent* of all voters in the state—more than 1.5 million people—voters that came from more heavily Democratic leaning, African American districts: Data cited in "Purges: A Growing Threat to the Right to Vote," Brennan Center for Justice Report, 2018, https://www.brennancenter.org/sites/default/files/publications/Purges_Growing_Threat_2018.pdf.

252 "I'm voting because most of my ancestors died for this," elderly voter, quoted in "Midterms 2018: The Crowded Scene at the Polls in Downtown Atlanta," *New Yorker*, November 6, 2018, https://www.newyorker.com/news/current/midterms-2018-the-crowded-scene-in-downtown-atlanta.

253 "I was numb": Stacey Abrams, *Our Time Is Now: Power, Purpose, and the Fight for a Fair America* (New York: Henry Holt, 2020), 17.

254 "Concession means to acknowledge an action is right, true, or proper:" Stacey Abrams, November 16, 2018, concession speech, reproduced in the *Atlanta Journal Constitution*, https://www.ajc.com/blog/politics/stacey-abrams-will-not-concede-because-the-erosion-our-democracy-not-right/JQqttbuF09NYkMQbIYx9BM.

Chapter Eighteen: Dr. Susan Moore Calls Out America's Unequal Health Care

256   "As a lifelong Detroiter, he had a special skill at telling our stories": Tonya Allen, quoted in Beth LeBlanc, "Detroit Consultant with No Known Health Issues or Recent Travel Dies After COVID-19 Diagnosis," *Detroit News*, March 24, 2020, https://www.detroitnews.com/story/news/local/detroit -city/2020/03/24/detroit-consultant-entrepreneur-dies-after -covid-19-diagnosis/2911918001.

257   "It seems like one after another after another, and it's just hitting close to home": Luther Keith, quoted in Erin Einhorn, "Detroit, Still Clawing Back from Financial Crisis, Reels as Coronavirus Claims Lives," *ABC News*, April 2, 2020, https://www.nbcnews .com/news/us-news/detroit-still-clawing-back-financial-crisis -reels-coronavirus-claims-lives-n1175191.

257   "It hit like a bomb": Michael Fowler, quoted in Ellen Barry, "Days After a Funeral in a Georgia Town, Coronavirus 'Hit Like a Bomb,'" *New York Times*, March 30, 2020, https://www.nytimes .com/2020/03/30/us/coronavirus-funeral-albany-georgia.html.

259   "You don't need it, you're not even short of breath": Dr. Susan Moore, quoted in Richard Hall, "'This Is How Black People Get Killed': Doctor Dies from Coronavirus After Posting Emotional Video from Hospital Bed Claiming Racist Treatment, *The Independent UK*, December 24, 2020,https://www.independent .co.uk/news/world/americas/susan-moore-coronavirus-racism -b1778765.html.

259   "He did not even listen to my lungs": Dr. Susan Moore, quoted in "Black US Doctor Dies of Covid Alleging Racist Hospital Care," BBC News, December 24, 2020, https://www.bbc.com/news /world-us-canada-55443339.

260   "Black workers face two of the most lethal preexisting conditions for coronavirus—racism and economic inequality": Economic Policy Institute Report, June 1, 2020, https://www.epi.org /publication/black-workers-covid.

261   "I told him you cannot tell me how I feel": Dr. Susan Moore quoted in "Black US Doctor Dies of Covid Alleging Racist Hospital Care."

261   "I was in so much pain from my neck. My neck hurt so bad": Dr. Susan Moore, quoted in Richard Hall, "'This Is How Black People Get Killed.'"

SOURCE NOTES

261 "I was crushed": Dr. Susan Moore, quoted in Fenit Nirappil, "A Black Doctor Alleged Racist Treatment Before Dying of Covid-19: 'This Is How Black People Get Killed,'" *Washington Post*, December 24, 2020, https://www.washingtonpost.com /health/2020/12/24/covid-susan-moore-medical-racism.

261 "He made me feel like a drug addict": Dr. Susan Moore, quoted in "Black Indiana Doctor Died of Coronavirus Weeks After Accusing Hospital of Racist Treatment," 6 ABC Action News Philadelphia, December 28, 2020,https://6abc.com/dr-susan -moore-md-covid-coronavirus-covid-19/9094278.

262 "You have to show proof that there is something wrong with you in order to get the medicine": Ibid.

263 "This is how Black people get killed": Dr. Susan Moore, quoted in "Hospital CEO's Response to Black Doctor's COVID-19 Death Prompts Backlash," ABC News, December 30, 2020, https://abcnews.go.com/US/hospital -ceos-response-black-doctors-covid-19-death/story?id =74971005.

264 "There was a separate entrance for blacks": David Barton Smith, *The Power to Heal: Civil Rights, Medicare, and the Struggle to Reform America's Health Care System* (Nashville: Vanderbilt University Press, 2016), 9.

264 "In those days": Ibid., 10.

265 "I remember when my uncle's friend": Ibid.

265 "of all the forms of inequality, injustice in health is the most shocking and the most inhuman because it often results in physical death": Martin Luther King Jr., quoted in Charlene Galarneau, "Getting Martin Luther King's Words Right," Physicians for a National Health Program, February 2018, https://pnhp.org/news/getting-martin-luther-kings-words-right.

266 "Free Blood Test; Free Treatment, By County Health Department and Government Doctors. YOU MAY FEEL WELL AND STILL HAVE BAD BLOOD. COME AND BRING ALL YOUR FAMILY": flyer, quoted in DeNeen L. Brown, "You've Got Bad Blood: The Horrors of the Tuskegee Syphilis Experiment," *Washington Post*, May 16, 2017, https:// www.washingtonpost.com/news/retropolis/wp/2017/05/16 /youve-got-bad-blood-the-horror-of-the-tuskegee-syphilis -experiment.

269 "Nearly every time she went to the hospital she had to advocate for herself": Henry Muhammed, Dr. Susan Moore's son, quoted in "Black Indiana Doctor Died of Coronavirus Weeks After Accusing Hospital of Racist Treatment," 6 ABC Action News Philadelphia, December 28, 2020, https://6abc.com/dr-susan -moore-md-covid-coronavirus-covid-19/9094278.

270 "She is me": Dr. Alicia Sanders quoted in "Black Indiana doctor died of coronavirus weeks after accusing hospital of racist treatment," Ibid.

Chapter Nineteen: The Black Lives Matter Movement Opens the Latest Battle for Racial Equality

271 "When I look at George Floyd, I look at my dad": Darnella Frazier, quoted in "George Floyd: What Witnesses Have Said in the Chauvin Trial," BBC News, April 18, 2021, https://www.bbc .com/news/world-us-canada-56581401.

271 "I was sad and kind of mad": Darnella Frazier's cousin, quoted in ibid.

271 "apologizing to George Floyd for not doing more and not physically interacting and not saving his life": Darnella Frazier, quoted in ibid.

273 "the sad part is, there's a section of America who is cheering and celebrating right now. and that makes me sick to my stomach. we GOTTA get it together y'all": Alicia Garza, quoted in Wesley Lowery, *They Can't Kill Us All: The Story of the Struggle for Black Lives* (New York: Little Brown and Company, 2016), 67.

274 "Black Lives Matter is our call to action": Patrice Cullors, quoted in "An Interview with the Founders of Black Lives Matter," *Ted*, October 2016, https://www.ted.com/talks/alicia_garza_patrisse _cullors_and_opal_tometi_an_interview_with_the_founders_of _black_lives_matter/transcript?language=en.

274 "I grew up in a neighborhood that was heavily policed": Opal Tometti, quoted in ibid.

274 "How do we live in a world that dehumanizes us and still be human?": Alicia Garza, quoted in Mychal Denzel Smith, "A Q&A with Alicia Garza, Co-Founder of #BlackLivesMatter," *The Nation*, March 24, 2015, https://www.thenation.com/article /archive/qa-alicia-garza-co-founder-blacklivesmatter.

274 "It's actually OK to be unique and have your own contributions": Ibid.

275 We knew that it was part of our sacred duty to step up": Melina Abdullah, quoted in Aleem Maqbool, "Black Lives Matter: From Social Media Post to Global Movement," BBC News, July 10, 2020, https://www.bbc.com/news/world-us-canada-53273381.

277 "That could be any of us": Lowery, *They Can't Kill Us All*, 25.

277 "It just felt different": Ibid., 26.

278 "In Ferguson, a wound bleeds": Ibid., 68.

280 "Lieutenant: Get over here.": Exchange recorded in "Investigation of the Ferguson Police Department," U.S. Department of Justice, Civil Rights Division, March 4, 2015, 17–18, https://www.justice .gov/sites/default/files/opa/press-releases/attachments/2015/03/04 /ferguson_police_department_report.pdf.

Chapter Twenty: Nikole Hannah-Jones Taps into the Power of History

288 "pay attention to what has happened in this country": Kimberlé Crenshaw, quoted in CNN, May 22, 2021, https://transcripts.cnn .com/show/cnr/date/2021-05-22/segment/04.

289 "that the United States of America and the state of Iowa are fundamentally or systemically racist or sexist": Text of Iowa law signed by Governor Kim Reynolds in July 2021: https://www .legis.iowa.gov/docs/publications/LGR/89/HF802.pdf.

290 "In most cases, the new American memory laws have been passed by state legislatures that, in the same session, have passed laws designed to make voting more difficult": Timothy Snyder, "The War on History Is a War on Democracy," *New York Times*, June 29, 2021, https://www.nytimes.com/2021/06/29/magazine /memory-laws.html.

291 "I've spent my entire life proving that I belong in elite white spaces that were not built for Black people": Nikole Hannah-Jones, quoted in Laurel Wamsley, "After Tenure Controversy, Nikole Hannah-Jones Will Join Howard Faculty Instead Of UNC," NPR, July 6, 2021, https://www.npr.org/2021/07/06 /1013315775/after-tenure-controversy-nikole-hannah-jones-will -join-howard-faculty-instead-of.

INDEX

★ ★ ★

INDEX

INDEX

INDEX

ABOUT THE AUTHORS

★ ★ ★

Dr. Michael Eric Dyson is an award-winning and *New York Times* bestselling author of over twenty books, a widely celebrated Vanderbilt University professor, a prominent public intellectual, an ordained Baptist minister, and a noted political analyst. A native of Detroit, Michigan, he currently lives in Nashville, Tennessee. This is his first book for teens.

Marc Favreau is the director of editorial programs at The New Press, the acclaimed author of *Crash* and *Spies*, and coeditor (with Ira Berlin and Steven F. Miller) of *Remembering Slavery: African Americans Talk About Their Personal Experiences of Slavery and Emancipation.* He lives in New York City and Martha's Vineyard, Massachusetts.